THE VOYAGES OF
CAPTAIN
JAMES
COOK

THE ILLUSTRATED ACCOUNTS OF THREE EPIC VOYAGES

THE VOYAGES OF
CAPTAIN
JAMES
COOK

NICHOLAS THOMAS, EDITOR

FROM THE WRITINGS OF JAMES COOK, JOHN HAWKESWORTH, GEORG FORSTER, AND JAMES KING

VOYAGEUR
PRESS

Contents

Part Three
1776–1780

THE VOYAGE OF THE *RESOLUTION* AND THE *DISCOVERY*

INTRODUCTION

CAPTAIN JAMES COOK is often considered the greatest of all sea explorers. His three voyages, undertaken between 1768 and 1780, dramatically extended the European understanding of the world, and in particular of the Pacific, Australia, and the Antarctic. But the expeditions were not only important because they replaced blank or misrecognized parts of maps with precisely delineated coastlines, and accurately situated many islands and archipelagos. The voyages were also important for geographical theory, for commerce, and for natural history. Their scientific findings were wide-ranging, and their human discoveries—the encounter with diverse peoples of the Pacific—were remarkable and had wide-ranging ramifications for European thought and culture.

Cook was famously of humble origins. Born in 1728 into a farming family near the present Yorkshire city of Middlesbrough, he moved first to the coastal settlement of Staithes and then to the port of Whitby, gaining experience in the coal trade. He joined the navy in 1755 and in due course gained renown for his ability and thoroughness as a surveyor. The brilliance of his Newfoundland charts led to his appointment as commander of the *Endeavour*.

The years following the Seven Years' War of 1756–1763 were peaceful. Science and the arts flourished and George III was supportive of the aspirations of the Royal Society. The opportunity to observe the Transit of Venus from a number of points around the world prompted international cooperation. A naval voyage was commissioned to observe the transit from the recently discovered island of Tahiti in the South Pacific. But naturally enough, the voyage had wider strategic aims. Britain was dynamic and commercially ambitious. There was considerable interest in the possibility that some southern continent might exist, perhaps comparable in its resources to China or India. The first nation to discover and inaugurate trade with such territories or nations would be decisively advantaged in the enduring competition among European states. Hence, following an extended stay at Tahiti, the *Endeavour* would turn south in search of the southern land, going on to circumnavigate New Zealand and trace the eastern Australian coast.

Over the course of the voyage, Cook formed a plan that would establish definitively whether any southern continent existed. He was given the opportunity to test the strategy during a second expedition which undertook grueling cruises through Antarctic waters. Though the finding was negative, Cook could consider the investigation of the southern oceans complete. The voyage moreover dramatically extended understandings of the islands of the Pacific tropics and had featured many brief and more extended meetings with the people of the islands, whose languages, cultures, and artifacts the voyagers were beginning to document and collect.

On Cook's return from the second voyage, it was anticipated that he might retire. But a third expedition was proposed to address a further major geographic conundrum: Was there a navigable northwest passage that would make it possible to sail from the North Atlantic to the North Pacific? Such a route would make a sea voyage to China faster and less hazardous than the routes around southern Africa and South America. Cook was unable to resist the challenge and accepted the command of a third great voyage. The expedition would feature further rich contacts with Pacific Islanders—as well as moments of tension and conflict. The effort to identify a navigable passage proved frustrating and exhausting. Passing through the Bering Strait and probing the

Cook spent his childhood in the agricultural settlement of Great Ayton, where this statue of the navigator as a boy marks his connection with the village.

waters of the Arctic, Cook encountered vast expanses of sea ice and withdrew, resolving to make a further attempt during the succeeding season. But in the Hawaiian archipelago he was drawn into relationships with a dynamic kingdom that he could not fully understand. Initially welcomed as an incarnation of one god, fortuitously supposed to be ascendant during that very season, on his return to the great island of Hawaii itself, following a storm, he posed a challenge to the king and relationships deteriorated, leading to an outbreak of violence at Kealakekua Bay in which the navigator was killed on February 14, 1779.

The voyages led swiftly to the inauguration of the trans-Pacific fur trade, to the colonization of Australia, and to the establishment of Christian missionaries on Tahiti. The flora and fauna of Australasia and many other regions were documented by scientists such as Joseph Banks, later President of the Royal Society and effectively the founder of the scientific botanic garden at Kew. The voyages had many artistic and literary impacts, as well. The published narratives—excerpted here—were dramatic and compelling, among the most popular of travel books in the period, and reprinted intermittently ever since. The voyages and their cross-cultural encounters also suggested questions and themes for philosophers and writers.

The voyages were as influential as they were in part because Cook and his scientists and associates were fine and engaging writers. They brought the places they visited, the dangers and drama of the voyage, to life in remarkably vivid terms. Nearly two hundred and fifty years later, their accounts communicate the hazards of these epoch-making expeditions, and the excitement of encounters with exotic peoples, in a manner at once real and thrilling.

Part 1
1768—1771
THE VOYAGE OF THE *ENDEAVOUR*

THE VOYAGE OF THE *ENDEAVOUR* had the ostensible purpose of observing the Transit of Venus from the island of Tahiti, known to Europeans as a result of its "discovery" by Samuel Wallis in June 1767. Yet Cook's voyage, like many precursors, had the larger purpose of searching for the Great Southern Land that had been an object of geographic speculation for centuries. The astronomical and navigational purposes of the voyage would anyway be eclipsed by their human interest, by the encounters with peoples who were new and exotic from European perspectives, who seized the imaginations of both the public and scientists.

Following brief visits to the well-known ports of Funchal (Madeira) and Rio, and encounters with the native peoples of Tierra del Fuego, Cook and his men spent nearly three months on Tahiti. In the course of preparing for the observation of the transit, they interacted extensively with the Islanders and began documenting their language, sociality, and customs. On leaving the Society Islands, with the Ra'iatean priest Tupaia, who wished to accompany Banks and Cook back to England, the ship headed west and south and reached New Zealand in early October 1769. Initial encounters at Poverty Bay broke down into lethal violence, but engagements elsewhere were marked by less tension. Cook circumnavigated and charted both the main North and South Islands and identified Queen Charlotte Sound as a good harbor to which he would return during both his second and third voyages.

The cruise up the eastern Australian coast was very different from the perspective of human interaction. At Botany Bay, from the end of April 1770, attempts were made to traffic with Aboriginal people, who tried to keep their distance from the Europeans. Following *Endeavour*'s near-wreck on the Great Barrier Reef, the ship was careened in the Endeavour River estuary and sufficient time was spent with the Guugu Yimithirr Australian Aboriginal tribe to record words and otherwise make observations. Fleeting contacts took place on New Guinea's south coast in the course of the passage to the Dutch East Indies. During and after the stay at Batavia, the impact of disease upon the crew was catastrophic—those who died included Tupaia and the boy referred to as his "servant."

While John Hawkesworth's 1773 *Account of the Voyages* of Cook's predecessors and the *Endeavour* was widely censured for inaccuracies as well as

PREVIOUS: This painting of Cook's 1770 Botany Bay landing was made at the time of Australian Federation in 1901. In fact, Cook did not stop his men from firing on the Aboriginal people, but was involved in shooting at them himself.

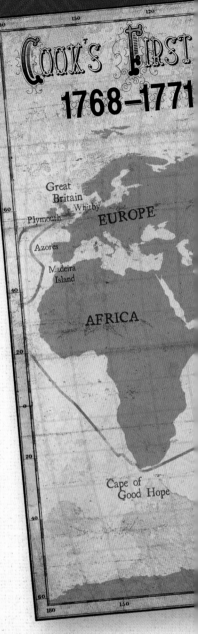

COOK'S FIRST
1768–1771

for including material considered licentious and impious, the book set a new standard in the literature of exploration and travel. Empowered by the ethnographic observations in Banks's and Cook's own journals, Hawkesworth's descriptions, though occasionally distorted, were vivid and detailed. The volumes were, moreover, the first in which the tradition of illustrating antiquities and natural specimens was extended to represent the "artificial curiosities" collected during the voyage.

Chapter 1

FROM THE THAMES TO MADEIRA

This extract from Cook's manuscript journal is matter-of-fact, but exemplifies the navigator's precise and practical approach to the business of fitting out the Endeavour *and the early stages of the voyage.*

RIVER THAMES, FRIDAY, MAY 27TH, TO FRIDAY, JULY 29TH [1768]. Moderate and fair weather; at 11 a.m. hoisted the Pendant, and took charge of the Ship, agreeable to my Commission of the 25th instant, she lying in the Bason in Deptford Yard. From this day to the 21st of July we were constantly employed in fitting the Ship, taking on board Stores and Provisions, etc. The same day we sailed from Deptford and anchored in Gallions reach, were we remained until the 30th. The transactions of Each Day, both while we lay here and at Deptford, are inserted in the Log Book, and as they contain nothing but common Occurrences, it was thought not necessary to insert them here.

JULY 30TH TO AUGUST 7TH. Saturday, July 30th, Weighed from Gallions, and made sail down the River, the same day Anchored at Gravesend, and the next Morning weighed from thence, and at Noon Anchored at the Buoy of the Fairway. On Wednesday, 3rd of August, Anchored in the Downs in 9 fathoms of water, Deal Castle North-West by West. On Sunday, 7th, I joined the Ship, discharged the Pilot, and the next day saild for Plymouth.

MONDAY, 8TH. Fresh Breezes and Cloudy weather the most part of these 24 hours. At 10 a.m. weighed and came to sail; at Noon the South Foreland bore North-East ½ North, distant 6 or 7 Miles. Wind West by North, North-West.

ABOVE: A model of the *Endeavour*, a Whitby-made "cat," or coal ship, designed to withstand the storms and shallows of the northeast England coast, and even be careened on a beach.

OVERLEAF: The Thames marked the starting point of the first voyage in 1768. In 1791, neoclassical Irish painter James Barry depicted the river as a god guided by English navigational instruments and propelled by Walter Raleigh, Francis Drake, and James Cook (bottom center). Mercury, god of commerce, flies past overhead, a nod to the driving force behind state-sponsored exploration.

TUESDAY, 9TH. Gentle breezes and Cloudy weather. At 7 p.m. the Tide being against us, Anchored in 13 fathoms of Water; Dungeness South-West by West. At 11 a.m. Weighed and made Sail down Channel; at Noon, Beachy Head, North by East ½ East, distant 6 Leagues, Latitude observed 50 degrees 30 minutes North. Wind North-West to North.

WEDNESDAY, 10TH. Variable: light Airs and Clear weather. At 8 p.m. Beachy Head North-East by East, distant 4 Leagues, and at 8 a.m. it bore North-East by North, 9 Leagues. Found the Variation of the Compass to be 23 degrees West; at Noon the Isle of Wight North-West by North. Wind West by North, North-East by East.

THURSDAY, 11TH. Light Airs and Clear weather. At 8 p.m. Dunnose North by West 5 Leagues, and at 4 a.m. it bore North-North-East ½ East, distant 5 Leagues. Wind Variable.

WEDNESDAY, 12TH. Light Airs and Calms all these 24 Hours. At Noon the Bill of Portland bore North-West ½ West, distant 3 Leagues. Latitude Observed 50 degrees 24 minutes North. Wind Easterly.

THURSDAY, 13TH. Ditto weather. At Noon the Start Point West 7 or 8 miles. Latitude Observed 50 degrees 12 minutes North, which must be the Latitude of the Start, as it bore West. Wind Variable.

SUNDAY, 14TH. Fine breezes and Clear weather. At ½ past 8 p.m. Anchored in the Entrance of Plymouth Sound in 9 fathoms water. At 4 a.m. weighed and worked into proper Anchoring ground, and Anchored in 6 fathoms, the Mewstone South-East, Mount Batten North-North-East ½ East, and Drake's Island North by West. Dispatched an Express to London for Mr. Banks and Dr. Solander to join the Ship, their Servants and Baggage being already on board. Wind North-Easterly.

MONDAY, 15TH. First and latter parts Moderate breezes and fair; Middle squally, with heavy showers of rain. I this day received an order to Augment the Ship's Company to 85 Men, which before was but 70. Received on board fresh Beef for the Ship's Company. Wind South-West to South-East.

TUESDAY, 16TH. First part moderate and Hazey; Middle hard Squalls with rain; the Latter moderate and fair. Received on board a supply of Bread, Beer, and Water. A Sergeant, Corporal, Drummer, and 9 Private Marines as part of the Complement. Wind South-South-East to North-East.

WEDNESDAY, 17TH. Little wind and Hazey weather. Sent some Cordage to the Yard in order to be Exchanged for Smaller. Several Shipwrights and Joiners from the Yard Employed on board refitting the Gentlemen's Cabins, and making a Platform over the Tiller, etc. Wind South-East to East by South.

THURSDAY, 18TH. Little wind and Cloudy. Struck down 4 guns into the Hold. Received on board 4 More, with 12 Barrels of Powder and several other Stores. Shipwrights and Joiners Employed on board. Wind Easterly.

FRIDAY, 19TH. Former part little wind with rain; remainder fair weather; a.m. Read to the Ship's Company the Articles of War and the Act of Parliament, they likewise were paid two Months' Wages in advance. I also told them that they were to Expect no additional pay for the performance of our intended Voyage; they were well satisfied, and Expressed great Cheerfulness and readiness to prosecute the Voyage. Received on board another Supply of Provisions, Rum, etc. Wind North-West to South-West.

* * *

MOORED IN FUNCHAL ROAD, MADEIRA, WEDNESDAY, [SEPTEMBER] 14TH. First part fine, Clear weather, remainder Cloudy, with Squals from the land, attended with Showers of rain. In the Night the Bend of the Hawsers of the Stream Anchor Slip'd owing to the Carelessness of the Person who made it fast. In the Morning hove up the Anchor in the Boat and carried it out to the Southward. In heaving the Anchor out of the Boat Mr. Weir, Master's Mate, was carried overboard by the Buoy rope and to the Bottom with the Anchor. Hove up the Anchor by the Ship as soon as possible, and found his Body intangled in the Buoy rope. Moor'd the Ship with the two Bowers in 22 fathoms Water; the Loo Rock West and the Brazen Head East. Saild His Majesty's Ship *Rose*. The Boats employed carrying the Casks a Shore for Wine, and the Caulkers caulking the Ship Sides. Wind Easterly.

THURSDAY, 15TH. Squals of Wind from the Land, with rain the most part of these 24 Hours. Received on board fresh Beef and Greens for the Ship's Company, and sent on shore all our Casks for Wine and Water, having a Shore Boat employed for that purpose. Wind North-East to South-East.

FRIDAY, 16TH. The most part fine, Clear weather. Punished Henry Stevens, Seaman, and Thomas Dunster, Marine, with 12 lashes each, for refusing to take their allowance of Fresh Beef. Employed taking on board Wine and Water. Wind Easterly.

SATURDAY, 17TH. Little wind, and fine Clear weather. Issued to the whole Ship's Company 20 pounds of Onions per Man. Employed as Yesterday. Wind Westerly.

SUNDAY, 18TH. Ditto Weather. P.M. received on board 270 pounds of fresh Beef, and a Live Bullock charged 613 pounds. Compleated our Wine and Water, having received of the former 3032 Gallons, of the Latter 10 Tuns. A.M. unmoor'd and prepar'd for Sailing. Funchall, in the Island of Madeira, by Observations made here by Dr. Eberton, F.R.S., lies in the latitude of 32 degrees 33 minutes 33 seconds North and longitude West from Greenwich 16 degrees 49 minutes, the Variation of the Compass 15 degrees 30 minutes West, decreasing as he says, which I much doubt; neither does this Variation agree with our own Observations. The Tides flow full, and Change North and South, and rise Perpendicular 7 feet at Spring Tides and 4 feet at Niep tides. We found the North point of the Diping Needle, belonging to the Royal Society, to Dip 77 degrees 18 minutes. The Refreshments for Shipping to be got at this place are Wine, Water, Fruit of Several Sorts, and Onions in Plenty, and some Sweatmeats; but Fresh Meat and Poultry are very Dear, and not to be had at any rate without Leave from the Governour. Wind southerly, East-South-East, South-West.

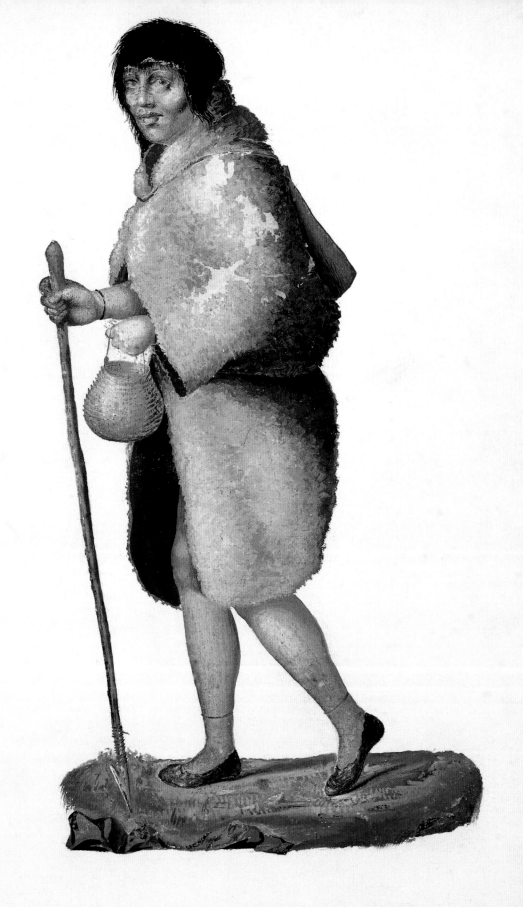

A WOMAN of the Island of TERRA DEL FUEGO.

Chapter 2

TRAGEDY AT TIERRA DEL FUEGO

---

*The literary gentleman John Hawkesworth, who was commissioned to write the offi-
cially sanctioned narrative of Byron's, Wallis's, and Cook's first voyage, drew on Joseph
Banks's journals as well as Cook's, as in the following "An Account of what happened
in ascending a Mountain to search for Plants." The experience revealed the severity
of the southern environment and the dangers of what had appeared, in prospect, a
straightforward walk up a hill.*

ON THE 16TH [OF JANUARY, 1769], early in the morning, Mr. Banks and Dr. Solander, with their attendants and servants, and two seamen to assist in carrying the baggage, accompanied by Mr. Monkhouse the Surgeon, and Mr. Green the Astronomer, set out from the ship, with a view to penetrate as far as they could into the country, and return at night. The hills, when viewed at a distance, seemed to be partly a wood, partly a plain, and above them a bare rock. Mr. Banks hoped to get through the wood, and made no doubt, but that, beyond it, he should, in a country which no botanist had ever yet visited, find alpine plants which would abundantly compensate his labour. They entered the wood at a small sandy beach, a little to the westward of the watering-place, and continued to ascend the hill, through the pathless wilderness, till three o'clock, before they got a near view of the places which they intended to visit. Soon after they reached what they had taken for a plain; but, to their great disappointment, found it a swamp, covered with low bushes of birch, about three feet high, interwoven with each other, and so stubborn that they could not be bent out of the way; it was therefore neces-

OPPOSITE: Joseph Banks's draftsman, Alexander Buchan, carefully represented the facial tattoos and dress of a Haush or Ona woman, among the indigenous people encountered at Tierra del Fuego.

At Tierra del Fuego the mariners began collecting "artificial curiosities"—that is, the artifacts of indigenous people, for the first time.

sary to lift the leg over them, which at every step was buried, ancle deep, in the soil. To aggravate the pain and difficulty of such travelling, the weather, which hitherto had been very fine, much like one of our bright days in May, became gloomy and cold; with sudden blasts of a most piercing wind, accompanied with snow. They pushed forward, however, in good spirits, notwithstanding their fatigue, hoping the worst of the way was past, and that the bare rock which they had seen from the tops of the lower hills was not more than a mile before them; but when they had got about two thirds over this woody swamp, Mr. Buchan, one of Mr. Banks's draughtmen, was unhappily seized with a fit. This made it necessary for the whole company to halt, and as it was impossible that he should go any farther, a fire was kindled, and those who were most fatigued were left behind to take care of him. Mr. Banks, Dr. Solander, Mr. Green, and Mr. Monkhouse went on, and in a short time reached the summit. As botanists, their expectations were here abundantly gratified; for they found a great variety of plants, which, with respect to the alpine plants in Europe, are exactly what those plants are with respect to such as grow in the plain.

The cold was now become more severe, and the snow-blasts more frequent; the day also was so far spent, that it was found impossible to get back to the ship before the next morning: to pass the night upon such a mountain, in such a climate, was not only comfortless, but dreadful; it was impossible however to be avoided, and they were to provide for it as well as they could.

Mr. Banks and Dr. Solander, while they were improving an opportunity which they had, with so much danger and difficulty, procured, by gathering the plants which they found upon the mountain, sent Mr. Green and Mr. Monkhouse back to Mr. Buchan and the people that were with him, with directions to bring them to a hill, which they thought lay in a better rout for returning to the wood, and which was therefore appointed as a general rendezvous. It was proposed, that from this hill they should push through the swamp, which seemed by the new rout not to be more than half a mile over, into the shelter of the wood, and there build their wigwam, and make a fire: this, as their way was all down hill, it seemed easy to accomplish. Their whole company assembled at the rendezvous, and, though pinched with the cold, were in health and spirits, Mr. Buchan himself having recovered his strength in a much greater degree than could have been expected. It was now near eight o'clock in the evening, but still good day-light, and they set forward for the nearest valley, Mr. Banks himself undertaking to bring up the rear, and see that no straggler was left behind: this may perhaps be thought a superfluous caution, but it will soon appear to be otherwise. Dr. Solander, who had more than once crossed the mountains which divide Sweden from Norway, well knew that extreme cold, especially when joined with fatigue, produces a torpor and sleepiness that are almost irresistible: he therefore conjured the company to keep moving, whatever pain it might cost them, and whatever relief they might be promised by an inclination to rest: Whoever sits down, says he, will sleep; and whoever sleeps, will wake no more. Thus, at once admonished and alarmed, they set forward; but while they were still upon the naked rock, and before they had got among the bushes, the cold became suddenly so intense, as to produce the effects that had been most dreaded. Dr. Solander himself was the first who found the inclination, against which he had warned others, irresistible; and insisted upon being suffered to lie down. Mr. Banks intreated and remonstrated in vain, down he lay upon the ground, though it was covered with snow; and it was with great difficulty that his friend kept him from sleeping. Richmond also, one of the black servants, began to linger, having suffered from the cold in the same manner as the Doctor. Mr. Banks, therefore, sent five of the company, among whom was Mr. Buchan, forward to get a fire ready at the first convenient place they could find; and

Cook's associates included some of the most advanced and influential scientists of his epoch, including Sir Joseph Banks, who participated in the first voyage as a young man and went on to become one of the Royal Society's longest-serving presidents.

himself, with four others, remained with the Doctor and Richmond, whom partly by persuasion and entreaty, and partly by force, they brought on; but when they had got through the greatest part of the birch and swamp, they both declared they could go no farther. Mr. Banks had recourse again to entreaty and expostulation, but they produced no effect: when Richmond was told, that if he did not go on he would in a short time be frozen to death; he answered, That he desired nothing but to lie down and die: the Doctor did not so explicitly renounce his life; he said he was willing to go on, but that he must first take some sleep, though he had before told the company that to sleep was to perish. Mr. Banks and the rest found it impossible to carry them, and there being no remedy they were both suffered to sit down, being partly supported by the bushes, and in a few minutes they fell into a profound sleep: soon after, some of the people who had been sent forward returned, with the welcome news that a fire was kindled about a quarter of a mile farther on the way. Mr. Banks then endeavoured to wake Dr. Solander and happily succeeded: but, though he had not slept five minutes, he had almost lost the use of his limbs, and the muscles were so shrunk that his shoes fell from his feet; he consented to go forward with such assistance as could be given him, but no attempts to relieve poor Richmond were successful. It being found impossible to make him stir, after some time had been lost in the attempt, Mr. Banks left his other black servant and a seaman, who seemed to have suffered least by the cold,

to look after him; promising, that as soon as two others should be sufficiently warmed, they should be relieved. Mr. Banks, with much difficulty, at length got the Doctor to the fire; and soon after sent two of the people who had been refreshed, in hopes that, with the assistance of those who had been left behind they would be able to bring Richmond, even though it should still be found impossible to wake him. In about half an hour, however, they had the mortification to see these two men return alone; they said, that they had been all round the place to which they had been directed, but could neither find Richmond nor those who had been left with him; and that though they had shouted many times, no voice had replied. This was matter of equal surprise and concern, particularly to Mr. Banks, who, while he was wondering how it could happen, missed a bottle of rum, the company's whole stock, which they now concluded to be in the knapsack of one of the absentees. It was conjectured, that with this Richmond had been rouzed by the two persons who had been left with him, and that, having perhaps drank too freely of it themselves, they had all rambled from the place where they had been left, in search of the fire, instead of waiting for those who should have been their assistants and guides. Another fall of snow now came on, and continued incessantly for two hours, so that all hope of seeing them again, at least alive, were given up; but about twelve o'clock, to the great joy of those at the fire, a shouting was heard at some distance. Mr. Banks, with four more, immediately went out, and found the seaman with just strength enough left to stagger along, and call out for assistance: Mr. Banks sent him immediately to the fire, and, by his direction, proceeded in search of the other two, whom he soon after found. Richmond was upon his legs, but not able to put one before the other; his companion was lying upon the ground, as insensible as a stone. All hands were now called from the fire, and an attempt was made to carry them to it; but this, notwithstanding the united efforts of the whole company, was found to be impossible. The night was extremely dark, the snow was now very deep, and, under these additional disadvantages, they found it very difficult to make way through the bushes and the bog for themselves, all of them getting many falls in the attempt. The only alternative was to make a fire upon the spot; but the snow which had fallen, and was still falling, besides what was every moment shaken in flakes from the trees, rendered it equally impracticable, to kindle one there, and to bring any part of that which had been kindled in the wood thither: they were, therefore, reduced to the sad necessity of leaving the unhappy wretches to their fate; having first made them a bed of boughs from the trees, and spread a covering of the same kind over them to a considerable height.

Having now been exposed to the cold and the snow near an hour and an half, some of the rest began to lose their sensibility; and one Briscoe, another of Mr. Banks's servants was so ill, that it was thought he must die before he could be got to the fire.

At the fire, however, at length they arrived; and passed the night in a situation, which, however dreadful in itself, was rendered more afflicting by the remembrance of what was past, and the uncertainty of what was to come. Of twelve, the number that set out together in health and spirits, two were supposed to be already dead; a third was so ill, that it was very doubtful whether he would be able to go forward in the morning; and a fourth, Mr. Buchan, was in danger of a return of his fits,

OPPOSITE: Detail from an engraving in John Hawkesworth's published *Account of the Voyages*, which presented Tierra del Fuegian life in classical, idealized terms.

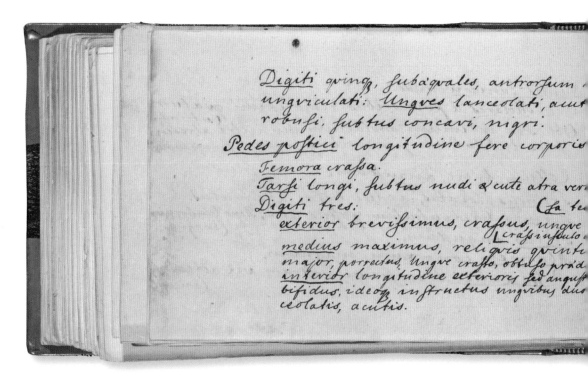

ABOVE: A "Solander slip" was a sheet of paper on which the description of a specimen was recorded, an innovation of Banks's botanist, Daniel Solander, and a reflection of the advanced and systematic nature of the voyage's efforts to document natural history.

by fresh fatigue after so uncomfortable a night: they were distant from the ship a long day's journey, through pathless woods, in which it was too probable they might be bewildered till they were overtaken by the next night; and, not having prepared for a journey of more than eight or ten hours, they were wholly destitute of provisions, except a vulture, which they happened to shoot while they were out, and which, if equally divided, would not afford each of them half a meal; and they knew not how much more they might suffer from the cold, as the snow still continued to fall. A dreadful testimony of the severity of the climate, as it was now the midst of summer in this part of the world, the twenty-first of December being here the longest day; and every thing might justly be dreaded from a phænomenon which, in the corresponding season, is unknown even in Norway and Lapland.

When the morning dawned, they saw nothing round them, as far as the eye could reach, but snow, which seemed to lie as thick upon the trees as upon the ground; and the blasts returned to frequently, and with such violence, that they found it impossible for them to set out: how long this might last they knew not, and they had but too much reason to apprehend that it would confine them in that desolate forest till they perished with hunger and cold.

After having suffered the misery and terror of this situation till six o'clock in the morning, they conceived some hope of deliverance by discovering the place of the sun through the clouds, which were become thinner, and began to break away. Their first care was to see whether the poor wretches whom they had been obliged to leave among the bushes were yet alive; three

Cauda longissima, vix corpore brevior, (ad au-
res enim illa reflecti potest,) teres, æqualiter
pilosa, basi valde crassa, sensim angu-
stata, primum porrecta, dein parum decli-
nans, apice leviter & arcu lato recurva.
Scrotum exsertum, inter femora pendulum.
Penis sub cauda retrospiciens, Præputio crasso,
exserto cinctus.
Vulva & Meatus urinarius comunem cum ano habent aperturam.
Regio Mamarum, sub postica parte abdomi-
nis, in juniore tantummodo visa, nuda erat,
mamis nondum exsertis.
Anus supra penem, sed quasi ex eodem orificio,
proprio tamen sphinctere cinctus.
94.

of the company were dispatched for that purpose, and very soon afterwards returned with the melancholy news, that they were dead.

Notwithstanding the flattering appearance of the sky, the snow still continued to fall so thick that they could not venture out upon their journey to the ship; but about 8 o'clock a small regular breeze sprung up, which, with the prevailing influence of the sun, at length cleared the air; and they soon after, with great joy, saw the snow fall in large flakes from the trees, a certain sign of an approaching thaw: they now examined more critically the state of their invalids; Briscoe was still very ill, but said, that he thought himself able to walk; and Mr. Buchan was much better than either he or his friends had any reason to expect. They were now, however, pressed by the calls of hunger, to which, after long fasting, every consideration of future good or evil immediately gives way. Before they set forward, therefore, it was unanimously agreed, that they should eat their vulture; the bird was accordingly skinned, and, it being thought best to divide it before it was fit to be eaten, it was cut into ten portions, and every man cooked his own as he thought fit. After this repast, which furnished each of them with about three mouthfuls, they prepared to set out; but it was ten o'clock before the snow was sufficiently gone off to render a march practicable. After a walk of about three hours they were very agreeably surprised to find themselves upon the beach, and much nearer to the ship than they had any reason to expect. Upon reviewing their track from the vessel, they perceived, that, instead of ascending the hill in a line, so as to penetrate into the country, they had made almost a circle round it. When they came on board, they congratulated each other upon their safety, with a joy that no man can feel who has not been exposed to equal danger; and as I had suffered great anxiety at their not returning in the evening of the day on which they set out, I was not wholly without my share.

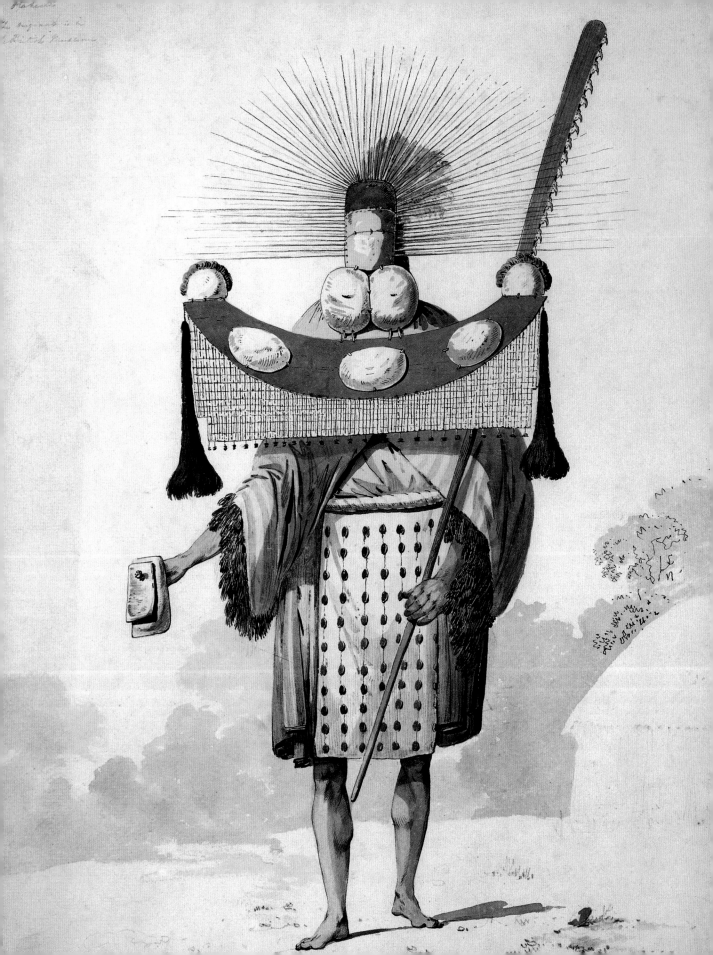

Chapter 3

TAHITI

ENCOUNTERING POLYNESIA

Cook's voyages were remarkable for extended contacts with many Islanders of the Pacific and native peoples of the Pacific Rim. Following the short meeting with Fuegians, those contacts were inaugurated by a stay of four months at Tahiti. Some of the mariners had already visited the island with Wallis in the Dolphin *in 1767, and they renewed friendships they had established with Islanders at that time.*

ABOUT ONE O'CLOCK, ON Monday the 10th of April [1769], some of the people who were looking out for the island to which we were bound, said they saw land ahead, in that part of the horizon where it was expected to appear; but it was so faint that, whether there was land in sight or not, remained a matter of dispute till sunset. The next morning, however, at six o'clock, we were convinced that those who said they had discovered land, were not mistaken; it appeared to be very high and mountainous, extending from W. by S ½ S. to W. by N. ½ N. and we knew it to be the same that Captain Wallis had called King George the III.'s Island. We were delayed in our approach to it by light airs and calms, so that in the morning of the 12th we were but little nearer than we had been the night before; but about seven a breeze sprung up, and before eleven several canoes were seen making towards the ship: there were but few of them, however, that would come near; and the people in those that did, could not be persuaded to come on board. In every canoe there were young plantains, and branches of a tree which the Indians call *E'Midho*; these, as we afterwards learnt, were brought as tokens of peace and amity, and the people in one of the canoes handed them up the ship's side, making signals at the same time with great earnestness, which we did not immediately understand; at length we guessed that they wished these symbols should be placed in

OPPOSITE: Among the rituals that most astonished the visitors was that of mourning, led by a "chief mourner" who wore this extraordinary and intricate costume featuring turtle shell, pearl shell, feathers, bark cloth, and a number of other elements.

Tahiti was selected as a suitable site from which to observe the Transit of Venus, following the island's discovery by Cook's predecessor, Samuel Wallis. His initial contacts with the Tahitians had been violent, but peace was then made.

some conspicuous part of the ship; we, therefore, immediately stuck them among the rigging, at which they expressed the greatest satisfaction. We then purchased their cargoes, consisting of cocoa-nuts, and various kinds of fruit, which after our long voyage were very acceptable.

We stood on with an easy sail all night, with soundings from 22 fathom to 12, and about seven o'clock in the morning we came to an anchor in 13 fathom, in Port-royal bay, called by the natives *Matavai*. We were immediately surrounded by the natives in their canoes, who gave us cocoa-nuts, fruit resembling apples, bread-fruit, and some small fishes, in exchange for beads and other trifles. They had with them a pig, which they would not part with for any thing but a hatchet, and therefore we refused to purchase it; because, if we gave them a hatchet for a pig now, we knew they would never afterwards sell one for less, and we could not afford to buy as many as it was probable we should want at that price. The bread-fruit grows on a tree that is about the size of a middling oak: its leaves are frequently a foot and an half long, of an oblong shape, deeply sinuated like those of the fig-tree, which they resemble in consistence and colour, and in the exuding of a white milky juice upon being broken. The fruit is about the size and shape of a child's head, and the surface is reticulated not much unlike a truffle: it is covered with a thin skin, and has a core about as big as the handle of a small knife: the eatable part lies between the skin and the core; it is as white as snow, and somewhat of the consistence of new bread: it must be roasted before it is eaten, being first divided into three or four parts: its taste is insipid, with a slight sweetness somewhat resembling that of the crumb of wheaten-bread mixed with a Jerusalem artichoke.

Among others who came off to the ship was an elderly man, whose name, as we learnt afterwards, was OWHAW, and who was immediately known to Mr. Gore, and several others who had been here with Captain Wallis; as I was informed that he had been very useful to them, I took him on board the ship with some others, and was particularly attentive to gratify him, as I hoped he might also be useful to us.

As our stay here was not likely to be very short, and as it was necessary that the merchandise which we had brought for traffic with the natives should not diminish in its value, which it would certainly have done, if every person had been left at liberty to give what he pleased for such things as he should purchase; at the same time that confusion and quarrels must necessarily have arisen from there being no standard at market: I drew up the following rules, and ordered that they should be punctually observed.

> *Rules to be observed by every person in or belonging to his Majesty's Bark the Endeavour, for the better establishing a regular and uniform trade for provision, &c. with the inhabitants of George's Island.*

"I. To endeavour, by every fair means, to cultivate a friendship with the natives; and to treat them with all imaginable humanity.

II. A proper person, or persons, will be appointed to trade with the natives for all manner of provisions, fruit, and other productions of the earth; and no officer or seaman, or other person belonging to the ship, excepting such as are so appointed, shall trade or offer to trade for any sort of provision, fruit, or other productions of the earth, unless they have leave so to do.

III. Every person employed on shore, on any duty whatsoever, is strictly to attend to the same; and if by any neglect he loseth any of his arms, or working tools, or suffers them to be stolen, the full value thereof will be charged against his pay, according to the custom of the navy in such cases, and he shall receive such farther punishment as the nature of the offence may deserve.

IV. The same penalty will be inflicted on every person who is found to embezzle, trade, or offer to trade, with any part of the ship's stores of what nature soever.

V. No sort of iron, or any thing that is made of iron, or any sort of cloth, or other useful or necessary articles, are to be given in exchange for any thing but provision."

"J. COOK."

As soon as the ship was properly secured, I went on shore with Mr. Banks and Dr. Solander, a party of men under arms, and our friend Owhaw. We were received from the boat by some hundreds of the inhabitants, whose looks at least gave us welcome, though they were struck with such awe, that the first who approached us crouched so low that he almost crept upon his hands and knees. It is remarkable that he, like the people in the canoes, presented to us the same symbol of peace that is known to have been in use among the ancient and mighty nations of the northern hemisphere, the green branch of a tree. We received it with looks and gestures of kindness and satisfaction; and observing that each of them held one in his hand, we immediately gathered every one a bough, and carried it in our hands in the same manner.

They marched with us about half a mile towards the place where the *Dolphin* had watered, conducted by Owhaw; they then made a full stop, and having laid the ground bare, by clearing away all the plants that grew upon it, the principal persons among them threw their green branches upon the naked spot, and made signs that we should do the same; we immediately showed our readiness to comply, and to give a greater solemnity to the rite, the marines were drawn up, and marching in order, each dropped his bough upon those of the Indians, and we followed their example. We then proceeded, and when we came to the watering-place it was intimated to us by signs, that we might occupy that ground, but it happened not to be fit for our purpose. During our walk they had shaken off their first timid sense of our superiority, and were become familiar: they went with us from the watering-place and took a circuit through the woods: as we went along, we distributed beads and other small presents among them, and had the satisfaction to see that they were much gratified. Our circuit was not less than four or five miles, through groves of trees, which were loaded with cocoa-nuts and bread-fruit, and afforded the most grateful shade. Under these trees were the habitations of the people, most of them being only a roof without walls, and the whole scene realized the poetical fables of Arcadia. We remarked however, not without some regret, that in all our walk we had seen only two hogs, and not a single fowl. Those of our company who had been here with the *Dolphin* told us, that none of the people whom we had yet seen were of the first class; they suspected that the chiefs had removed, and upon carrying us to the place where what they called the Queen's palace had stood, we found that no traces of it were left. We determined therefore to return in the morning, and endeavour to find out the *Noblesse* in their retreats.

This unique sculpture, perhaps originally part of a lintel, was probably collected during Cook's and Banks's tour of Tahiti in late June 1769. Now in the collections of the Museum of Archaeology and Anthropology in Cambridge, it is the first work of sculpture from Oceania collected by any European that remains extant today.

In the morning, however, before we could leave the ship, several canoes came about us, most of them from the westward, and two of them were filled with people, who by their dress and deportment appeared to be of a superior rank: two of these came on board, and each singled out his friend; one of them, whose name we found to be MATAHAH, fixed upon Mr. Banks, and the other upon me: this ceremony consisted in taking off great part of their clothes and putting them upon us. In return for this, we presented each of them with a hatchet and some beads. Soon after they made signs for us to go with them to the places where they lived, pointing

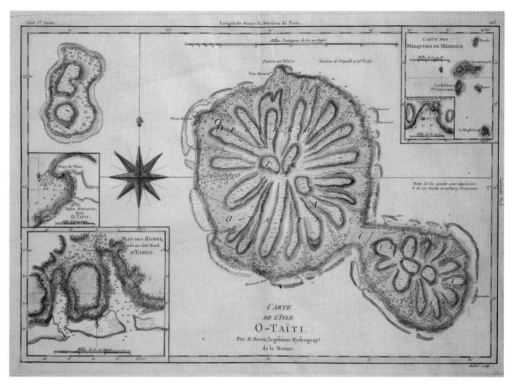

Following his tour of the island, Cook produced this vivid map that was subsequently printed in several editions of his voyages.

to the S.W.; and as I was desirous of finding a more commodious harbour, and making farther trial of the disposition of the people, I consented.

I ordered out two boats, and with Mr. Banks and Dr. Solander, the other gentlemen, and our two Indian friends, we embarked for our expedition. After rowing about a league, they made signs that we should go on shore, and gave us to understand that this was the place of their residence. We accordingly landed, among several hundreds of the natives, who conducted us into a house of much greater length than any we had seen. When we entered, we saw a middle-aged man, whose name we afterwards discovered to be TOOTAHAH; mats were immediately spread, and we were desired to sit down over against him. Soon after we were seated, he ordered a cock and hen to be brought out, which he presented to Mr. Banks and me; we accepted the present, and in a short time each of us received a piece of cloth, perfumed after their manner, by no means disagreeably, which they took great pains to make us remark. The piece presented to Mr. Banks was eleven yards long and two wide; in return for which, he gave a laced silk neckcloth, which he happened to have on, and a linen pocket handkerchief: Tootahah immediately dressed himself in this new finery, with an air of perfect complacency and satisfaction. But it is now time that I should take some notice of the ladies.

* * *

ABOVE: In the 1990s it was discovered that the Raiatean priest Tupaia was the artist of a series of sketches previously thought to have been made by an untrained European artist during Cook's first voyage. This particular piece represents Tahitian houses and important trees and plants, including breadfruit, coconut palms, and pandanus, from which mats were woven.

SOON AFTER THE interchanging of our presents with Tootahah, they attended us to several large houses, in which we walked about with great freedom: they shewed us all the civility of which, in our situation, we could accept; and, on their part, seemed to have no scruple that would have prevented its being carried farther. The houses, which as I have observed before, are all open, except a roof, afforded no place of retirement; but the ladies, by frequently pointing to the mats upon the ground, and sometimes seating themselves and drawing us down upon them, left us no room to doubt of their being much less jealous of observation than we were.

We now took leave of our friendly Chief, and directed our course along the shore; when we had walked about a mile, we met, at the head of a great number of people, another Chief, whose name was TUBOURAI TAMAIDE, with whom we were also to ratify a treaty of peace, with the ceremony of which we were now become better acquainted. Having received the branch which he presented to us, and given another in return, we laid our hands upon our left breasts, and pronounced the word *Taio*, which we supposed to signify friend; the Chief then gave us to understand, that if we chose to eat, he had victuals ready for us. We accepted his offer, and dined very heartily upon fish, bread-fruit, cocoa-nuts and plantains, dressed after their manner; they eat some of their fish raw, and raw fish was offered to us, but we declined that part of the entertainment.

During this visit a wife of our noble host, whose name was TOMIO, did Mr. Banks the honour to place herself upon the same matt, close by him. Tomio was not in the first bloom of her youth, nor did she appear to have been ever remarkable for her beauty: he did not therefore, I believe, pay her the most flattering attention: it happened too, as a farther mortification to this lady, that seeing a very pretty girl among the crowd, he, not adverting to the dignity of his companion, beckoned her to come to him: the girl, after some entreaty, complied, and sat down on the other side of him; he loaded her with beads, and every showy trifle that would please her: his Princess, though she was somewhat mortified at the preference that was given to her rival, did not discontinue her civilities, but still assiduously supplied him with the milk of the cocoa-nut, and such other dainties as were in her reach. This scene might possibly have become more curious and interesting, if it had not been suddenly interrupted by an interlude of a more serious kind. Just at this time, Dr. Solander and Mr. Monkhouse complained that their pockets had been picked. Dr. Solander had lost an opera glass in a shagreen case, and Mr. Monkhouse his snuff-box. This incident unfortunately put an end to the good-humour of the company. Complaint of the injury was made to the Chief; and, to give it weight, Mr. Banks started up, and hastily struck the but end of his firelock upon the ground: this action, and the noise that accompanied it, struck the whole assembly with a panic, and every one of the natives ran out of the house with the utmost precipitation, except the Chief, three women, and two or three others, who appeared by their dress to be of a superior rank.

The Chief, with a mixture of confusion and concern, took Mr. Banks by the hand, and led him to a large quantity of cloth, which lay at the other end of the house: this he offered to him piece by piece, intimating by signs, that if that would atone for the wrong which had been done, he might take any part of it, or, if he pleased, the whole. Mr. Banks put it by, and gave him to understand, that he wanted nothing but what had been dishonestly taken away. Toubourai Tamaide then went hastily out, leaving Mr. Banks with his wife Tomio, who during the whole scene of terror and confusion had kept constantly at his side, and intimating his desire that he should wait there till his return. Mr. Banks accordingly sat down, and conversed with her, as well as he could by signs, about half an hour. The chief then came back with the snuff-box and the case of the opera glass in his hand, and, with a joy in his countenance that was painted with a strength of expression which distinguishes these people from all others, delivered them to the owners. The case of the opera glass, however, upon being opened, was found to be empty; upon this discovery, his countenance changed in a moment; and catching Mr. Banks again by the hand, he rushed out of the house, without uttering any sound, and led him along the shore, walking with great rapidity: when they had got about a mile from the house, a woman met him and gave him a piece of cloth, which he hastily took from her, and continued to press forward with it in his hand. Dr. Solander and Mr. Monkhouse had followed them, and they came at length to a house where they were received by a woman, to whom he gave the cloth, and intimated to the gentlemen that they should give her some beads. They immediately complied; and the beads and cloth being deposited upon the floor, the woman went out, and in about half an hour returned with the opera glass, expressing the same joy upon the occasion that had before been expressed by the Chief. The beads were now returned, with an inflexible resolution not to accept them; and the cloth was, with with the same pertinacity, forced upon Dr. Solander, as a recompence for the injury that had been done him. He could not avoid accepting the cloth, but insisted in his turn upon giving a new present of beads to the woman. It will not perhaps be easy to account for all the steps that were taken in the recovery of this glass and snuff-box; but this cannot be thought strange, considering that the scene of action was among a people whose language, policy and connections are even now but imperfectly known; upon the whole, however, they show an intelligence and influence which would do honour to any system of government, however regular and improved. In the evening, about six o'clock, we returned to the ship.

M. A. Rooker delt from a Sketch by W. Wilson.

The great *marae* of Mahaiatea on Tahiti's western coast, shown in a missionary view from the end of the eighteenth century, was one of the Tahitian temples Cook and his companions visited.

J. Landseer sculp.t

TAHITI

ENCOUNTERING CUSTOM

Tahiti would become renowned, even notorious among Europeans, for the opulence of its climate, the civility of its people, and the supposed licentiousness of their customs. A description of an extraordinary scene of apparently "customary" public sexual intercourse led to Hawkesworth's Account being censured for indecency; the occasion was probably rather a parody of the sailors' eagerness to seek sexual favors in exchange for iron and other trade goods. But the visitors also made serious efforts to describe and interpret intriguing practices, such as the funeral ceremony involving the spectacularly costumed "chief mourner."

FRIDAY, THE 12TH OF MAY [1769], was distinguished by a visit from some ladies whom we had never seen before, and who introduced themselves with some very singular ceremonies. Mr. Banks was trading in his boat at the gate of the fort as usual, in company with Tootahah, who had that morning paid him a visit, and some other of the natives; between nine and ten o'clock, a double canoe came to the landing-place, under the awning of which sat a man and two women: the Indians that were about him made signs that he should go out to meet them, which he hasted to do; but by the time he could get out of the boat, they had advanced within ten yards of him: they then stopped, and made signs that he should do so too, laying down about a dozen young plantain trees, and some other small plants: he complied, and the people having made a lane between them, the man, who appeared to be a servant, brought them to Mr. Banks by one of each at a time; passing and repassing six times, and always pronouncing a short sentence when he delivered them. Tupia, who stood by Mr. Banks, acted as his master of the ceremonies, and receiving the branches as they were brought, laid them

OPPOSITE: This color litho depicting Cook's arrival in Tahiti in 1769 was created to accompany the 1910 edition of *The Life and Voyages of Captain James Cook*, a selection edited by C. G. Cash.

Adzes such as these, with basalt blades affixed to the handles with fine sinnet (a coconut-fiber string), were used in canoe construction and woodworking.

down in the boat. When this was done, another man brought a large bundle of cloth, which having opened, he spread piece by piece upon the ground, in the space between Mr. Banks and his visitors; there were nine pieces and having laid three pieces one upon another, the foremost of the women, who seemed to be the principal, and who was called OORATTOOA, stepped upon them, and taking up her garments all round her to the waist, turned about, with great composure and deliberation, and with an air of perfect innocence and simplicity, three times; when this was done, she dropped the veil, and stepping off the cloth, three more pieces were laid on, and she repeated the ceremony, then stepping off as before; the last three were laid on, and the ceremony was repeated in the same manner the third time. Immediately after this the cloth was rolled up, and given to Mr. Banks, as a present from the lady, who, with her friend, came up and saluted him. He made such presents to them both as he thought would be most acceptable, and after having staid about an hour they went away. In the evening, the Gentlemen at the fort had a visit from Oberea, and her favourite female attendant, whose name was OTHEOTHEA, an agreeable girl, whom they were the more pleased to see, because, having been some days absent, it had been reported that she was either sick or dead.

On the 13th, the market being over about ten o'clock, Mr. Banks walked into the woods with his gun, as he generally did, for the benefit of the shade in the heat of the day: as he was returning back, he met Tubourai Tamaide, near his occasional dwelling, and stopping to spend a little time with him, he suddenly took the gun out of Mr. Banks's hand, cocked it, and, holding it up in the air, drew the trigger: fortunately for him, it flashed in the pan: Mr. Banks immediately took it from him, not a little surprised how he had acquired sufficient knowlege of a gun to discharge it, and reproved him with great severity for what he had done. As it was of infinite importance to keep the Indians totally ignorant of the management of fire-arms, he had taken every opportunity of intimating that they could never offend him so highly as by even touching his piece; it was now proper to enforce this prohibition, and he therefore added threats to his

The mariners were astonished by Tahitian tattoo, and many sailors, in fact, had themselves tattooed during the visit, possibly with these particular implements, which were collected and later presented by Cook to his Admiralty patron, the Earl of Sandwich.

reproof: the Indian bore all patiently; but the moment Mr. Banks crossed the river, he set off with all his family and furniture for his house at Eparre. This being quickly known from the Indians at the fort, and great inconvenience being apprehended from the displeasure of this man, who upon all occasions had been particularly useful, Mr. Banks determined to follow him without delay, and solicit his return: he set out the same evening, accompanied by Mr. Mollineux, and found him sitting in the middle of a large circle of people, to whom he had probably related what had happened, and his fears of the consequences; he was himself the very picture of grief and dejection, and the same passions were strongly marked in the countenances of all the people that surrounded him. When Mr. Banks and Mr. Mollineux went into the circle, one of the women expressed her trouble, as Terapo had done upon another occasion, and struck a shark's tooth into her head several times, till it was covered with blood. Mr. Banks lost no time in putting an end to this universal distress; he assured the Chief, that every thing which had passed should be forgotten, that there was not the least animosity remaining on one side, nor any thing to be feared on the other. The Chief was soon soothed into confidence and complacency, a double canoe was ordered to be got ready, they all returned together to the fort before supper, and as a pledge of perfect reconciliation, both he and his wife slept all night in Mr. Banks's tent: their presence, however, was no palladium; for, between eleven and twelve o'clock, one of the natives attempted to get into the fort by scaling the walls, with a design, no doubt, to steal whatever he should happen to find; he was discovered by the centinel, who happily did not fire, and he ran away much faster than any of our people could follow him. The iron, and iron-tools, which were in continual use at the armourer's forge, that was set up within the works, were temptations to theft which none of these people could withstand.

On the 14th, which was Sunday, I directed that Divine Service should be performed at the fort: we were desirous that some of the principal Indians should be present, but when the hour came, most of them were returned home. Mr. Banks, however, crossed the river, and brought back Tubourai Tamaide and his wife Tomio, hoping that it would give occasion to some enquiries on their part, and some instruction on ours: having seated them, he placed himself between them, and during the whole service, they very attentively observed his behaviour, and very exactly imitated it; standing, sitting, or kneeling, as they saw him do: they were conscious that we were employed about somewhat serious and important, as appeared by their calling to the Indians without the fort to be silent; yet when the service was over, neither of them asked any questions, nor would they attend to any attempt that was made to explain what had been done.

Such were our Matins; our Indians thought fit to perform Vespers of a very different kind. A young man, near six feet high, performed the rites of Venus with a little girl about eleven or twelve years of age, before several of our people, and a great number of the natives, without the least sense of its being indecent or improper, but, as appeared, in perfect conformity to the custom of the place. Among the spectators were several women of superior rank, particularly Oberea, who may properly be said to have assisted at the ceremony; for they gave instructions to the girl how to perform her part, which, young as she was, she did not seem much to stand in need of.

This incident is not mentioned as an object of idle curiosity, but as it deserves consideration in determining a question which has been long debated in philosophy; Whether the shame attending certain actions, which are allowed on all sides to be in themselves innocent, is implanted in Nature, or superinduced by custom? If it has its origin in custom, it will, perhaps, be found difficult to trace that custom, however general, to its source; if in instinct, it will be equally difficult to discover from what cause it is subdued or at least over-ruled among these people, in whose manners not the least trace of it is to be found.

* * *

ON THE 5TH, we kept his Majesty's birth-day; for though it is the 4th, we were unwilling to cele- brate it during the absence of the two parties who had been sent out to observe the Transit. We had several of the Indian Chiefs at our entertainment, who drank his Majesty's health by the name of Kihiargo, which was the nearest imitation they could produce of King George.

About this time died an old woman of some rank, who was related to Tomio, which gave us an opportunity to see how they disposed of the body, and confirmed us in our opinion that these people, contrary to the present custom of all other nations now known, never bury their dead. In the middle of a small square, neatly railed in with bamboo, the awning of a canoe was raised upon two posts, and under this the body was deposited upon such a frame as has before been described: it was covered with fine cloth, and near it was placed bread-fruit, fish, and other provisions: we supposed that the food was placed there for the spirit of the deceased, and consequently, that these Indians had some confused notion of a separate state; but upon our applying for further information to Tubourai Tamaide, he told us, that the food was placed there as an offering to their gods. They do not, however, suppose, that the gods eat, any more than the Jews supposed that Jehovah could dwell in a house: the offering is made here upon the same principle as the Temple was built at Jerusalem, as an expression of reverence and gratitude, and a solicitation of the more immediate presence of the Deity. In the front of the area was a kind of stile, where the relations

This breastplate, or
taumi, of feathers, shells,
and wicker was the work of a
Society Islander of high status.

of the deceased stood to pay the tribute of their sorrow; and under the awning were innumerable small pieces of cloth, on which the tears and blood of the mourners had been shed; for in their paroxysms of grief it is a universal custom to wound themselves with the shark's tooth. Within a few yards two occasional houses were set up, in one of which some relations of the deceased constantly resided, and in the other the chief mourner, who is always a man, and who keeps there a very singular dress in which a ceremony is performed that will be described in its turn. Near the place where the dead are thus set up to rot, the bones are afterwards buried.

What can have introduced among these people the custom of exposing their dead above ground, till the flesh is consumed by putrefaction, and then burying the bones, it is perhaps impossible to guess; but it is remarkable, that Ælian and Apollonius Rhodius impute a similar practice to the ancient inhabitants of Colchis, a country near Pontus in Asia, now called Mingrelia; except that among them this manner of disposing of the dead did not extend to both sexes: the women they buried; but the men they wrapped in a hide, and hung up in the air by a chain. This practice among the Colchians is referred to a religious cause. The principal objects of their worship were the Earth and the Air; and it is supposed that, in consequence of some superstitious notion, they devoted their dead to both. Whether the natives of Otaheite had any

ABOVE: This panorama was taken by Mark Adams from Point Venus, the site of Cook's encampment and several momentous early encounters between Europeans and Tahitians during the late eighteenth and early nineteenth centuries.

notion of the same kind we were never able certainly to determine; but we soon discovered, that the repositories of their dead were also places of worship. Upon this occasion it may be observed, that nothing can be more absurd than the notion that the happiness or misery of a future life depends, in any degree, upon the disposition of the body when the state of probation is past; yet that nothing is more general than a solicitude about it. However cheap we may hold any funereal rites which custom has not familiarized, or superstition rendered sacred, most men gravely deliberate how to prevent their body from being broken by the mattock and devoured by the worm, when it is no longer capable of sensation; and purchase a place for it in holy ground, when they believe the lot of its future existence to be irrevocably determined. So strong is the association of pleasing or painful ideas with certain opinions and actions which affect us while we live, that we involuntarily act as if it was equally certain that they would affect us in the same manner when we are dead, though this is an opinion that nobody will maintain. Thus it happens, that the desire of preserving from reproach even the name that we leave behind us, or of procuring it honour, is one of the most powerful principles of action, among the inhabitants of the most speculative and enlightened nations. Posthumous reputation, upon every principle, must be acknowledged to have no influence upon the dead; yet the desire of obtaining and securing it, no force of reason, no habits of thinking can subdue, except in those whom habitual baseness and guilt have rendered indifferent to honour and shame while they lived. This indeed seems to be among the happy imperfections of our nature, upon which the general good of society in a certain measure depends; for as some crimes are supposed to be prevented by hanging the body of the criminal in chains after he is dead, so in consequence of the same association of ideas, much good is procured to society, and, much evil prevented, by a desire of preventing disgrace or procuring honour to a name, when nothing but a name remains.

* * *

ON THE 10TH, the ceremony was to be performed, in honour of the old woman whose sepulchral tabernacle has just been described, by the chief mourner; and Mr. Banks had so great a curiosity to see all the mysteries of the solemnity, that he determined to take a part in it, being told, that he could be present upon no other condition. In the evening, therefore, he repaired to the place where the body lay, and was received by the daughter of the deceased, and several other persons, among whom was a boy about fourteen years old, who were to assist in the ceremony. Tubourai Tamaide was to be the principal mourner; and his dress, which was extremely fantastical, though not unbecoming, is represented by a figure in one of the plates. Mr. Banks was stripped of his European clothes, and a small piece of cloth being tied round his middle, his body was smeared with charcoal and water, as low as the shoulders, till it was as black as that of a negroe: the same operation was performed upon several others, among whom were some women, who were reduced to a state as near to nakedness as himself; the boy was blacked all over, and then the procession set forward. Tubourai Tamaide uttered something, which was supposed to be a prayer, near the body; and did the same when he came up to his own house: when this was done, the procession was continued towards the fort, permission having been obtained to approach it upon this occasion. It is the custom of the Indians to fly from these processions with the utmost precipitation, so that as soon as those who were about the fort, saw it at a distance, they hid themselves in the woods. It proceeded from the fort along the shore, and put to flight another body of Indians, consisting of more than an hundred, every one hiding himself under the first shelter that he could find: it then crossed the river, and entered the woods, passing several houses, all which were deserted, and not a single Indian could be seen during the rest of the procession, which continued more than half an hour. The office that Mr. Banks performed, was called that of the Nineveh, of which there were two besides himself; and the natives having all disappeared, they came to the chief mourner, and said imatata, there are no people, after which the company was dismissed to wash themselves in the river, and put on their customary apparel.

Chapter 5

NEW ZEALAND

ENCOUNTERING WARRIORS

The Endeavour *made her way south in search of the Great South Land. On reaching New Zealand, visited some 130 years earlier by the Dutch navigator Abel Tasman, he was concerned to identify the limits of the landmasses and circumnavigated both main islands. Again, the discovery of people was most challenging. The Maori were related to the Polynesians of the tropics but resisted initial contacts vigorously.*

ON THE NEXT DAY, Friday, October the 6th [1769], we saw land from the mast-head, bearing W. by N. and stood directly for it; in the evening it could just be discerned from the deck, and appeared large. The variation this day was, by azimuth and amplitude, 15° 4' ½ E. and by observation made of the sun and moon, the longitude of the ship appeared to be 180° 55' W. and by the medium of this and subsequent observations, there appeared to be an error in the ship's account of longitude during her run from Otaheite of 3° 16', she being so much to the westward of the longitude resulting from the log. At midnight, I brought to and sounded, but had no ground with one hundred and seventy fathom.

On the 7th, it fell calm, we therefore approached the land slowly, and in the afternoon, when a breeze sprung up, we were still distant seven or eight leagues. It appeared still larger as it was more distinctly seen, with four or five ranges of hills, rising one over the other, and a chain of mountains above all, which appeared to be of an enormous height. This land became the subject of much eager conversation; but the general opinion seemed to be that we had found the *Terra australis incognita*. About five o'clock we saw the opening of a bay, which seemed to run pretty far

OPPOSITE: The voyagers found *ta moko*, Maori tattoo, daunting—particularly the full-face designs worn by many men. One of the voyage artists, Sidney Parkinson, created this vivid study, one the first European images of what is now a world-famous form of body art. European audiences were fascinated by such images of the Maori, and artworks made during the voyages were reprinted many times.

inland, upon which we hauled our wind and stood in for it; we also saw smoke ascending from different places on shore. When night came on, however, we kept plying off and on till day-light, when we found ourselves to the leeward of the bay, the wind being at north: we could now perceive that the hills were cloathed with wood, and that some of the trees in the valleys were very large. By noon we fetched in with the south west point; but not being able to weather it, tacked and stood off: at this time we saw several canoes standing cross the bay, which in a little time made to shore, without seeming to take the least notice of the ship; we also saw some houses, which appeared to be small, but neat; and near one of them a considerable number of the people

Like many of his precursors, Cook's first voyage had the larger purpose of searching for the Great Southern Land—*Terra australis incognita*—that had long been an object of geographic speculation. This seventeenth-century map of the Americas by the Flemish cartographer Jodocus Hondius proposes a depiction of the hypothetical continent.

Maori fortifications on top of an arched rock in Mercury Bay with a war canoe in the foreground. Though the feature still existed in the 1860s, it collapsed sometime later.

collected together, who were sitting upon the beach, and who, we thought, were the same that we had seen in the canoes. Upon a small peninsula, at the north east head, we could plainly perceive a pretty high and regular paling, which inclosed the whole top of a hill; this was also the subject of much speculation, some supposing it to be a park of deer, others an inclosure for oxen and sheep. About four o'clock in the afternoon, we anchored on the north west side of the bay, before the entrance of a small river, in ten fathom water, with a fine sandy bottom, and at about half a league from the shore. The sides of the bay are white cliffs of a great height; the middle is low land, with hills gradually rising behind, one towering above another, and terminating in the chain of mountains which appeared to be far inland.

In the evening I went on shore, accompanied by Mr. Banks and Dr. Solander, with the pinnace and yawl, and a party of men. We landed abreast of the ship, on the east side of the river, which was here about forty yards broad; but seeing some natives on the west side whom I wished to speak with, and finding the river not fordable, I ordered the yawl in to carry us over, and left the pinnace at the entrance. When we came near the place where the people were assembled, they all ran away; however, we landed, and leaving four boys to take care of the yawl, we walked up to some huts which were about two or three hundred yards from the water-side. When we had got some distance from the boat, four men, armed with long lances, rushed out of the woods, and running up to attack the boat, would certainly have cut her off, if the people in the pinnace had not discovered them, and called to the boys to drop down the stream: the boys instantly obeyed; but being closely pursued by the Indians, the Cockswain of the pinnace, who had the charge of the boats, fired a musquet over their heads; at this they stopped and looked round them, but in a few minutes renewed the pursuit, brandishing their lances in a threatening manner: the Cockswain then fired a second musquet over their heads, but of this they took no notice; and one of them lifting up his spear to dart it at the boat, another piece was fired, which shot him dead. When he fell, the other three stood motionless for some minutes, as if petrified with astonishment; as soon as they recovered, they went back, dragging after them the dead body, which however they soon left, that it might not incumber their flight. At the report of the first musquet we drew together, having straggled to a little distance from each other, and made the best of our way back to the boat; and crossing the river, we soon saw the Indian lying dead upon the ground. Upon examining the body, we found that he had been shot through the heart: he was a man of the middle size and stature; his complexion was brown, but not very dark; and one side of his face was tattowed in spiral lines of a very regular figure: he was covered with a fine cloth, of a manufacture altogether new to us, and it was tied on exactly according to the representation in Valentyn's Account of Abel Tasman's Voyage, vol. iii. part 2. page 50. His hair also was tied in a knot on the top of his head, but had no feather in it. We returned immediately to the ship, where we could hear the people on shore talking with great earnestness, and in a very loud tone, probably about what had happened, and what should be done.

In the morning, we saw several of the natives where they had been seen the night before, and some walking with a quick pace towards the place where we had landed, most of them unarmed; but three or four with long pikes in their hands. As I was desirous to establish an intercourse with them, I ordered three boats to be manned with seamen and marines, and proceeded towards the shore, accompanied by Mr. Banks, Dr. Solander, the other Gentlemen, and Tupia; about fifty of them seemed to wait for our landing, on the opposite side of the river, which we thought a sign of fear, and seated themselves upon the ground: at first, therefore, myself, with only Mr. Banks, Dr. Solander, and Tupia, landed from the little boat, and advanced towards them; but we had not proceeded many paces before they all started up, and every man produced either a long pike, or a small weapon of green Talc, extremely well polished, about a foot long, and thick enough to weigh four or five pounds: Tupia called to them in the language of Otaheite; but they answered only by flourishing their weapons, and making signs to us to depart; a musquet was then fired wide of them, and the ball struck the water, the river being still between us: they saw the effect, and desisted from their threats; but we thought it prudent to retreat till the marines could be landed. This was soon done; and they marched, with a jack carried before them, to a little bank, about fifty yards from the water-side; here they were drawn up, and I again advanced, with Mr. Banks and Dr. Solander; Tupia, Mr. Green, and Mr. Monkhouse, being with us. Tupia was again directed to speak to them, and it was with great pleasure that we perceived he was perfectly understood, he and the natives speaking only different dialects of the same language. He told them that we wanted provision and water, and would give them iron in exchange, the properties of which he explained as well as he was able. They were willing to trade, and desired that we would come over to them for that purpose: to this we consented,

OPPOSITE: Though the Dutch explorer Abel Tasman had visited and named New Zealand in 1642, Cook was the first to circumnavigate both main islands. This chart records the indigenous names for the North Island, Te Ahi o Maui (Maui's fire), and for the South Island, Te Wai Pounamu (the Greenstone Land).

S. Parkinson del.   T. Chambers Sc.

A New Zealand Warrior in his Proper Dress, &
Compleatly Armed, According to their Manner.

ABOVE: The priest Tupaia depicted Joseph Banks exchanging a sheet of paper for a crayfish in northern New Zealand. The Maori on the left wears a feather cloak, an indication of high status. Tupaia accompanied Cook as a navigator but died of malaria in the present-day Jakarta.

OPPOSITE: The Europeans found the Maori formidably impressive. This man bears a long club of the type known as *tewhatewha*, a number of which were collected by the voyagers.

provided they would lay by their arms; which, however, they could by no means be persuaded to do. During this conversation, Tupia warned us to be upon our guard, for that they were not our friends: we then pressed them in our turn to come over to us; and at last one of them stripped himself, and swam over without his arms: he was almost immediately followed by two more, and soon after by most of the rest, to the number of twenty or thirty; but these brought their arms with them. We made them all presents of iron and beads; but they seemed to set little value upon either, particularly the iron, not having the least idea of its use; so that we got nothing in return but a few feathers: they offered indeed to exchange their arms for ours, and, when we refused, made many attempts to snatch them out of our hands. As soon as they came over, Tupia repeated his declaration, that they were not our friends, and again warned us to be upon our guard; their attempts to snatch our weapons, therefore, did not succeed; and we gave them to understand by Tupia, that we should be obliged to kill them if they offered any farther violence. In a few minutes, however, Mr. Green happening to turn about, one of them snatched away his hanger, and retiring to a little distance, waved it round his head, with a shout of exultation: the rest now began to be extremely insolent, and we

The pohutukawa tree, with its bright red flowers, is an emblem of New Zealand's beaches and coasts. This engraving of *Metrosideros excelsa* depicts a specimen collected during the first voyage.

saw more coming to join them from the opposite side of the river. It was therefore become necessary to repress them, and Mr. Banks fired at the man who had taken the hanger with small shot, at the distance of about fifteen yards: when the shot struck him, he ceased his cry; but instead of returning the hanger, continued to flourish it over his head, at the same time slowly retreating to a greater distance. Mr. Monkhouse seeing this, fired at him with ball, and he instantly dropped. Upon this the main body, who had retired to a rock in the middle of the river upon the first discharge, began to return; two that were near to the man who had been killed, ran up to the body, one seized his weapon of green Talc, and the other endeavoured to secure the hanger, which Mr. Monkhouse had but just time to prevent. As all that had retired to the rock were now advancing, three of us discharged our pieces, loaded only with small shot, upon which they swam back for the shore; and we perceived, upon their landing, that two or three of them were wounded. They retired slowly up the country, and we reimbarked in our boats.

As we had unhappily experienced that nothing was to be done with these people at this place, and finding the water in the river to be salt, I proceeded in the boats round the bead of the bay in search of fresh water, and with a design, if possible, to surprise some of the natives, and take them on board, where by kind treatment and presents I might obtain their friendship, and by their means establish an amicable correspondence with their countrymen.

To my great regret, I found no place where I could land, a dangerous surf every where beating upon the shore; but I saw two canoes coming in from the sea, one under sail, and the other worked with paddles. I thought this a favourable opportunity to get some of the people into my possession without mischief, as those in the canoe were probably fishermen and without arms, and I had three boats full of men. I therefore disposed the boats so as most effectually to intercept them in their way to the shore; the people in the canoe that was paddled perceived us so soon, that by making to the nearest land with their utmost strength, they escaped us; the other sailed on till she was in the midst of us, without discerning what we were; but the moment she discovered us, the people on board struck their sail, and took to their paddles, which they plied so briskly that she out-ran the boat. They were however within hearing, and Tupia called out to them to come along side, and promised for us that they should come to no hurt: they chose, however, rather to trust to their paddles than our promises, and continued to make from us with all their power. I then ordered a musquet to be fired over their heads, as the least exceptionable expedient to accomplish my design, hoping it would either make them surrender or leap into the water. Upon the discharge of the piece, they ceased paddling; and all of them, being seven in number, began to strip, as we imagined to jump overboard; but it happened otherwise. They immediately

ABOVE RIGHT: *Patu* hand clubs in this form were made of wood, whalebone, and greenstone, as well as, in the case of the example shown, basalt. While these were deadly weapons used in hand-to-hand fighting, they were also aesthetically refined and much admired for their balance and finish.

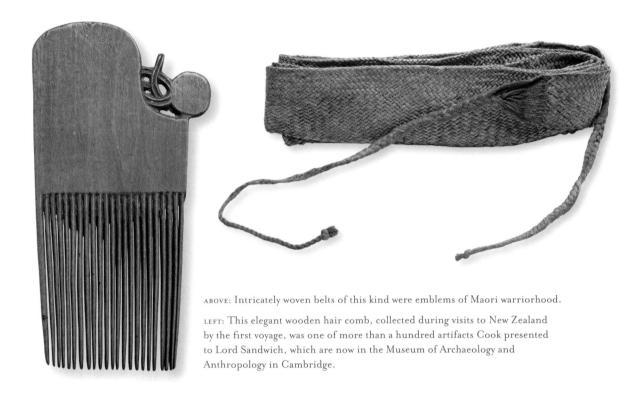

ABOVE: Intricately woven belts of this kind were emblems of Maori warriorhood.

LEFT: This elegant wooden hair comb, collected during visits to New Zealand by the first voyage, was one of more than a hundred artifacts Cook presented to Lord Sandwich, which are now in the Museum of Archaeology and Anthropology in Cambridge.

formed a resolution not to fly, but to fight; and when the boat came up, they began the attack with their paddles, and with stones and other offensive weapons that were in the boat, so vigorously, that we were obliged to fire upon them in our own defence: four were unhappily killed, and the other three who were boys, the eldest about nineteen, and the youngest about eleven, instantly leaped into the water; the eldest swam with great vigour, and resisted the attempts of our people to take him into the boat by every effort that he could make: he was however at last overpowered, and the other two were taken up with less difficulty. I am conscious that the feeling of every reader of humanity will censure me for having fired upon these unhappy people, and it is impossible that, upon a calm review, I should approve it myself. They certainly did not deserve death for not chusing to confide in my promises; or not consenting to come on board my boat, even if they had apprehended no danger; but the nature of my service required me to obtain a knowlege of their country, which I could no otherwise effect than by forcing my way into it in a hostile manner, or gaining admission through the confidence and good-will of the people. I had already tried the power of presents without effect; and I was now prompted, by my desire to avoid further hostilities, to get some of them on board, as the only method left of convincing them that we intended them no harm, and had it in our power to contribute to their gratification and convenience. Thus far my intentions certainly were not criminal; and though in the contest, which I had not the least reason to expect, our victory might have been complete without so great an expence of life; yet in such situations, when the command to fire has been given, no man can restrain its excess, or prescribe its effect.

Among the New Zealand plants Sydney Parkinson documented was *Phormium tenax*, or flax, from which Maori made prestigious cloaks. Banks was very interested in this useful plant, which was later introduced to Europe.

Chapter 6

NEW ZEALAND

CONSTERNATION AND CANNIBALISM

Cook and his companions were impressed by the Maori but astonished and troubled to discover a "horrid custom" among them: they consumed the bodies of slain enemies. Cook struggled to make sense of what seemed their positive and negative characteristics, as well as of his geographical discoveries up to this stage of the voyage.

[JANUARY 1770] THE SHORE at this place seemed to form several bays, into one of which I proposed to carry the ship, which was become very foul, in order to careen her, and at the same time repair some defects, and recruit our wood and water.

With this view, I kept plying on and off all night, having from eighty to sixty-three fathom. At day-break the next morning, I stood for an inlet which runs in S.W.; and at eight I got within the entrance, which may be known by a reef of rocks, stretching from the north west point, and some rocky islands which lie off the south east point. At nine o'clock, there being little wind, and what there was being variable, we were carried by the tide or current within two cables' length of the north west shore, where we had fifty-four fathom water, but by the help of our boats we got clear. Just at this time we saw a sea-lion rise twice near the shore, the head of which exactly resembled that of the male which has been described in the Account of Lord Anson's Voyage. We also saw some of the natives in a canoe cross the bay, and a village situated upon the point of an island which lies seven or eight miles within the entrance. At noon, we were the length of this island, but there being little wind, the boats were ordered ahead to tow. About one o'clock, we hauled close round the south west end of the island; and the inhabitants of the village which was built upon it, were immediately up in arms. About two, we anchored in a very safe and convenient cove, on the north west side of the bay, and facing the south west end of the island, in eleven fathom water, with soft ground, and moored with the stream anchor.

OPPOSITE: Queen Charlotte Sound, at the northern end of the South Island, was a perfect place of respite. Cook would return there several times over the course of the three voyages.

We were about four long cannon shot distant from the the [*sic*] village or Heppah, from which four canoes were immediately dispatched, as we imagined to reconnoitre, and if they should find themselves able, to take us. The men were all well armed, and dressed nearly as they are represented in the figure published by Tasman; two corners of the cloth which they wrapped round the body were passed over the shoulders from behind, and being brought down to the upper edge of it before, were made fast to it just under the breast; but few, or none, had feathers in their hair. They rowed round the ship several times, with their usual tokens of menace and defiance, and at last began the assault by throwing some stones: Tupia expostulated with them, but apparently to very little purpose; and we began to fear that they would oblige us to fire at them, when a very old man in one of the boats expressed a desire of coming on board. We gladly encouraged him in his design, a rope was thrown into his canoe, and she was immediately alongside of the ship: the old man rose up, and prepared to come up the ship's side, upon which all the rest expostulated with great vehemence against the attempt, and at last laid hold of him, and held him back: he adhered however to his purpose with a calm but steady perseverance, and having at length disengaged himself, he came on board. We received him with all possible expressions of friendship and kindness, and after some time dismissed him, with many presents to his companions. As soon as he was returned on board his canoe, the people in all the rest began to dance, but whether as a token of enmity or friendship we could not certainly determine, for we had seen them dance in a disposition both for peace and war. In a short time, however, they retired to their fort, and soon after I went on shore, with most of the gentlemen, at the bottom of the cove, a-breast of the ship.

We found a fine stream of excellent water, and wood in the greatest plenty, for the land here was one forest, of vast extent. As we brought the seine with us, we hauled it once or twice, and with such success that we caught near three hundred weight of fish of different sorts, which was equally distributed among the ship's company.

At day-break, while we were busy in careening the ship, three canoes came off to us, having on board above a hundred men, besides several of their women, which we were pleased to see, as in general it is a sign of peace; but they soon afterwards became very troublesome, and gave us reason to apprehend some mischief from them to the people that were in our boats alongside the ship. While we were in this situation, the long-boat was sent ashore with some water casks, and some of the canoes attempting to follow her, we found it necessary to intimidate them by firing some small shot: we were at such a distance that it was impossible to hurt them, yet our reproof had its effect, and they desisted from the pursuit. They had some fish in their canoes which they now offered to sell, and which, though it stunk, we consented to buy: for this purpose a man in a small boat was sent among them, and they traded for some time very fairly. At length, however, one of them watching his opportunity snatched at some paper which out market-man held in his hand, and missing it, immediately put himself in a posture of defence, flourishing his patoo-patoo, and making show as if he was about to strike; some small shot were then fired at him from the ship, a few of which struck him upon the knee: this put an end to our trade, but the Indians still continued near the ship, rowing round her many times, and conversing with Tupia, chiefly concerning the traditions they had among them with respect to the antiquities of their country. To this subject they were led by the enquiries which Tupia had been directed to make, whether they had ever seen such a vessel as ours, or had ever heard that any such had been upon

The art of *waka* (canoe) construction has been revived in New Zealand. Long Maori canoes are vigorously paddled, as seen in this Glenn Jowitt photograph.

their coast. These enquiries were all answered in the negative, so that tradition has preserved among them no memorial of Tasman; though, by an observation made this day, we find that we are only fifteen miles south of Murderer's bay, our latitude being 41° 5' 32", and Murderer's bay, according to his account, being 40° 50'.

The women in these canoes, and some of the men, had a head-dress which we had not before seen. It consisted of a bunch of black feathers, made up in a round form, and tied upon the top of the head, which it intirely covered, and made it twice as high, to appearance, as it was in reality.

After dinner, I went in the pinnace with Mr. Banks, Dr. Solander, Tupia, and some others, into another cove, about two miles distant from that in which the ship lay: in our way we saw something floating upon the water, which we took for a dead seal, but upon rowing up to it, found it to be the body of a woman, which to all appearance had been dead some days. We proceeded to our cove, where we went on shore, and found a small family of Indians, who appeared to be greatly terrified at our approach, and all ran away except one. A conversation between this person and Tupia soon brought back the rest, except an old man and a child, who still kept aloof, but stood

Aoraki/Mount Cook is the highest point in New Zealand. The first Europeans to see it were likely members of Abel Tasman's first Pacific voyage in 1642. The mountain, however, had been known to the Maori since their arrival there in the 1300s. Aoraki was given the English name Mount Cook in 1851 by Captain John Lort Stokes. Cook, it seems, never laid eyes on the peak.

peeping at us from the woods. Of these people, our curiosity naturally led us to enquire after the body of the woman which we had seen floating upon the water: and they acquainted us, by Tupia, that she was a relation, who had died a natural death; and that, according to their custom, they had tied a stone to the body, and thrown it into the sea, which stone, they supposed, had by some accident been disengaged.

This family, when we came on shore, was employed in dressing some provisions: the body of a dog was at this time buried in their oven, and many provision baskets stood near it. Having cast our eyes carelessly into one of these, as we passed it, we saw two bones pretty cleanly picked, which did not seem to be the bones of a dog, and which, upon a nearer examination, we discovered to be those of a human body. At this sight we were struck with horror, though it was only a confirmation of what we had heard many times since we arrived upon this coast. As we could have no doubt but the bones were human, neither could we have any doubt but that the flesh which covered them had been eaten. They were found in a provision basket; the flesh that remained appeared manifestly to have been dressed by fire, and in the gristles at the end, were the marks of the teeth which had gnawed them: to put an end however to conjecture, founded upon circumstances and appearances, we directed Tupia to ask what bones they were; and the Indians, without the least hesitation, answered, the bones of a man: they were then asked what was become of the flesh, and they replied that they had eaten it; but, said Tupia, why did you not eat the body of the woman which we saw floating upon the water: the woman, said they, died of disease; besides, she was our relation, and we eat only the bodies of our enemies, who are killed in battle. Upon enquiry who the man was whose bones we had found, they told us, that about five days before, a boat belonging to their enemies came into the bay, with many persons on board, and that this man was one of seven whom they had killed. Though stronger evidence of this horrid practice prevailing among the inhabitants of this coast will scarcely be required, we have still stronger to give. One of us asked if they had any human bones with the flesh remaining upon them, and upon their answering us that all had been eaten, we affected to disbelieve that the bones were human, and said that they were the bones of a dog; upon which one of the Indians with some eagerness took hold of his own fore-arm, and thrusting it towards us, said, that the bone which Mr. Banks held in his hand had belonged to that part of a human body; at the same time, to convince us that the flesh had been eaten, he took hold of his own arm with his teeth, and made shew of eating: he also bit and gnawed the bone which Mr. Banks had taken, drawing it through his mouth, and shewing, by signs, that it had afforded a delicious repast; the bone was then returned to Mr. Banks, and he brought it away with him. Among the persons of this family, there was a woman who had her arms, legs, and thighs frightfully cut in several places; and we were told that she had inflicted the wounds upon herself, in token of her grief for the loss of her husband, who had been lately killed and eaten by their enemies, who had come from some place to the eastward, towards which the Indians pointed.

The ship lay at the distance of somewhat less than a quarter of a mile from the shore, and in the morning we were awakened by the singing of the birds: the number was incredible, and they seemed to strain their throats in emulation of each other. This wild melody was infinitely superior to any that we had ever heard of the same kind; it seemed to be like small bells, most exquisitely tuned, and perhaps the distance, and the water between, might be no small advantage to the sound. Upon enquiry, we were informed that, the birds here always began to sing about two hours after midnight, and continuing their musick till sun-rise, were, like our nightingales, silent the rest of the day. In the forenoon, a small canoe came off from the Indian village to the ship, and among those that were in it, was the old man who had first come on board at our arrival in the bay. As soon as it came alongside, Tupia renewed the conversation, that had passed the day before, concerning their practice of eating human flesh, during which they repeated what they had told us already: but, said Tupia, where are the heads? do you eat them too? Of the heads, said the old man, we eat only the brains and the next time I come I will bring some of them to convince you that what we have told you is truth. After some farther conversation between these people and Tupia, they told him that they expected their enemies to come very shortly, to revenge the death of the seven men whom they had killed and eaten.

On the 18th, the Indians were more quiet than usual, no canoe came near the ship, nor did we see one of them moving on the shore, their fishing, and other usual occupations being totally suspended. We thought they expected an attack on this day, and therefore attended more diligently to what passed on shore; but we saw nothing to gratify our curiosity.

After breakfast, we went out in the pinnace, to take a view of the bay, which was of vast extent, and consisted of numberless small harbours and coves, in every direction: we confined our excursion, however, to the western side, and the country being an impenetrable forest where we landed, we could see nothing worthy of notice: we killed, however, a good number of shaggs, which we saw sitting upon their nests in the trees, and which, whether roasted or stewed, we considered as very good provision. As we were returning, we saw a single man in a canoe fishing; we rowed up to him, and to our great surprize he took not the least notice of us, but even when we were alongside of him, continued to follow his occupation, without adverting to us any more than if we had been invisible. He did not, however, appear to be either sullen or stupid: we requested him to draw up his net, that we might examine it, and he readily complied: it was of a circular form, extended by two hoops, and about seven or eight feet in diameter: the top was open, and sea-ears were fastened to the bottom as a bait: this he let down so as to lie upon the ground, and when he thought fish enough were assembled over it, he drew it up by a very gentle and even motion, so that the fish rose with it, scarcely sensible that they were lifted, till they came very near the surface of the water, and then were brought out in the net by a sudden jerk. By this simple method he had caught abundance of fish, and indeed they are so plenty in this bay, that the catching them requires neither much labour nor art.

* * *

THUS FAR OUR NAVIGATION has certainly been unfavourable to the notion of a southern continent, for it has swept away at least three-fourths of the positions upon which it has been founded. The principal navigators, whose authority has been urged on this occasion, are Tasman, Juan Fernandes, Hermite, the commander of a Dutch squadron, Quiros, and Roggewein; and the track of the *Endeavour* has demonstrated that the land seen by these persons, and supposed to be part of a continent, is not so; it has also totally subverted the theoretical arguments which have been brought to prove that the existence of a southern continent is necessary to preserve an equilibrium between the two hemispheres; for upon this principle what we have already proved to be water, would render the southern hemisphere too light. In our rout to the northward, after doubling Cape Horn, when we were in the latitude of 40°, our longitude was 110°; and in our return to the southward, after leaving Ulietea, when we were again in latitude 40°, our longitude was 145°; the difference is 35°. When we were in latitude 30° the difference of longitude between the two tracks was 21°, which continued till we were as low as 20°; but a single view of the chart will convey a better idea of this than the most minute description: yet as upon a view of the chart it will appear that there is a large space extending quite to the Tropics, which neither we, nor any other navigators to our knowlege have explored, and as there will appear to be room enough for the Cape of a southern continent to extend northward into a low southern latitude, I shall give my reasons for believing there is no Cape, of any southern continent, to the northward of 40° south.

Notwithstanding what has been laid down by some geographers in their maps, and alleged by Mr. Dalrymple, with respect to Quiros, it is improbable in the highest degree that he saw to the southward of two islands, which he discovered in latitude 25 or 26, and which I suppose may lie between the longitude of 130° and 140° W. any signs of a continent, much less any thing which, in his opinion, was a known or indubitable sign of such land; for if he had, he would certainly have sailed southward in search of it, and if he had sought, supposing the signs to have been indubitable, he must have found: the discovery of a southern continent was the ultimate object of Quiros's voyage, and no man appears to have had it more at heart; so that if he was in latitude 26° S. and

The view across Poverty Bay on New Zealand's east coast, the site of Cook's first violent encounters with Maori, and of the present-day town of Gisborne.

in longitude 146° W. where Mr. Dalrymple has placed the islands he discovered, it may fairly be inferred that no part of a southern continent extends to that latitude.

It will, I think, appear with equal evidence from the accounts of Roggewein's voyage, that between the longitudes of 130° and 150° W. there is no main land to the northward of 35° S. Mr. Pingre, in a treatise concerning the transit of Venus, which he went out to observe, has inserted an extract of Roggewein's voyage, and a map of the South Seas; and for reasons which may be seen at large in his work, supposes him, after leaving Easter Island, which he places in latitude 28 ½ S. longitude 123° W. to have steered S.W. as high as 34° S. and afterwards W.N.W.; and if this was indeed his rout, the proof that there is no main land to the northward of 35° S. is irre-fragable. Mr. Dalrymple indeed supposes his rout to have been different, and that from Easter Isle he steered N.W. taking a course afterwards very little different from that of La Maire; but I think it is highly improbable that a man, who at his own request was sent to discover a southern continent, should take a course in which La Maire had already proved no continent could be found: it must however be confessed, that Roggewein's track cannot certainly be ascertained, because in the accounts that have been published of his voyage, neither longitudes nor latitudes are mentioned. As to myself I saw nothing that I thought a sign of land, in my rout either to the northward, southward, or westward, till a few days before I made the east coast of New Zealand: I did indeed frequently see large flocks of birds, but they were generally such as are found at a very remote distance from any coast; and it is also true that I frequently saw pieces of rock-weed, but I could not infer the vicinity of land from these, because I have been informed, upon indubi-table authority, that a considerable quantity of the beans called *ox-eyes*, which are known to grow no where but in the West Indies, are every year thrown up on the coast of Ireland, which is not less than twelve hundred leagues distant.

AUSTRALIA

DISCOVERING NOMADS

The Australian continent was already known to Europeans through the Dutch visits to the western coasts and William Dampier's reports from fleeting contacts in northern Australia. Cook established the great land's extent by charting the eastern coast. He also described Aboriginal Australians more fully than any previous observer, but failed to establish the rapport with them that had come more easily in Polynesia.

IN THE COURSE OF THE 13TH [April 1770], being in latitude 39° 23' S. longitude 204° 2' W. I found the variation to be 12° 27' E. and in the morning of the 14th, it was 11° 30'; this day we also saw some flying fish. On the 15th, we saw an egg bird and a gannet, and as these are birds that never go far from the land, we continued to sound all night, but had no ground with 130 fathom. At noon on the 16th, we were in latitude 39° 45' S. longitude 208° W. At about two o'clock the wind came about to the W.S.W. upon which we tacked and stood to the N.W.; soon after a small land-bird perched upon the rigging, but we had no ground with 120 fathom. At eight we wore and stood to the southward till twelve at night, and then wore and stood to the N.W. till four in the morning, when we again stood to the southward, having a fresh gale at W.S.W. with squalls and dark weather till nine, when the weather became clear, and there being little wind, we had an opportunity to take several observations of the sun and moon, the mean result of which gave 207° 56' W. longitude: our latitude at noon was 39° 36' S. We had now a hard gale from the southward, and a great sea from the same quarter, which obliged us to run under our fore-sail and mizen all night, during which we sounded every two hours, but had no ground with 120 fathom.

OPPOSITE: Sunset over Botany Bay. Cook initially bestowed the name "Sting-Ray Harbour" on the inlet, but a name change was inspired by the many findings of an expedition by Banks, Solander, and Herman Spöring, another of the voyage's botanists.

Cook's landing site, the south shore of Botany Bay, as it is today, photographed by Mark Adams.

In the morning of the 18th, we saw two Port Egmont hens, and a pintado bird, which are certain signs of approaching land, and indeed by our reckoning we could not be far from it, for our longitude was now one degree to the westward of the east side of Van Diemen's land, according to the longitude laid down by Tasman, whom we could not suppose to have erred much in so short a run as from this land to New Zealand, and by our latitude we could not be above fifty or fifty-five leagues from the place whence he took his departure. All this day we had frequent squalls and a great swell. At one in the morning we brought to and sounded, but had no ground with 130 fathom; at six we saw land extending from N.E. to W. at the distance of five or six leagues, having eighty fathom water with a fine sandy bottom.

We continued standing westward, with the wind at S.S.W. till eight, when we made all the sail we could, and bore away along the shore N.E. for the eastermost land in sight, being at this time in latitude 37° 58' S. and longitude 210° 39' W. The southermost point of land in sight, which bore from us W. ¼ S. I judged to lie in latitude 38°, longitude 211° 7', and gave it the name of POINT HICKS, because Mr. Hicks, the First Lieutenant, was the first who discovered it. To the southward of this Point no land was to be seen, though it was very clear in that quarter, and by our longitude, compared with that of Tasman, not as it is laid down in the printed charts, but in the extracts from Tasman's journal, published by Rembrantse, the body of Van Diemen's land ought to have borne due south; and indeed, from the sudden falling of the sea after the wind abated, I had reason to think it did; yet as I did not see it, and as I found this coast trend N.E. and S.W. or rather more to the eastward, I cannot determine whether it joins to Van Diemen's land or not.

At noon, we were in latitude 37° 50', longitude 210° 29' W. The extreams of the land extended from N.W. to E.N.E and a remarkable point bore N. 20 E. at the distance of about four leagues. This point rises in a round hillock, very much resembling the Ram Head at the entrance of Plymouth Sound, and therefore I called it by the same name. The variation by an azimuth, taken this morning, was 3° 7' E.; and what we had now seen of the land, appeared low and level: the sea shore was a white sand, but the country within was green and woody. About one o'clock, we saw three water spouts at once; two were between us and the shore, and the third at some distance, upon our larboard quarter: this phænomenon is so well known, that it is not necessary to give a particular description of it here.

At six o'clock in the evening, we shortened sail, and brought to for the night, having fifty-six fathom water, and a fine sandy bottom. The northermost land in sight then bore N. by E. ½ E. and a small island lying close to a point on the main bore W. distant two leagues. This point, which I called CAPE HOWE, may be known by the trending of the coast, which is north on the one side, and south west on the other; it may also be known by some round hills upon the main, just within it.

Of several dozen spears seized at Botany Bay in order to disarm the Aboriginal people of the locality, only four are extant today and reside in the Museum of Archaeology and Anthropology in Cambridge.

We brought to for the night, and at four in the morning made sail along shore to the northward. At six, the northermost land in sight bore N.N.W. and we were at this time about four leagues from the shore. At noon, we were in latitude 36° 51' S. longitude 209° 53' W. and about three leagues distant from the shore. The weather being clear, gave us a good view of the country, which has a very pleasing appearance: it is of a moderate height, diversified by hills and vallies, ridges and plains, interspersed with a few lawns of no great extent, but in general covered with wood: the ascent of the hills and ridges is gentle, and the summits are not high. We continued to sail along the shore to the northward, with a southerly wind, and in the afternoon we saw smoke in several places, by which we knew the country to be inhabited. At six in the evening, we shortened sail, and sounded: we found forty-four fathom water, with a clear sandy bottom, and stood on under an easy sail till twelve, when we brought to for the night, and had ninety fathom water.

At four in the morning, we made sail again, at the distance of about five leagues from the land, and at six, we were abreast of a high mountain, lying near the shore, which, on account of

its figure, I called MOUNT DROMEDARY: under this mountain the shore forms a point, to which I gave the name of POINT DROMEDARY, and over it there is a peaked hillock. At this time, being in latitude 36° 18' S. longitude 209° 55' W. we found the variation to be 10° 42' E.

Between ten and eleven, Mr. Green and I took several observations of the sun and moon, the mean result of which gave 209° 17' longitude W. By an observation made the day before, our longitude was 210° 9' W. from which, 20' being subtracted, there remains 209° 49' the longitude of the ship this day at noon, the mean of which, with this day's observation, gives 209° 33', by which I fix the longitude of this coast. At noon, our latitude was 35° 49' S. Cape Dromedary bore S. 30 W. at the distance of twelve leagues, and an open bay, in which were three or four small islands, bore N.W. by W. at the distance of five or six leagues. This bay seemed to afford but little shelter from the sea winds, and yet it is the only place where there appeared a probability of finding anchorage upon the whole coast. We continued to steer along the shore N. by E. and N.N.E. at the distance of about three leagues, and saw smoke in many places near the beach. At five in the evening, we were abreast of a point of land which rose in a perpendicular cliff, and which, for that reason, I called POINT UPRIGHT. Our latitude was 35° 35' S. when this point bore from us due west, distant about two leagues: in this situation, we had about thirty-one fathom water with a sandy bottom. At six in the evening, the wind falling, we hauled off E.N.E. and at this time the northermost land in sight bore N. by E. ½ E. At midnight, being in seventy fathom water, we brought to till four in the morning, when we made sail in for the land; but at day-break, found our situation nearly the same as it had been at five in the evening before, by which it was apparent that we had been driven about three leagues to the southward, by a tide or current, during the night. After this we steered along the shore N.N.E. with a gentle breeze at S.W. and were so near the land as to distinguish several of the natives upon the beach, who appeared to be of a black, or very dark colour. At noon, our latitude, by observation, was 35° 27' S. and longitude 209° 23' W. Cape Dromedary bore S. 28 W. distant nineteen leagues, a remarkable peaked hill, which resembled a square dove-house, with a dome at the top, and which for that reason I called the PIGEON HOUSE, bore N. 32° 30' W. and a small low island, which lay close under the shore, bore N.W. distant about two or three leagues. When I first discovered this island, in the morning, I was in hopes, from its appreareance, that I should have found shelter for the ship behind it, but when we came near it, it did not promise security even for the landing of a boat: I should however have attempted to send a boat on shore, if the wind had not veered to that direction, with a large hollow sea rolling in upon the land from the S.E. which indeed had been the case ever since we had been upon it. The coast still continued to be of a moderate height, forming alternately rocky points and sandy beaches; but within, between Mount Dromedary and the Pigeon House, we saw high mountains, which, except two, are covered with wood: these two lie inland behind the Pigeon House, and are remarkably flat at the top, with steep rocky cliffs all round them, as far as we could see. The trees which almost every where clothe this country, appear to be large and lofty. This day the variation was found to be 9° 50' E. and for the two last days, the latitude, by observation,

OPPOSITE: Among the plants first recorded and collected by the mariners during the visit to Botany Bay were some that have since become icons of the Australian environment, including *Banksia integrifolia*, named after Joseph Banks.

was twelve or fourteen miles to the southward of the ship's account, which could have been the effect of nothing but a current setting in that direction. About four in the afternoon, being near five leagues from the land, we tacked and stood off S.E. and E. and the wind having veered in the night, from E. to N.E. and N. we tacked about four in the morning, and stood in, being about nine or ten leagues from the shore. At eight, the wind began to die away, and soon after it was calm. At noon, our latitude, by observation, was 35° 38', and our distance from the land about six leagues. Cape Dromedary bore S. 37 W. distant seventeen leagues, and the Pigeon House N. 40 W.: in this situation we had seventy-four fathom water. In the afternoon, we had variable light airs and calms, till six in the evening, when a breeze sprung up at N. by W.: at this time, being about four or five leagues from the shore, we had seventy fathom water. The Pigeon House bore N. 45 W. Mount Dromedary S. 30 W. and the northermost land in sight N. 19 E.

We stood to the north east till noon the next day, with a gentle breeze at N.W. and then we tacked and stood westward. At this time, our latitude, by observation, was 35° 10' S. and longitude 208° 51' W. A point of land which I had discovered on George's day, and which therefore I called CAPE GEORGE, bore W. distant nineteen miles, and the Pigeon House, (the latitude and longitude of which I found to be 35° 19' S. and 209° 42' W.) S. 75 W. In the morning, we had found the variation, by amplitude, to be 7° 50' E. and by several azimuths 7° 54' E. We had a fresh breeze at N.W. from noon till three; it then came to the west, when we tacked and stood to the northward. At five in the evening, being about five or six leagues from the shore, with the Pigeon House bearing W.S.W. distant about nine leagues, we had eighty-six fathom water; and at eight, having thunder and lightning, with heavy squalls, we brought to in 120 fathom.

At three in the morning, we made sail again to the northward, having the advantage of a fresh gale at S.W. At noon, we were about three or four leagues from the shore, and in latitude 34° 22' S. longitude 208° 36' W. In the course of this day's run from the preceding noon, which was forty-five miles north east, we saw smoke in several places near the beach. About two leagues to the northward of Cape George, the shore seemed to form a bay, which promised shelter from the north east winds, but as the wind was with us, it was not in my power to look into it without beating up, which would have cost me more time than I was willing to spare. The north point of this bay, on account of its figure, I named LONG NOSE; its latitude is 35° 6', and about eight leagues north of it there lies a point, which, from the colour of the land about it, I called RED POINT: its latitude is 34° 29', and longitude 208° 45' W. To the northwest of Red Point, and a little way inland, stands a round hill, the top of which looks like the crown of a hat. In the afternoon of this day, we had a light breeze at N.N.W. till five in the evening, when it fell calm: at this time, we were between three and four leagues from the shore, and had forty-eight fathom water: the variation by azimuth was 8° 48' E. and the extremities of this land were from N.E. by N. to S.W. by S. Before it was dark, we saw smoke in several places along the shore, and a fire two or three times afterwards. During the night we lay becalmed, driving in before the sea till one in the morning, when we got a breeze from the land, with which we steered N.E. being then in thirty-eight fathom. At noon, it veered to N.E. by N. and we were then in latitude 34° 10 S. longitude 208° 27' W.: the land was distant about five leagues, and extended from S. 37 W. to N. ½ E. In this latitude, there are some white cliffs, which rise perpendicularly from the sea to a considerable height. We stood off the shore till two o'clock, and then tacked and stood in till

A memorial to Joseph Banks is located on the Botany Bay foreshore.

six, when we were within four or five miles of it, and at that distance had fifty fathom water. The extremities of the land bore from S. 28 W. to N. 25° 30 E. We now tacked and stood off till twelve, then tacked and stood in again till four in the morning, when we made a trip off till daylight; and during all this time we lost ground, owing to the variableness of the winds. We continued at the distance of between four and five miles from the shore, till the afternoon, when we came within two miles, and I then hoisted out the pinnace and yawl to attempt a landing, but the pinnace proved to be so leaky that I was obliged to hoist her in again. At this time we saw several of the natives walking briskly along the shore, four of whom carried a small canoe upon their shoulders: we flattered ourselves that they were going to put her into the water, and come off to the ship, but finding ourselves disappointed, I determined to go on shore in the yawl, with as many as it would carry: I embarked therefore, with only Mr. Banks, Dr. Solander, Tupia, and four rowers: we pulled for that part of the shore where the Indians appeared, near which four small canoes were lying at the water's edge.

The Indians sat down upon the rocks, and seemed to wait for our landing; but to our great regret, when we came within about a quarter of a mile, they ran away into the woods: we determined however to go ashore, and endeavour to procure an interview, but in this we were again disappointed, for we found so great a surf beating upon every part of the beach, that landing with our little boat was altogether impracticable: we were therefore obliged to be content with gazing at such objects as presented themselves from the water: the canoes, upon a near view, seemed very much to resemble those of the smaller sort at New Zealand. We observed, that among the trees on shore, which were not very large, there was no underwood; and could distinguish that many of them were of the palm kind, and some of them cabbage trees: after many a wishful look we were obliged to return, with our curiosity rather excited than satisfied, and about five in the evening got on board the ship. About this time it fell calm, and our situation was by no means agreeable: we were now not more than a mile and a half from

the shore, and within some breakers, which lay to the southward; but happily a light breeze came off the land, and carried us out of danger: with this breeze we stood to the northward, and at day-break we discovered a bay, which seemed to be well sheltered from all winds, and into which therefore I determined to go with the ship. The pinnace being repaired, I sent her, with the Master, to sound the entrance, while I kept turning up, having the wind right out. At noon, the mouth of the bay bore N.N.W. distant about a mile, and seeing a smoke on the shore, we directed our glasses to the spot, and soon discovered ten people, who, upon our nearer approach, left their fire, and retired to a little eminence, whence they could conveniently observe our motions. Soon after two canoes, each having two men on board, came to the shore just under the eminence, and the men joined the rest on the top of it. The pinnace, which had been sent ahead to sound, now approached the place, upon which all the Indians retired farther up the hill, except one, who hid himself among some rocks near the landing-place. As the pinnace proceeded along the shore, most of the people took the same route, and kept abreast of her at a distance; when she came back, the master told us, that in a cove a little within the harbour, some of them had come down to the beach, and invited him to land by many signs and words of which he knew not the meaning; but that all of them were armed with long pikes, and a wooden weapon shaped somewhat like a cimeter. The Indians who had not followed the boat, seeing the ship approach, used many threatening gestures, and brandished their weapons; particularly two, who made a very singular appearance, for their faces seemed to have been dusted with a white powder, and their bodies painted with broad streaks of the same colour, which passing obliquely over their breasts and backs, looked not unlike the cross-belts worn by our soldiers; the same kind of streaks were also drawn round their legs and thighs like

LEFT: Cook Island is visible off the coast of Fingal Head, New South Wales. Cook first spotted these features on May 16, 1770. There is some controversy as to whether Fingal Head is really the feature that Cook dubbed Point Danger.

broad garters: each of these men held in his hand the weapon that had been described to us as like a cimeter, which appeared to be about two feet and a half long, and they seemed to talk to each other with great earnestness.

We continued to stand into the bay, and early in the afternoon anchored under the south shore, about two miles within the entrance, in six fathom water, the south point bearing S.E. and the north point East. As we came in we saw, on both points of the bay, a few huts, and several of the natives, men, women, and children. Under the south head we saw four small canoes, with each one man on board, who were very busily employed in striking fish with a long pike or spear: they ventured almost into the surf, and were so intent upon what they were doing, that although the ship passed within a quarter of a mile of them, they scarcely turned their eyes towards her; possibly being deafened by the surf, and their attention wholly fixed upon their business or sport, they neither saw nor heard her go past them.

The place where the ship had anchored was abreast of a small village, consisting of about six or eight houses; and while we were preparing to hoist out the boat, we saw an old woman, followed by three children, come out of the wood; she was loaded with fire-wood, and each of the children had also its little burden: when she came to the houses three more children, younger than the others, came out to meet her: she often looked at the ship, but expressed neither fear nor surprise: in a short time she kindled a fire, and the four canoes came in from fishing. The men landed and having hauled up their boats, began to dress their dinner, to all appearance wholly unconcerned about us, though we were within half a mile of them. We thought it remarkable that of all the people we had yet seen, not one had the least appearance of clothing, the old woman herself being destitute even of a fig-leaf.

After dinner the boats were manned, and we set out from the ship, having Tupia of our party. We intended to land where we saw the people, and began to hope that as they had so little regarded the ship's coming into the bay, they would as little regard our coming on shore: in this, however, we were disappointed; for as soon as we approached the rocks, two of the men came down upon them to dispute our landing, and, the rest ran away. Each of the two champions was armed with a lance about ten feet long, and a short stick which he seemed to handle as if it was a machine to assist him in managing or throwing the lance: they called to us in a very loud tone, and in a harsh dissonant language, of which neither we nor Tupia understood a single word: they brandished their weapons, and seemed resolved to defend their coast to the uttermost, though they were but two, and we were forty. I could not but admire their courage, and being very unwilling that hostilities should commence with such inequality of force between us, I ordered the boat to lie upon her oars: we then parlied by signs for about a quarter of an hour, and to bespeak their good-will, I threw them nails, beads, and other trifles, which they took up and seemed to be well pleased with. I then made signs that I wanted water, and, by all the means that I could devise, endeavoured to convince them that we would do them no harm: they now waved to us, and I was willing to interpret it as an invitation; but upon our putting the boat in, they came again to oppose us. One appeared to be a youth about nineteen or twenty, and the other a man of middle age: as I had now no other resource I fired a musquet between them. Upon the report, the youngest dropped a bundle of lances upon the rock, but recollecting himself in an instant he snatched them up again with great haste: a stone was then thrown at us, upon which I ordered a musquet to be fired with small shot, which struck the eldest upon the legs, and he immediately ran to one of the houses, which was distant about an hundred yards: I now hoped that our contest was over, and we immediately landed; but we had scarcely left the boat when he returned, and we then perceived that he had left the rock only to fetch a shield or target for his defence. As soon as he came up, he threw a lance at us, and his comrade another; they fell where we stood thickest, but happily hurt nobody. A third musquet with small shot was then fired at them, upon which one of them threw another lance, and both immediately ran away: if we had pursued, we might probably have taken one of them; but Mr. Banks suggesting that the lances might be poisoned, I thought it not prudent to venture into the woods. We repaired immediately to the huts, in one of which we found the children, who had hidden themselves behind a shield and some bark; we peeped at them, but left them in their retreat, without their knowing that they had been discovered, and we threw into the house when we went away some beads, ribbons, pieces of cloth, and other presents, which

Casuarina equistefoliaI, coastal she-oak, is found from Southeast Asia to the Pacific Islands and is highly characteristic of the New South Wales coast.

we hoped would procure us the good-will of the inhabitants when they should return; but the lances which we found lying about, we took away with us, to the number of about fifty: they were from six to fifteen feet long, and all of them had four prongs in the manner of a fish-gig, each of which was pointed with fish-bone, and very sharp: we observed that they were smeared with a viscous substance of a green colour, which favoured the opinion of their being poisoned, though we afterwards discovered that it was a mistake: they appeared, by the sea-weed that we found sticking to them, to have been used in striking fish. Upon examining the canoes that lay upon the beach, we found them to be the worst we had ever seen: they were between twelve and fourteen feet long, and made of the bark of a tree in one piece, which was drawn together and tied up at each end, the middle being kept open by sticks which were placed across them from gunwale to gunwale as thwarts. We then searched for fresh water, but found none, except in a small hole which had been dug in the sand.

Having reimbarked in our boat, we deposited our lances on board the ship, and then went over to the north point of the bay, where we had seen several of the inhabitants when we were entering it, but which we now found totally deserted. Here however we found fresh water, which trickled down from the top of the rocks, and stood in pools among the hollows at the bottom; but it was situated so as not to be procured for our use without difficulty.

Chapter 8

THE BARRIER REEF

---

*Nowhere did Cook come nearer to grief than during the cruise up the coast of what
is now north Queensland. The ship was badly damaged and the effort to preserve
her desperate. An enforced stay for repairs in the estuary of what would be called
the Endeavour River was enriched by cautious further meetings with Indigenous
Australians, and by the first European sighting of the kangaroo.*

[JUNE 1770] HITHERTO WE HAD SAFELY NAVIGATED this dangerous coast, where the sea in all parts conceals shoals that suddenly project from the shore, and rocks that rise abruptly like a pyramid from the bottom, for an extent of two and twenty degrees of latitude, more than one thousand three hundred miles; and therefore hitherto none of the names which distinguish the several parts of the country that we saw, are memorials of distress; but here we became acquainted with misfortune, and we therefore called the point which we had just seen farthest to the northward, CAPE TRIBULATION.

This Cape lies in latitude 16° 6' S. and longitude 214° 39' W. We steered along the shore N. by W. at the distance of between three and four leagues, having from fourteen to twelve, and ten fathom water: in the offing we saw two islands, which lie in latitude 16° S. and about six or seven leagues from the main. At six in the evening, the northermost land in sight bore N. by W. ½ W. and two low woody islands, which some of us took to be rocks above water, bore N. ½ W. At this time we shortened sail, and hauled off shore E.N.E. and N.E. by E. close upon a wind, for it was my design to stretch off all night, as well to avoid the danger we saw ahead, as to see whether any islands lay in the offing, especially as we were now near the latitude assigned to the islands which were discovered by Quiros, and which some geographers, for what reason I know not, have thought fit to join to this land. We had the advantage of a fine breeze, and a clear moonlight night, and in standing off from six till near nine o'clock, we deepened our water from fourteen to twenty-one fathom, but while we were at supper it suddenly shoaled, and we fell into twelve, ten, and eight fathom, within the space of a few minutes; I immediately ordered every body to their station, and all was ready to put about and come to an anchor, but meeting at the next cast of the lead with deep water again, we concluded that we had gone over the tail of the shoals which we

The *Endeavour* undergoes repair following the near-wreck on the Great Barrier Reef.

had seen at sun-set, and that all danger was past: before ten, we had twenty and one and twenty fathom, and this depth continuing, the gentlemen left the deck in great tranquility, and went to bed; but a few minutes before eleven, the water shallowed at once from twenty to seventeen fathom, and before the lead could be cast again, the ship struck, and remained immoveable, except by the heaving of the surge, that beat her against the craggs of the rock upon which she lay. In a few moments every body was upon the deck, with countenances which sufficiently expressed the horrors of our situation. We had stood off the shore three hours and a half, with a pleasant breeze, and therefore knew that we could not be very near it, and we had too much reason to conclude that we were upon a rock of coral, which is more fatal than any other, because the points of it are sharp, and every part of the surface so rough as to grind away whatever is rubbed against it, even with the gentlest motion. In this situation all the sails were immediately taken in, and the boats hoisted out to examine the depth of water round the ship: we soon discovered that our fears had not aggravated our misfortune, and that the vessel had been lifted over a ledge of the rock, and lay in a hollow within it: in some places there was from three to four fathom, and in others not so many feet. The ship lay with her head to the N.E.; and at the distance of about thirty yards on the starboard side, the water deepened to eight, ten, and twelve fathom. As soon as the long-boat was out, we struck our yards and top-masts, and carried out the stream anchor on the starboard bow, got the coasting anchor and cable into the boat, and were going to carry it out the same way; but upon sounding a second time round the ship, the water was found to be deepest astern: the anchor therefore was carried out from the starboard quarter instead of the starboard bow, that is, from the stern instead of the head, and having taken ground, our utmost force was applied to the capstern, hoping that if the anchor did not come home, the ship would be got off, but to our great misfortune and disappointment we could not move her: during all this

time she continued to beat with great violence against the rock, so that it was with the utmost difficulty that we kept upon our legs; and to complete the scene of distress, we saw by the light of the moon the sheathing boards from the bottom of the vessel floating away all round her, and at last her false keel, so that every moment was making way for the sea to rush in which was to swallow us up. We had now no chance but to lighten her, and we had lost the opportunity of doing that to the greatest advantage, for unhappily we went on shore just at high water, and by this time it had considerably fallen, so that after she should be lightened so as to draw as much less water as the water had sunk, we should be but in the same situation as at first; and the only alleviation of this circumstance was, that as the tide ebbed the ship settled to the rocks, and was not beaten against them with so much violence. We had indeed some hope from the next tide, but it was doubtful whether she would hold together so long, especially as the rock kept grating her bottom under the starboard bow with such force as to be heard in the fore store-room. This however was no time to indulge conjecture, nor was any effort remitted in despair of success: that no time might be lost, the water was immediately started in the hold, and pumped up; six of our guns, being all we had upon the deck, our iron and stone ballast, casks, hoop staves, oil jars, decayed stores, and many other things that lay in the way of heavier materials, were thrown overboard with the utmost expedition, every one exerting himself with an alacrity almost approaching to cheerfulness, without the least repining or discontent; yet the men were so far imprest with a sense of their situation, that not an oath was heard among them, the habit of profaneness, however strong, being instantly subdued, by the dread of incurring guilt when death seemed to be so near.

While we were thus employed, day broke upon us, and we saw the land at about eight leagues distance, without any island in the intermediate space,

LEFT: Present-day Cooktown is the site of the Endeavour River estuary. Here in 1770, the badly damaged *Endeavour* was hauled up in order to be repaired.

upon which, if the ship should have gone to pieces, we might have been set ashore by the boats, and from which they might have taken us by different turns to the main: the wind however gradually died away, and early in the forenoon it was a dead calm; if it had blown hard, the ship must inevitably have been destroyed. At eleven in the forenoon we expected high water, and anchors were got out, and every thing made ready for another effort to heave her off if she should float, but to our inexpressible surprize and concern she did not float by a foot and a half, though we had lightened her near fifty ton, so much did the day-tide fall short of that in the night. We now proceeded to lighten her still more, and threw overboard every thing that it was possible for us to spare: hitherto she had not admitted much water, but as the tide fell, it rushed in so fast, that two pumps, incessantly worked, could scarcely keep her free. At two o'clock, she lay heeling two or three streaks to starboard, and the pinnace, which lay under her bows, touched the ground: we had now no hope but from the tide at midnight, and to prepare for it we carried out our two bower anchors, one on the starboard quarter, and the other right a-stern, got the blocks and tackle which were to give us a purchase upon the cables in order, and brought the falls, or ends of them, in abaft, straining them tight, that the next

effort might operate upon the ship, and by shortening the length of the cable between that and the anchors, draw her off the ledge upon which she rested, towards the deep water. About five o'clock in the afternoon, we observed the tide begin to rise, but we observed at the same time that the leak increased to a most alarming degree, so that two more pumps were manned, but unhappily only one of them would work: three of the pumps however were kept going, and at nine o'clock the ship righted, but the leak had gained upon us so considerably, that it was imagined she must go to the bottom as soon as she ceased to be supported by the rock: this was a dreadful circumstance, so that we anticipated the floating of the ship not as an earnest of deliverance, but as an event that would probably precipitate our destruction. We well knew

Having completed the survey of the eastern Australian coast, Cook formally took possession (on what was called Possession Island) of the entire territory in the name of King George III, though not with the degree of formality and ceremony represented in this later painting.

that our boats were not capable of carrying us all on shore, and that when the dreadful crisis should arrive, as all command and subordination would be at an end, a contest for preference would probably ensue, that would increase the horrors even of shipwreck, and terminate in the destruction of us all by the hands of each other; yet we knew that if any should be left on board to perish in the waves, they would probably suffer less upon the whole than those who should get on shore, without any lasting or effectual defence against the natives, in a country, where

The great South Sea Caterpillar, transform'd into a Bath Butterfly.

Description of the New Bath Butterfly taken from the Philosophical Transactions for 1795 — "This Insect first crawl'd into notice, from among the Weeds & Mud on the Banks of the South Sea: & being afterwards placed in a Warm Situation by the Royal Society, was changed by the heat of the Sun into its present form — it is noticed & Valued Solely on account of the beautiful Red which encircles its Body, & the Shining Spot on its Breast: a Distinction which never fails to render Caterpillars valuable.

Joseph Banks was widely lampooned as a foppish dilettante, and indeed lived the life of a rakish aristocrat, but he was also a dedicated natural historian who went on to become the most important scientific entrepreneur of his epoch.

even nets and firearms would scarcely furnish them with food; and where, if they should find the means of subsistence, they must be condemned to languish out the remainder of life in a desolate wilderness, without the possession, or even hope, of any domestic comfort, and cut off from all commerce with mankind, except the naked savages who prowled the desert, and who perhaps were some of the most rude and uncivilized upon the earth.

To those only who have waited in a state of such suspense, death has approached in all his terrors; and as the dreadful moment that was to determine our fate came on, every one saw his own sensations pictured in the countenances of his companions: however, the capstan and windlace were manned with as many hands as could be spared from the pumps, and the ship floating about twenty minutes after ten o'clock, the effort was made, and she was heaved into deep water. It was some comfort to find that she did not now admit more water than she had done upon the rock; and though, by the gaining of the leak upon the pumps, there was no less than three feet nine inches water in the hold, yet the men did not relinquish their labour, and we held the water as it were at bay; but having now endured excessive fatigue of body and agitation of mind for more than four and twenty hours, and having but little hope of succeeding at last, they began to flag: none of them could work at the pump more than five or six minutes together, and then, being totally exhausted, they threw themselves down upon the deck, though a stream of water was running over it from the pumps between three and four inches deep; when those who succeeded them had worked their spell, and were exhausted in their turn, they threw themselves down in the same manner, and the others started up again, and renewed their labour; thus relieving each other till an accident was very near putting an end to their efforts at once. The planking which lines the inside of the ship's bottom is called the cieling, and between this, and the outside planking, there is a space of about eighteen inches: the man who till this time had attended the well to take the depth of water, had taken it only to the cieling, and gave the measure accordingly; but   he being now relieved, the person who came in his stead, reckoned the depth to the outside planking, by which it appeared in a few minutes to have gained upon the pumps eighteen inches, the difference between the planking without and within. Upon this, even the bravest was upon the point of giving up his labour with his hope, and in a few minutes every thing would have been

This cannon was dropped overboard in a desperate effort to lighten the *Endeavour* while the ship was stuck on the Great Barrier Reef. Later retrieved, it is now in Te Papa, the National Musuem of New Zealand in Wellington.

involved in all the confusion of despair. But this accident, however dreadful in its first consequences, was eventually the cause of our preservation: the mistake was soon detected, and the sudden joy which every man felt upon finding his situation better than his fears had suggested, operated like a charm, and seemed to possess him with a strong belief that scarcely any real danger remained. New confidence and new hope, however founded, inspired new vigour; and though our state was the same as when the men first began to slacken in their labour, through weariness and despondency, they now renewed their efforts with such alacrity and spirit, that before eight o'clock in the morning the leak was so far from having gained upon the pumps, that the pumps had gained considerably upon the leak. Every body now talked of getting the ship into some harbour, as a thing not to be doubted, and as hands could be spared from the pumps, they were employed in getting up the anchors: the stream anchor and best bower we had taken on board; but it was found impossible to save the little bower, and therefore it was cut away at a whole cable: we lost also the cable of the stream anchor among the rocks; but in our situation these were trifles which scarcely attracted our notice. Our next business was to get up the fore-topmast and fore-yard, and warp the ship to the southeast, and at eleven, having now a breeze from the sea, we once more got under sail and stood for the land.

It was however impossible long to continue the labour by which the pumps had been made to gain upon the leak, and as the exact situation of it could not be discovered, we had no hope of stopping it within. In this situation, Mr. Monkhouse, one of my midshipmen, came to me and proposed an expedient that he had once seen used on board a merchant ship, which sprung a leak that admitted above four feet water an hour, and which by this expedient was brought safely from Virginia to London; the master having such confidence in it, that he took her out of harbour,

Painter John Hamilton Mortimer depicted Cook, Banks, and the Earl of Sandwich—sometime Lord of the Admiralty and Cook's patron, who likely commissioned this painting—the botanist Solander, and Dr. John Hawkesworth, the literary gentleman who would write the official narrative of the first voyage.

knowing her condition, and did not think it worth while to wait till the leak could be otherwise stopped. To this man, therefore, the care of the expedient, which is called fothering the ship, was immediately committed, four or five of the people being appointed to assist him, and he performed it in this manner: He took a lower studding sail, and having mixed together a large quantity of oakham and wool, chopped pretty small, he stitched it down in handfuls upon the sail, as lightly as possible, and over this he spread the dung of our sheep and other filth; but horse dung, if we had had it, would have been better. When the sail was thus prepared, it was hauled under the ship's bottom by ropes, which kept it extended, and when it came under the leak, the suction which carried in the water carried in with it the oakham and wool from the surface of the sail, which in other parts the water was not sufficiently agitated to wash off. By the success of this expedient our leak was so far reduced, that instead of gaining upon three pumps, it was easily kept under with one. This was a new source of confidence and comfort; the people could scarcely have expressed more joy if they had been already in port; and their views were so far from being limited to running the ship ashore in some harbour, either of an island or the main, and building a vessel out of her materials, to carry us to the East Indies, which had so lately been the utmost object of our hope, that nothing was now thought of but ranging along the shore in search of a convenient place to repair the damage she had sustained, and then prosecuting the voyage upon the same plan as if nothing had happened. Upon this occasion I must observe, both in justice and gratitude to the ship's company, and the Gentlemen on board, that although in the midst of our distress every one seemed to have a just sense of his danger, yet no passionate exclamations, or frantic gestures, were to be heard or seen; every one appeared to have the perfect possession of his mind, and every one exerted himself to the uttermost, with a quiet and patient perseverance, equally distant from the tumultuous violence of terror, and the gloomy inactivity of despair.

In the mean time, having light airs at E.S.E. we got up the main-topmast, and main-yard, and kept edging in for the land, till about six o'clock in the evening, when we came to an anchor in seventeen fathom water, at the distance of seven leagues from the shore, and one from the ledge of rocks upon which we had struck.

This ledge or shoal lies in latitude 15° 45' S. and between six and seven leagues from the main. It is not however the only shoal on this part of the coast, especially to the northward; and at this time we saw one to the southward, the tail of which we passed over, when we had uneven soundings about two hours before we struck. A part of this shoal is always above water, and has the appearance of white sand: a part also of that upon which we had lain is dry at low water, and in that place consists of sand stones; but all the rest of it is a coral rock.

While we lay at anchor for the night, we found that the ship made about fifteen inches water an hour, from which no immediate danger was to be apprehended; and at six o'clock in the morning, we weighed and stood to the N.W. still edging in for the land with a gentle breeze at S.S.E. At nine we passed close without two small islands that lie in latitude 15° 41' S. and about four leagues from the main: to reach these islands had, in the height of our distress, been the object of our hope, or perhaps rather of our wishes, and therefore I called them HOPE ISLANDS.

OPPOSITE: *Melaleuca* is a north Australian paperbark, one of many species first formally described by Solander following the voyage.

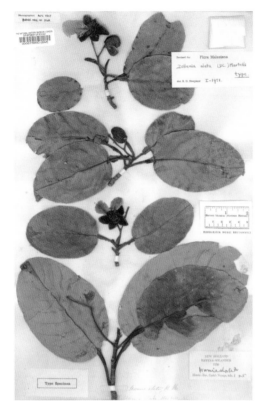

At noon we were about three leagues from the land, and in latitude 15° 37' S.; the northermost part of the main in sight bore N. 30 W.; and Hope Islands extended from S. 30 E. to S. 40 E. In this situation we had twelve fathom water, and several sand-banks without us. At this time the leak had not increased; but that we might be prepared for all events, we got the sail ready for another fothering. In the afternoon, having a gentle breeze at S.E. by E. I sent out the Master with two boats, as well to sound ahead of the ship, as to look out for a harbour where we might repair our defects, and put the ship in a proper trim. At three o'clock, we saw an opening that had the appearance of an harbour, and stood off and on while the boats examined it; but they soon found that there was not depth of water in it sufficient for the ship. When it was near sunset, there being many shoals about us, we anchored in four fathom, at the distance of about two miles from the shore, the land extending from N. ½ E. to S. by E. ½ E. The pinnace was still out with one of the mates; but at nine o'clock she returned, and reported, that about two leagues to leeward she had discovered just such a harbour as we wanted, in which there was a sufficient rise of water, and every other convenience that could be desired, either for laying the ship ashore, or heaving her down.

In consequence of this information, I weighed at six o'clock in the morning, and having sent two boats ahead, to lie upon the shoals that we saw in our way, we ran down to the place; but notwithstanding our precaution, we were once in three fathom water. As soon as these shoals were passed, I sent the boats to lie in the channel that led to the harbour, and by this time it began to blow. It was happy for us that a place of refuge was at hand; for we soon found that the ship would not work, having twice missed stays: our situation, however, though it might have been much worse, was not without danger; we were entangled among shoals, and I had great reason to fear being driven to leeward, before the boats could place themselves so as to prescribe our course. I therefore anchored in four fathom, about a mile from the shore, and then made the signal for the boats to come on board. When this was done I went myself and buoyed the channel, which I

ABOVE: *Dillenia alata* is better known as red beech or the golden guinea tree, a large northeast Australian rainforest tree. This specimen was collected by Banks's assistant, botanist Daniel Solander, during the period at the Endeavour River, and now resides at the Natural History Museum in London.

OPPOSITE: This "three-banded bull fish" was painted by Sydney Parkinson, most likely while the *Endeavour* was careened in the mouth of the Endeavour River. Found on the Great Barrier Reef, the fish is today known as a pennant bannerfish (*Heniochus chrysostomus*).

chætodon macrolepidotus L.

This sketch made during the sojourn in north Queensland reveals Parkinson struggling to come to grips with the unfamiliar proportions of the kangaroo. Parkinson's sketches were the first European images of the animal.

found very narrow; the harbour also I found smaller than I expected, but most excellently adapted to our purpose; and it is remarkable, that in the whole course of our voyage we had seen no place which, in our present circumstances, could have afforded us the same relief. At noon, our latitude was 15° 26' S. During all the rest of this day, and the whole night, it blew too fresh for us to venture from our anchor and run into the harbour; and for our farther security, we got down the top-gallant yards, unbent the mainsail and some of the small sails; got down the fore-top-gallant mast, and the gibb boom, and sprit-sail, with a view to lighten the ship forwards as much as possible, in order to come at her leak, which we supposed to be somewhere in that part; for in all the joy of our unexpected deliverance, we had not forgot that at this time there was nothing but a lock of wool between us and destruction. The gale continuing, we kept our station all the 15th. On the 16th, it was somewhat more moderate; and about six o'clock in the morning, we hove the cable short, with a design to get under sail, but were obliged to desist, and veer it out again. It is remarkable that the sea breeze, which blew fresh when we anchored, continued to do so almost every day while we stayed here; it was calm only while we were upon the rock, except once; and even the gale that afterwards wafted us to the shore, would then certainly have beaten us to pieces. In the evening of the preceding day, we had observed a fire near the beach over against us; and as it would be necessary for us to stay sometime in this place, we were not without hope of making

Joseph Banks's collections were organized systematically
according to the most advanced classifications of the period.

an acquaintance with the people. We saw more fires upon the hills to-day, and with our glasses discovered four Indians going along the shore, who stopped, and made two fires; but for what purpose it was impossible we should guess.

The scurvy now began to make its appearance among us, with many formidable symptoms. Our poor Indian, Tupia, who had some time before complained that his gums were sore and swelled, and who had taken plentifully of our lemon juice by the Surgeon's direction, had now livid spots upon his legs, and other indubitable testimonies that the disease had made a rapid progress, notwithstanding all our remedies, among which the bark had been liberally administered.

Mr. Green, our astronomer, was also declining; and these, among other circumstances, imbittered the delay which prevented our going ashore.

In the morning of the 17th, though the wind was still fresh, we ventured to weigh, and push in for the harbour; but in doing this we twice run the ship aground: the first time she went off without any trouble, but the second time she stuck fast. We now got down the fore yard, fore topmasts, and booms, and taking them overboard, made a raft of them alongside of the ship. The tide was happily rising, and about one o'clock in the afternoon, she floated. We soon warped her into the harbour, and having moored her alongside of a steep beach to the south, we got the anchors, cables, and all the hawsers on shore before night.

Chapter 9

AUSTRALIAN REFLECTIONS

Cook had begun his voyage as a formidably intelligent but practical and narrowly focused man—a maker of maps more than a scientist or scholar. Though he remained temperamentally pragmatic throughout his adult life, he became increasingly interested in humanity. Among early expressions of his interest in making sense of what he had seen is a passage considering the "happiness" he observed in the lives of indigenous Australians. This passage from his journal was not published in the form in which he wrote it until more than one hundred years after his death.

[AUGUST 1770] FROM WHAT I HAVE SAID of the Natives of New Holland they may appear to some to be the most wretched People upon Earth; but in reality they are far more happier than we Europeans, being wholy unacquainted not only with the Superfluous, but with the necessary Conveniences so much sought after in Europe; they are happy in not knowing the use of them. They live in a Tranquility which is not disturbed by the Inequality of Condition. The earth and Sea of their own accord furnishes them with all things necessary for Life. They covet not Magnificient Houses, Household-stuff, etc.; they live in a Warm and fine Climate, and enjoy every wholesome Air, so that they have very little need of Cloathing; and this they seem to be fully sencible of, for many to whom we gave Cloth, etc., left it carelessly upon the Sea beach and in the Woods, as a thing they had no manner of use for; in short, they seem'd to set no Value upon anything we gave them, nor would they ever part with anything of their own for any one Article we could offer them. This, in my opinion, Argues that they think themselves provided with all the necessarys of Life, and that they have no Superfluities.

I shall conclude the account of this Country with a few observations on the Currents and Tides upon the Coast, because I have mentioned in the Course of this Journal that the latter hath sometimes set one way and sometimes another, which I shall Endeavour to account for in

OPPOSITE: This watercolor of a well-known eastern Australian bush flower was completed by Banks's draftsman, John Frederick Miller, in London after an outline made by Sydney Parkinson during the voyage.

the best manner I can. From the Latitude of 32 degrees, or above downwards to Sandy Cape in the Latitude of 24 degrees 46 minutes, we constantly found a Current setting to the Southward at the rate of 10 or 15 Miles per Day, more or less, according to the distance we were from the land, for it runs stronger in shore than in the Offing. All this time I had not been able to satisfy myself whether the flood-tide came from the Southward, Eastward, or Northward, but judged it to come from the South-East; but the first time we anchor'd upon the coast, which was in the Latitude of 24 degrees 30 minutes, and about 10 Leagues to the South-East of Bustard Bay, we found there the flood to come from the North-West. On the Contrary, 30 Leagues further to the North-West, on the South side of Keppel Bay, we found the Flood to come from the East, and at the Northern part of the said Bay we found it come from the Northward, but with a much Slower Motion than the Easterly Tide. Again, on the East side of the Bay of Inlets we found the flood to set strong to the Westward as far as the Op'ning of Broad sound, but on the North side of that sound the flood come with a Slow motion from the North-West; and when at Anchor before Repulse bay we found the flood to come from the northward. We need only admit the flood tide to come from the East or South-East, and then all these seeming Contradictions will be found to be conformable to reason and experience. It is well known that where there are deep Inlets, large Creeks, etc., into low lands, that it is not occasioned by fresh water Rivers; there is a very great indraught of the Flood Tide, the direction of which will be determin'd according to the possition or direction of the Coast which forms the

Entrance into such Inlets; and this direction the Tide must follow, let it be ever so contrary to their general Course out at Sea, and where the Tides are weak, as they are in general upon this Coast, a large Inlet will, if I may so call it, attract the Flood tide for many Leagues. Any one need only cast an Eye over the Chart to be made sencible of what I have advanced. To the Northward of Whitsundays Passage there are few or no large Inlets, and consequently the Flood sets to the Northward or North-West, according to the direction of the Coast, and Ebb the Contrary; but this is to be understood at a little distance from land, or where there is no Creeks or Inlets, for where such are, be they ever so small, they draw the flood from the Southward, Eastward, and Northward, and, as I found by experience, while we lay in Endeavour River. Another thing I have observed upon the Tides which ought to be remarked, which is that there is only one high Tide in 24 Hours, and that is the night Tide. On the Spring Tides the difference between the

While some people on the larger Melanesian islands had an inland orientation, the coasts, lagoons, and seas were nevertheless vitally important to subsistence, travel, and trade. This man was photographed by Glenn Jowitt in the Solomon Islands in 1998.

perpendicular rise of the night and day Tides is not less than 3 feet, which is a great deal where the Tides are so inconsiderable, as they are here. This inequality of the Tide I did not observe till we run ashore; perhaps it is much more so to the Northward than to the Southward. After we had got within the Reefs the second time we found the Tides more considerable than at any time before, except in the Bay of Inlets. It may be owing to the water being confin'd in Channels between the Shoals, but the flood always set to the North-West to the extremity of New Wales, from thence West and South-West into the India Seas.

Chapter 10

TAKING STOCK

Cook proceeded through Torres Strait and in October 1770 reached Batavia (now Jakarta), then capital of the Dutch East Indies. He was back in a world known to Europeans, regularly connected to Europe through commerce. He prepared a dispatch for the Admiralty, summarizing the voyage and his findings, and proposing a second expedition that would resolve for once and for all the question of whether there was any great southern continent.

TO PHILIP STEPHENS, ESQ.

Sir,

Please to acquaint my Lords Commissioners of the Admiralty that I left Rio de Janeiro the 8th of December, 1768, and on the 16th of January following arrived in Success Bay in Straits La Maire, where we recruited our Wood and Water; on the 21st of the same month we quitted Straits La Maire, and arrived at George's Island on the 13th of April. In our Passage to this Island I made a far more Westerly Track than any Ship had ever done before; yet it was attended with no discovery until we arrived within the Tropick, where we discovered several Islands. We met with as Friendly a reception by the Natives of George's Island as I could wish, and I took care to secure ourselves in such a manner as to put it out of the power of the whole Island to drive us off. Some days preceeding the 3rd of June I sent Lieutenant Hicks to the Eastern part of this Island, and Lieutenant Gore to York Island, with others of the Officers (Mr. Green having furnished them with Instruments), to observe the Transit of Venus, that we may have the better Chance of succeeding should the day prove unfavourable; but in this We were so fortunate that the observations were everywhere attended with every favourable Circumstance. It was the 13th of July before I was ready to quitt this Island, after which I spent near a month in exploring some other Islands which lay to the Westward, before we steer'd to the Southward. On the 14th of August we discovered

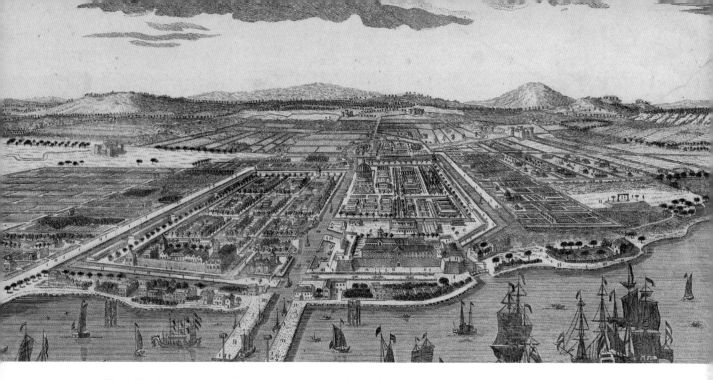

Dutch Batavia, present-day Jakarta, circa 1780. It was here while en route home from the first voyage that Cook stopped to dispatch a summary of his findings to the Admiralty.

a small Island laying in the Latitude of 22 degrees 27 minutes South, Longitude 150 degrees 47 minutes West. After quitting this Island I steered to the South, inclining a little to the East, until we arrived in the Latitude 40 degrees 12 minutes South, without seeing the least signs of Land. After this I steer'd to the Westward, between the Latitude of 30 and 40 degrees until the 6th of October, on which day we discovered the East Coast of New Zeland, which I found to consist of 2 large Islands, extending from 34 to 48 degrees of South Latitude, both of which I circumnavigated. On the 1st of April, 1770, I quitted New Zeland, and steer'd to the Westward, until I fell in with the East Coast of New Holland, in the Latitude of 30 degrees South. I coasted the shore of this Country to the North, putting in at such places as I saw Convenient, until we arrived in the Latitude of 15 degrees 45 minutes South, where, on the night of the 10th of June, we struck upon a Reef of Rocks, were we lay 23 Hours, and received some very considerable damage. This proved a fatal stroke to the remainder of the Voyage, as we were obliged to take shelter in the first Port we met with, were we were detain'd repairing the damage we had sustain'd until the 4th of August, and after all put to Sea with a leaky Ship, and afterwards coasted the Shore to the Northward through the most dangerous Navigation that perhaps ever ship was in, until the 22nd of same month, when, being in the Latitude of 10 degrees 30 minutes South, we found a Passage into the Indian Sea between the Northern extremity of New Holland and New Guinea. After getting through the Passage I stood for the Coast of New Guinea, which we made on the 29th; but as we found it absolutely necessary to heave the Ship down to Stop her leaks before we proceeded home, I made no stay here, but quitted this Coast on the 30th of September, and made the best of my way to Batavia, where we Arrived on the 10th instant, and soon after obtained leave of the Governor and Council to be hove down at Onrust, where we have but just got alongside of the Wharf in order to take out our Stores, etc.

I send herewith a copy of my Journal, containing the Proceedings of the whole Voyage, together with such Charts as I have had time to Copy, which I judge will be sufficient for the present to illustrate said Journal. In this Journal I have with undisguised truth and without gloss inserted the whole Transactions of the Voyage, and made such remarks and have given such discriptions of things as I thought was necessary in the best manner I was Capable off. Altho' the discoverys made in this Voyage are not great, yet I flatter myself they are such as may Merit the Attention of their Lordships; and altho' I have failed in discovering the so much talked of Southern Continent (which perhaps do not exist), and which I myself had much at heart, yet I am confident that no part of the Failure of such discovery can be laid to my charge. Had we been so fortunate not to have run a shore much more would have been done in the latter part of the Voyage than what was; but as it is, I presume this Voyage will be found as compleat as any before made to the South Seas on the same account. The plans I have drawn of the places I have been at were made with all the Care and accuracy that time and Circumstances would admit of. Thus far I am certain that the Latitude and Longitude of few parts of the World are better settled than these. In this I was very much assisted by Mr. Green, who let slip no one opportunity for making of Observations for settling the Longitude during the whole Course of the Voyage; and the many Valuable discoveries made by Mr. Banks and Dr. Solander in Natural History, and other things useful to the learned world, cannot fail of contributing very much to the Success of the Voyage. In justice to the Officers and the whole Crew, I must say they have gone through the fatigues and dangers of the whole Voyage with that cheerfulness and Allertness that will always do Honour to British Seamen, and I have the satisfaction to say that I have not lost one Man by sickness during the whole Voyage. I hope that the repairs wanting to the Ship will not be so great as to detain us any length of time. You may be assured that I shall make no unnecessary delay either here or at any other place, but shall make the best of my way home. I have the Honour to be with the greatest respect,

Sir,

Your most Obedient Humble Servant,

(Signed) JAMES COOK.

Endeavour Bark, at Onrust, near Batavia, the 23rd of October, 1770.

I HAVE made mention . . . of 2 Spanish Ships touching at Georges Island some months before our Arrival there. Upon our arrival at Batavia we were inform'd that 2 French Ships, commanded by the Sieur de Bougainville, had put in there about 2 years before us in their way home from the South Seas. We were told many Circumstances relating to the 2 Ships, all tending to prove beyond a doubt that they were the same 2 as were at George's Island as above mentioned, which we then conjectur'd to be Spaniards, being lead into that mistake by the Spanish Iron, etc., we saw among the Natives, and by Toobouratomita pitching upon the

Colours of that Nation for those they wore, in which he might very easily be mistaken; but as to the Iron, etc., there might be no mistake, for we were told that either one or both of these Ships had put into the River de la Plata, where they disposed of all their European goods brought for that purpose, and purchased others to Trade with the Islanders in the South Sea; and I think we were told that they also touched upon the Spanish Main in the South Sea. As a proof of their having been trading with the Spaniards, Bougainville's Ship had on board a great Quantity of Spanish Dollars at the time she arrived at and left Batavia, some days after our arrival at the Cape of Good Hope. I was told by some French Officers, lately come from the Island Mauritius, that Orette, the Native of George's Island which Bougainville brought away with him, was now at the Maritius, and that they were going to fit out a Ship to carry him to his Native country, where they intend to make a Settlement; 100 Troops for that purpose were to go out in the same Ship. This account is confirmed by a French Gentleman we have on board, who has very lately been at the Maritius. As I have no reason to doubt the truth of this account, it leads me to consider the rout that this Ship must take, which I think can be no other than that of Tasmans as far as the Coast of New Zeland; and if she fall in with that Coast to the Southward of Cape Farewell will very probably put into Admiralty Bay, or Queen Charlotte's sound, as Tasman's track will in some measure point out to her one or the other of these places. I think it is not likely she will venture through the Strait, even suppose she discovers it, but will follow Tasman's Track to the North Cape, where no doubt she will leave him, and follow the direction of the Coast to the South-East, as it will not be out of her way; by which means she will fall in with the most fertile part of that Country, and as they cannot know anything of the *Endeavour*'s voyage, they will not hesitate a moment to declare themselves the first discoverers. Indeed, I cannot see how they can think otherwise, unless the Natives inform them to the contrary, which they may not choose to understand. The French Officers before spoke of would not allow that George's Island was first discover'd by the Dolphin, though no doubt Bougainville did; but it was not for the Interest of his Country, nor perhaps his own, to own it. Thus this Island, though of little value, may prove a Bone of Contention between the 2 Nations, especially if the French make a Settlement upon it, and the Dolphin's voyage, and this of ours, published by Authority to fix the prior right of discovery beyond disputes.

Now I am upon the Subject of discoveries, I hope it will not be taken amiss if I give it as my opinion that the most feasable method of making further discoveries in the South Sea is to enter it by the way of New Zeland, first touching and refreshing at the Cape of Good Hope; from thence proceed to the Southward of New Holland for Queen Charlotte's Sound, where again refresh Wood and water, taking care to be ready to leave that place by the latter end of September, or beginning of October at farthest, when you would have the whole Summer before you, and after getting through the Strait, might, with the prevailing Westerly Winds, run to the Eastward in as high a Latitude as you please, and if you meet with no lands would have time enough to get round Cape Horne before the Summer was too far spent; but if after meeting with no Continent, and you had other objects in view, then haul to the Northward, and after visiting some of the Islands already discovered, after which proceed with the trade wind back to the Westward in search of those before mentioned—thus the discoveries in the South Sea would be compleat.

Part 2
1772—1775

THE VOYAGE OF THE *RESOLUTION*
AND THE *ADVENTURE*

THE VOYAGES OF RESOLUTION and *Adventure* (July 1772–July 1775) featured epic forays into Antarctic waters and a genuinely unprecedented series of meetings with Islanders. The aim was to determine once and for all whether any great southern land in temperate latitudes existed. Cook's method was to investigate far southern waters during the southern summers while spending the colder months further exploring the Pacific tropics, obtaining rest and refreshment. This involved two major east-to-west cruises through many archipelagos during the southern winters of 1773 and 1774. Islands such as Rapanui and the Marquesas that were known to Europeans but had not been visited since 1722 and 1595, respectively, were called at. Others, such as Niue, were discovered for the first time. There were extended visits to parts of Vanuatu and New Caledonia, bringing Melanesian peoples, cultures, and environments into view, and there were further encounters in the Society Islands and New Zealand.

This succession of encounters resulted in a far richer understanding of the Pacific than Europeans previously had, though building on knowledge gained by Spaniards in the late sixteenth and early seventeenth centuries. Islanders, too, especially in the Society Islands and New Zealand, began to have a richer knowledge of Europeans. Some mariners were now able to speak Tahitian and had some competence in Tongan and Maori, among other Polynesian languages. A much fuller sense of the affinities among various Polynesian peoples emerged, as did a sense of their distinctness from various peoples of western Oceania. The participation in the voyage of Johann Reinhold Forster (1729–1798) and Georg Forster (1754–1794), imaginative, exceptionally learned, and controversial father-and-son naturalists, made the ethnographic and historical record from this expedition exceptionally rich. Georg Forster's *Voyage round the World* (1777) is unambiguously the finest of the Cook voyage narratives, and a great and influential work of scientific travel writing. Equally, William Hodges (1744–1797) was the most gifted and remarkable of any of the voyage artists, and produced many images of people, scenes, and inhabited landscapes that are richly informative.

Although the *Resolution* and *Adventure* were separated during a storm in November 1773, neither ship experienced anything like the crisis of the *Endeavour*'s near-wreck on the Great Barrier Reef. Both reached home safely.

PREVIOUS: On Cook's second voyage, the people at Tanna were more receptive to the European visitors than those at Niue and Erramanga. The Forsters, among others, were able to venture inland and get a sense of settlements and agriculture.

From the mariners' perspective, the catastrophe of the voyage was not a nautical one but a human one. A boatload off the *Adventure* grievously offended Maori, and were consequently massacred and their bodies consumed. Until this time, cannibalism in New Zealand was a frightful rumor. This proof that it was actually practiced, and the fact that Europeans were among the victims, profoundly shocked the travelers and prompted considerable reflection upon the nature of humanity and customs around the world.

Following the controversy over Hawkesworth's version of the first-voyage narrative, Cook was determined to be author of the book recounting the second voyage, and he duly wrote *A Voyage Towards the South Pole and around the World* (1777), a plainly written and unsensational, but nevertheless remarkable, narrative of a sea-voyage rich in findings and encounters.

~ Chapter 1 ~

COOK'S PLAN

This extract from the "General Introduction" to Cook's Voyage Towards the South Pole *summarized the approach to discovery and the choice of ships.*

SOON AFTER MY RETURN home in the *Endeavour*, it was resolved to equip two ships, to complete the discovery of the Southern Hemisphere. The nature of this voyage required ships of a particular construction, and the *Endeavour* being gone to Falkland's Isles as a store-ship, the Navy-board was directed to purchase two such ships as were most suitable for this service.

At this time various opinions were espoused by different people, touching the size and kind of vessels most proper for such a voyage. Some were for having large ships, and proposed those of forty guns, or East India Company's ships. Others preferred large good sailing frigates, or three-decked ships, employed in the Jamaica trade, fitted with round-houses. But of all that was said and offered to the Admiralty's consideration on this subject, as far as has come to my knowledge, what, in my opinion, was most to the purpose, was suggested by the Navy-board.

***

AS THE GREATEST danger to be apprehended and provided against, on a voyage of discovery, especially to the most distant parts of the globe, is that of the ship's being liable to be run a-ground on an unknown, desert, or perhaps savage coast; so no consideration should be set in competition with that of her being of a construction of the safest kind, in which the officers may, with the least hazard, venture upon a strange coast. A ship of this kind must not be of a great draught of water, yet of a sufficient burden and capacity to carry a proper quantity of provisions and necessaries for her complement of men, and for the time requisite to perform the voyage.

She must also be of a construction that will bear to take the ground; and of a size, which in case of necessity, may be safely and conveniently laid on shore, to repair any accidental damage

OPPOSITE: Cook's ship on the second voyage was the *Resolution*, a refitted Whitby coal ship or "cat," like the *Endeavour*.

Before the second voyage, William Hodges painted Cook.

or defect. These properties are not to be found in ships of war of forty guns, nor in frigates, nor in East India Company's ships, nor in large three-decked West India ships, nor indeed in any other but North-country-built ships, or such as are built for the coal-trade, which are peculiarly adapted to this purpose.

In such a vessel an able sea-officer will be most venturesome, and better enabled to fulfil his instructions, than he possibly can (or indeed than would be prudent for him to attempt) in one of any other *sort* or *size*.

Upon the whole, I am firmly of opinion, that no ships are so proper for discoveries in distant unknown parts, as those constructed as was the *Endeavour*, in which I performed my former voyage. For no ships of any other kind can contain stores and provisions sufficient (in proportion to the necessary number of men,) considering the length of time it will be necessary they should last. And, even if another kind of ship could stow a sufficiency, yet on arriving at the parts for discovery, they would still, from the nature of their construction and size, be *less fit* for the purpose.

Hence, it may be concluded, so little progress had been hitherto made in discoveries in the Southern Hemisphere. For all ships which attempted it before the *Endeavour*, were unfit for it; although the officers employed in them had done the utmost in their power.

It was upon this consideration that the *Endeavour* was chosen for that voyage. It was to those properties in her that those on board owed their preservation; and hence we were enabled to prosecute discoveries in those seas so much longer than any other ship ever did, or could do. And, although discovery was not the first object of that voyage, I could venture to traverse a far greater space of sea, til then unnavigated; to discover greater tracts of country in high and low south latitudes, and to persevere longer in exploring and surveying more correctly the extensive coasts of those new-discovered countries, than any former navigator perhaps had done during one voyage.

The Cape of Good Hope at the southern tip of Africa played prominently in the voyages of James Cook, and indeed in the navigations of many explorers. On the second voyage Cook was instructed to proceed from Madeira, "there to take in a supply of wine," to the Cape of Good Hope, where he would "refresh the ships' companies" and take aboard more supplies.

In short, these properties in the ships, with perseverance and resolution in their commanders, will enable them to execute their orders; to go beyond former discoverers; and continue to Britain the reputation of taking the lead of nations, in exploring the globe.

These considerations concurring with Lord Sandwich's opinion on the same subject, the Admiralty determined to have two such ships as are here recommended. Accordingly two were purchased of Captain William Hammond of Hull. They were both built at Whitby, by the same person who built the *Endeavour*, being about fourteen or sixteen months old at the time they were purchased, and were, in my opinion, as well adapted to the intended service, as if they had been built for the purpose. The largest of the two was four hundred and sixty-two tons burden. She was named *Resolution*, and sent to Deptford to be equipped. The other was three hundred and thirty-six tons burden. She was named *Adventure*, and sent to be equipped at Woolwich.

* * *

ON THE 28TH OF NOVEMBER, 1771, I was appointed to the command of the *Resolution*; and Tobias Furneaux (who had been second lieutenant with Captain Wallis) was promoted, on this occasion, to the command of the *Adventure*.

At Plymouth I received my instructions, dated the 25th of June, directing me to take under my command the *Adventure*; to make the best of my way to the island of Madeira, there to take in a supply of wine, and then proceed to the Cape of Good Hope, where I was to refresh the ships' companies, and to take on board such provisions and necessaries as I might stand in need of. After leaving the Cape of Good Hope, I was to proceed to the southward, and endeavour to fall in with Cape Circumcision, which was said by Monsieur Bouvet to lie in the latitude of 54° S. and in about 11° 20' E. longitude from Greenwich. If I discovered this cape, I was to satisfy myself whether it was a part of the continent which had so much engaged the attention of geographers and former navigators, or a part of an island. If it proved to be the former, I was to employ myself diligently in exploring as great an extent of it as I could, and to make such notations thereon, and observations of every kind, as might be useful either to navigation or commerce, or tend to the promotion of natural knowledge. I was also directed to observe the genius, temper, disposition, and number of the inhabitants, if there were any, and endeavour, by all proper means, to cultivate a friendship and alliance with them; making them presents of such things as they might value; inviting them to traffic, and shewing them every kind of civility and regard. I was to continue to employ myself on this service, and making discoveries either to the eastward or westward, as my situation might render most eligible; keeping in as high a latitude as I could, and prosecuting my discoveries as near to the South Pole as possible, so long as the condition of the ships, the health of their crews, and the state of their provisions, would admit of; taking care to reserve as much of the latter as would enable me to reach some known port, where I was to procure a sufficiency to bring me home to England. But if Cape Circumcision should prove to be part of an island only, or if I should not be able to find the said Cape, I was in the first case to make the necessary survey of the island, and then to stand on to the southward, so long as I judged there was a likelihood of falling in with the continent, which I was also to do in the latter case, and then to proceed to the eastward in further search of the said continent, as well as to make discoveries of such islands as might be situated in that unexplored part of the southern hemisphere; keeping in high latitudes, and prosecuting my discoveries, as above mentioned, as near the pole as possible until I had circumnavigated the globe; after which I was to proceed to the Cape of Good Hope, and from thence to Spithead.

In the prosecution of these discoveries, wherever the season of the year rendered it unsafe for me to continue in high latitudes, I was to retire to some known place to the northward, to refresh my people, and refit the ships; and to return again to the southward as soon as the season of the year would admit of it. In all unforeseen cases, I was authorised to proceed according to my own discretion; and in case the *Resolution* should be lost or disabled, I was to prosecute the voyage on board the *Adventure*.

I gave a copy of these instructions to Captain Furneaux, with an order directing him to carry them into execution; and, in case he was separated from me, appointed the island of Madeira for the first place of rendezvous; Port Praya in the island of St Jago for the second; Cape of Good Hope for the third; and New Zealand for the fourth.

OPPOSITE: The brilliant but fractious German naturalist Johann Reinhold Forster took Joseph Banks's place on the second voyage. This painting of a giant devil ray, probably caught in Atlantic waters, was one of many natural history illustrations made by Forster's son Georg, who would in due course become more famous than his father as a scientific traveler, writer, and radical.

250.

Raia rostrata.

Chapter 2

INTO THE ANTARCTIC

---

*Following a passage to the South Atlantic and a period in Cape Town, the ships
made their first attempt to venture into far southern latitudes. The mariners were
astonished by the severity of the weather and by massive "ice islands."*

HAVING AT LENGTH FINISHED my business at the Cape, and taken leave of the governor and some others
of the chief officers, who, with very obliging readiness, had given me all the assistance I could desire,
on the 22d of November we repaired on board; and at three o'clock in the afternoon weighed, and
came to sail with the wind at N. by W. As soon as the anchor was up, we saluted the port with fifteen
guns, which was immediately returned; and after making a few trips, got out of the bay by seven
o'clock, at which time the town bore S.E. distant four miles. After this we stood to the westward
all night, in order to get clear of the land, having the wind at N.N.W. and N.W., blowing in squalls
attended with rain, which obliged us to reef our topsails. The sea was again illuminated for some
time, in the same manner as it was the night before we arrived in Table Bay.

Having got clear of the land, I directed my course for Cape Circumcision. The wind continued at N.W. a moderate gale, until the 24th, when it veered round to the eastward. On the noon
of this day, we were in the latitude of 35° 25' S., and 29' west of the Cape; and had abundance of
albatrosses about us, several of which were caught with hook and line; and were very well relished
by many of the people, notwithstanding they were at this time served with fresh mutton. Judging
that we should soon come into cold weather, I ordered slops to be served to such as were in want;
and gave to each man the fearnought jacket and trowsers allowed them by the Admiralty.

1772 DECEMBER

The wind continued easterly for two days, and blew a moderate gale, which brought us
into the latitude of 39° 4', and 2° of longitude west of the Cape, thermometer 52-½ The
wind now came to W. and S.W.; and on the 29th fixed at W.N.W., and increased to
a storm, which continued, with some few intervals of moderate weather, till the 6th of
December, when we were in the latitude of 48° 41' S., and longitude 18° 24' E. This gale,
which was attended with rain and hail, blew at times with such violence that we could

carry no sails; by which means we were driven far to the eastward of our intended course, and no hopes were left me
of reaching Cape Circumcision. But the greatest misfortune that attended us, was the loss of great part
of our live stock, which we had brought from the
Cape, and which consisted of sheep, hogs, and
geese. Indeed this sudden transition from warm,
mild weather, to extreme cold and wet, made
every man in the ship feel its effects. For by this
time the mercury in the thermometer had fallen
to 38; whereas at the Cape it was generally at
67 and upwards. I now made some addition to
the people's allowance of spirit, by giving them a
dram whenever I thought it necessary, and ordered
Captain Furneaux to do the same. The night proved
clear and serene, and the only one that was so since
we left the Cape; and the next morning the rising sun
gave us such flattering hopes of a fine day, that we were
induced to let all the reefs out of the top-sails, and to
get top-gallant yards across, in order to make the most
of a fresh gale at north. Our hopes, however, soon van-
ished; for before eight o'clock, the serenity of the sky was

William Hodges, the greatest of the
artists to travel with Cook, produced
evocative landscapes. He later went on
to produce important works in India.

changed into a thick haze, accompanied with rain. The gale increasing obliged us to
hand the main-sail, close-reef our top-sails, and to strike top-gallant yards. The barom-
eter at this time was unusually low, which foreboded an approaching storm, and this
happened accordingly. For, by one o'clock p.m. the wind, which was at N.W., blew with
such strength as obliged us to take in all our sails, to strike top-gallant-masts, and to get
the spritsail-yard in. And I thought proper to wear, and lie-to, under a mizzen-stay-sail,
with the ships' heads to the N.E. as they would bow the sea, which ran prodigiously
high, better on this tack.

At eight o'clock next morning, being the 8th, we wore, and lay on the other tack;
the gale was a little abated, but the sea ran too high to make sail, any more than the fore-
top-mast-stay-sail. In the evening, being in the latitude of 49° 40 S., and 1-½° E. of the
Cape, we saw two penguins and some sea or rock-weed, which occasioned us to sound,
without finding ground at 100 fathoms. At eight p.m. we wore, and lay with our heads
to the N.E. till three in the morning of the 9th, then wore again to the southward, the
wind blowing in squalls attended with showers of snow. At eight, being something more
moderate, I made the *Adventure* signal to make sail; and soon after made sail ourselves
under the courses and close-reefed top-sails. In the evening, took in the top-sails and
main-sail, and brought-to under fore-sail and mizzen; thermometer at 36°. The wind
still at N.W. blew a fresh gale, accompanied with a very high sea. In the night had a
pretty smart frost with snow.

Cape Town, at the time a Dutch settlement, was Cook's last point of contact with Europeans prior to the venture south into Antarctic waters. This piece was painted by William Hodges.

In the morning of the 10th we made sail under courses and top-sails close-reefed; and made the signal for the *Adventure* to make sail and lead. At eight o'clock saw an island of ice to the westward of us, being then in the latitude of 56° 40' S. and longi-tude 2° 0' E. of the Cape of Good Hope. Soon after the wind moderated, and we let all the reefs out of the top-sails, got the spritsail-yard out, and top-gallant-mast up. The weather coming hazy, I called the *Adventure* by signal under my stern, which was no

sooner done, than the haze increased so much with snow and sleet, that we did not see an island of ice, which we were steering directly for, till we were less than a mile from it. I judged it to be about 50 feet high, and half a mile in circuit. It was flat at top, and its sides rose in a perpendicular direction, against which the sea broke exceedingly high. Captain Furneaux at first took this ice for land, and hauled off from it, until called back by signal. As the weather was foggy, it was necessary to proceed with caution. We therefore reefed our top-sails, and at the same time sounded, but found no ground with 150 fathoms. We kept on to the southward with the wind at north till night, which we spent in making short trips, first one way and then another, under an easy sail; thermometer these 24 hours from 36-½ to 31.

At day-light in the morning of the 11th, we made sail to the southward with the wind at west, having a fresh gale, attended with sleet and snow. At noon we were in the latitude of 51° 50' S., and longitude 21° 3' E., where we saw some white birds about the size of pigeons, with blackish bills and feet. I never saw any such before; and Mr. Forster had no knowledge of them. I believe them to be of the peterel tribe, and natives of these icy seas. At this time we passed between two ice islands, which lay at a little distance from each other.

In the night the wind veered to N.W. which enabled us to steer S.W. On the 12th we had still thick hazy weather, with sleet and snow; so that we were obliged to proceed with great caution on account of the ice islands. Six of these we passed this day; some of them near two miles in circuit, and sixty feet high. And yet, such was the force and height of the waves, that the sea broke quite over them. This exhibited a view which for a few moments was pleasing to the eye; but when we reflected on the danger, the mind was filled with horror. For were a ship to get against the weather-side of one of these islands when the sea runs high, she would be dashed to pieces in a moment. Upon our getting among the ice islands, the albatrosses left us; that is, we saw but one now and then. Nor did our other companions, the pintadoes, sheerwaters, small grey birds, fulmars, &c., appear in such numbers; on the other hand, penguins began to make their appearance. Two of these birds were seen to-day.

The wind in the night veered to west, and at last fixed at S.W., a fresh gale, with sleet and snow, which froze on our sails and rigging as it fell, so that they were all hung with icicles. We kept on to the southward, passed no less than eighteen ice islands, and saw more penguins. At noon on the 13th, we were in the latitude of 54° S., which is the latitude of Cape Circumcision, discovered by M. Bouvet in 1739; but we were ten degrees of longitude east of it; that is, near 118 leagues in this latitude. We stood on to the S.S.E. till eight o'clock in the evening, the weather still continuing thick and hazy, with sleet and snow. From noon till this time, twenty ice islands, of various extent, both for height and circuit, presented themselves to our view. At eight o'clock we sounded, but found no ground with 150 fathom of line.

OVERLEAF: The "ice islands" were massive, unlike anything that the mariners had previously encountered.

We now tacked and made a trip to the northward till midnight, when we stood again to the southward; and at half an hour past six o'clock in the morning of the 14th, we were stopped by an immense field of low ice; to which we could see no end, either to the east, west, or south. In different parts of this field were islands or hills of ice, like those we found floating in the sea; and some on board thought they saw land also over the ice, bearing S.W. by S. I even thought so myself; but changed my opinion upon more narrowly examining these ice hills, and the various appearances they made when seen through the haze. For at this time it was both hazy and cloudy in the horizon; so that a distant object could not be seen distinct. Being now in the latitude of 54° 50' S. and longitude 21° 34' E., and having the wind at N.W. we bore away along the edge of the ice, steering S.S.E. and S.E., according to the direction of the north side of it, where we saw many whales, penguins, some white birds, pintadoes, &c.

At eight o'clock we brought-to under a point of the ice, where we had smooth water: and I sent on board for Captain Furneaux. After we had fixed on rendezvouses in case of separation, and some other matters for the better keeping company, he returned on board, and we made sail again along the ice. Some pieces we took up along-side, which yielded fresh water. At noon we had a good observation, and found ourselves in latitude 54° 55' S.

We continued a south-east course along the edge of the ice, till one o'clock, when we came to a point round which we hauled S.S.W., the sea appearing to be clear of ice in that direction. But after running four leagues upon this course, with the ice on our starboard side, we found ourselves quite imbayed; the ice extending from N.N.E. round by the west and south, to east, in one compact body. The weather was indifferently clear; and yet we could see no end to it. At five o'clock we hauled up east, wind at north, a gentle gale, in order to clear the ice. The extreme east point of it, at eight o'clock, bore E. by S., over which appeared a clear sea. We however spent the night in making short boards, under an easy sail. Thermometer, these 24 hours, from 32 to 30.

Next day, the 15th, we had the wind at N.W., a small gale, thick foggy weather, with much snow; thermometer from 32 to 27; so that our sails and rigging were all hung with icicles. The fog was so thick at times, that we could not see the length of the ship; and we had much difficulty to avoid the many islands of ice that surrounded us. About noon, having but little wind, we hoisted out a boat to try the current, which we found set S.E. near ¾ of a mile an hour. At the same time, a thermometer, which in the open air was at 32°, in the surface of the sea was at 30°; and, after being immerged 100 fathoms deep for about fifteen or twenty minutes, came up at 34°, which is only 2° above freezing. Our latitude at this time was 55° 8'.

The thick fog continued till two o'clock in the afternoon of the next day, when it cleared away a little, and we made sail to the southward, wind still at N.W. a gentle gale. We had not run long to the southward before we fell in with the main field of ice extending from S.S.W. to E. We now bore away to east along the edge of it; but at night hauled off north, with the wind at W.N.W., a gentle gale, attended with snow.

At four in the morning on the 17th, stood again to the south; but was again obliged to bear up on account of the ice, along the side of which we steered betwixt E. and S.S.W., hauling into every bay or opening, in hopes of finding a passage to the south. But we found every where the ice closed. We had a gentle gale at N.W. with showers of snow. At noon we were, by observation, in the latitude of 55° 16' S. In the evening the weather was clear and serene. In the course of this day we saw many whales, one seal, penguins, some of the white birds, another sort of peterel, which is brown and white, and not much unlike a pintado; and some other sorts already known. We found the skirts of the loose ice to be more broken than usual; and it extended some distance beyond the main field, insomuch that we sailed amongst it the most part of the day; and the high ice islands without us were innumerable. At eight o'clock we sounded, but found no ground with 250 fathoms of line. After this we hauled close upon a wind to the northward, as we could see the field of ice extend as far as N.E. But this happened not to be the northern point; for at eleven o'clock we were obliged to tack to avoid it.

At two o'clock the next morning we stood again to the northward, with the wind at N.W. by W., thinking to weather the ice upon this tack; on which we stood but two hours, before we found ourselves quite imbayed, being then in latitude 55° 8', longitude 24° 3'. The wind veering more to the north, we tacked and stood to the westward under all the sail we could carry, having a fresh breeze and clear weather, which last was of short duration. For at six o'clock it became hazy, and soon after there was thick fog; the wind veered to the N.E., freshened and brought with it snow and sleet, which froze on the rigging as it fell. We were now enabled to get clear of the field of ice: but at the same time we were carried in amongst the ice islands, in a manner equally dangerous, and which with much difficulty we kept clear of.

Dangerous as it is to sail among these floating rocks (if I may be allowed to call them so) in a thick fog, this, however, is preferable to being entangled with immense fields of ice under the same circumstances. The great danger to be apprehended in this latter case, is the getting fast in the ice; a situation which would be exceedingly alarming. I had two men on board that had been in the Greenland trade; the one of them in a ship that lay nine weeks, and the other in one that lay six weeks, fast in this kind of ice, which they called packed ice. What they called field ice is thicker; and the whole field, be it ever so large, consists of one piece. Whereas this which I call field-ice, from its immense extent, consists of many pieces of various sizes, both in thickness and surface, from thirty or forty feet square to three or four, packed close together, and in places heaped one upon another. This, I am of opinion, would be found too hard for a ship's side, that is not properly armed against it. How long it may have lain, or will lie here, is a point not easily determined. Such ice is found in the Greenland seas all the summer long; and I think it cannot be colder there in the summer, than it is here. Be this as it may, we certainly had no thaw; on the contrary, the mercury in Fahrenheit's thermometer kept generally below the freezing point, although it was the middle of summer.

Chapter 3

IN DUSKY SOUND

Exhausted by a four-month Antarctic cruise, the ships' companies were delight-
ed to reach southern New Zealand in March 1773. The calm waters of Dusky
Sound provided an idyllic environment in which to rest and refresh. This extract
is from Georg Forster's lyrical Voyage round the World, *the best-written of any*
Cook-voyage narrative, notable particularly for its fine and detailed natural his-
tory and its sympathetic observation of Pacific Islanders, such as the small Maori
group encountered during this visit.

AFTER AN INTERVAL of one hundred and twenty-two days, and a run of above three thousand five hundred leagues, out of sight of land, we entered Dusky Bay on the 26th of March about noon. This bay
is situated a little to the northward of Cape West, and captain Cook, in his voyage in the *Endeavour*,
had discovered and named it without entering into it. The soundings gave about 40 fathoms in the
entrance, but as we advanced, we had no ground with 60, and therefore were obliged to push on
farther. The weather was delightfully fair, and genially warm, when compared to what we had lately
experienced; and we glided along by insensible degrees, wafted by light airs, past numerous rocky
islands, each of which was covered with wood and shrubberies, where numerous evergreens were
sweetly contrasted and mingled with the various shades of autumnal yellow. Flocks of aquatic birds
enlivened the rocky shores, and the whole country resounded with the wild notes of the feathered
tribe. We had long and eagerly wished for the land and its vegetable productions, and therefore
could not but eye the prospect before us with peculiar delight, and with emotions of joy and satisfaction which were strongly marked in the countenance of each individual.

About three o'clock in the afternoon, we dropped an anchor under a point of an island,
where we were in some measure sheltered from the sea, and so near the shore, as to reach it with
a hawser. The sloop was no sooner in safety, than every sailor put his hook and line overboard,
and in a few moments numbers of fine fish were hauled up on all parts of the vessel, which
heightened the raptures we had already felt at our entrance into this bay. The real good taste
of the fish, joined to our long abstinence, inclined us to look upon our first meal here, as the
most delicious we had ever made in our lives. The view of rude sceneries in the style of *Rosa*, of

This engraving derives from Hodges' sketches of the Maori family of Dusky Sound.

antediluvian forests which cloathed the rock, and of numerous rills of water, which every where rolled down the steep declivity, altogether conspired to complete our joy; and so apt is mankind, after a long absence from land, to be prejudiced in favour of the wildest shore, that we looked upon the country at that time, as one of the most beautiful which nature unassisted by art could produce. Such are the general ideas of travellers and voyagers long exhausted by distresses; and with such warmth of imagination they have viewed the rude cliffs of Juan Fernandez, and the impenetrable forests of Tinian!

Immediately after dinner two boats were sent out to reconnoitre different parts of the bay, and chiefly to look for a safe harbour for our vessel, the first anchoring-place being open, inconvenient, and only serving the necessity of the moment. We improved these opportunities of pursuing our researches in natural history, and separated in order to profit by both excursions. Each of the parties found convenient and well-sheltered harbours, with plenty of wood and water; and wherever they went they met with such abundance of fish and water-fowl, that they entertained hopes

of a constant supply of refreshments during their stay in these parts. This prospect prevailed upon Capt. Cook, who had but cursorily examined the southern extremities of New-Zeeland in his former voyage, to spend some time there, in order to gain a more competent knowledge of its situation and productions. On our part, we perceived a new store of animal and vegetable bodies, and among them hardly any that were perfectly similar to the known species, and several not analogous even to the known genera. With these therefore we hoped to be wholly employed during our stay, in spight of the approach of autumn, which seemed to threaten the vegetable creation.

Early the next morning, a small boat having been sent out towards the shore, returned in three hours time with as many fishes, caught by the hook, as supplied a plentiful dinner to all on board. The best and most savoury fish was a species of the cod, which, from its external colour, our sailors called a coal-fish: besides this we caught several species of excellent flat cavalhas (*sciænæ*), some scorpens, mullets, horse-mackrel, and many other sorts of a fine taste, which were entirely unknown in Europe. At nine o'clock we got under sail and went into Pickersgill harbour, one of those examined the preceding day, where the ship was moored head and stern in a small creek, and so near the shore, that we could reach it by means of a stage of a few planks. Nature had assisted us for this purpose with a large tree, projecting in an horizontal position over the water, of which we placed the top on our gunwale, connecting our planks with it. This situation facilitated all our operations, and was particularly adapted to the conveniency of wooding and watering, for our sloop's yards were locked in the branches of surrounding trees, and about half a musket shot a-stern we had a fine stream of fresh water.

* * *

ON THE FIRST day after our arrival we found a beautiful tree in flower, something related to the myrtle-genus, of which an infusion had been drank instead of tea in Capt. Cook's former voyage. We immediately repeated the experiment with great eagerness, as we had not yet seen any plant which was fit to be used at our tables. Its leaves were finely aromatic, astringent, and had a particular pleasant flavour at the first infusion; but this fine taste went off at the next filling up of the

ABOVE: Mark Adams' photographs reveal the extent to which William Hodges adapted the realities of the terrain in order to produce a pleasing, romantic image of the waterfall of Cascade Cove (following page).

OPPOSITE: Cook first visited the Marlborough Sounds, in the northeast of New Zealand's South Island, during the first voyage. It was here that the crew found the grass that helped cure their scurvy.

Hodges' magnificent painting evokes the rugged topography, including the waterfall at Cascade Cove, and the dramatic and changing light of Dusky Sound. The Maori family was actually encountered on a nearby island, not in the vicinity of the waterfall.

tea-pot, and a great degree of bitterness was then extracted. We therefore never suffered it to be twice infused. The use of this plant, which became general among our crew, probably contributed greatly to restore their strength, and to remove all scorbutic symptoms. A plant, which might be of service to future navigators, deserved to be drawn, in order that they might know it again. We have therefore very readily permitted Captain Cook to make use of our drawing of it, from which a plate has been engraved by order of the Admiralty, intended to accompany his own account of this voyage. In a fine soil in thick forests it grows to a considerable tree, sometimes thirty or forty feet high, and above a foot in diameter; on a hilly arid exposure I have, on the contrary, found it as a little shrub, six inches high, which bore flowers and seed; but its usual size is about eight or ten feet, and about three inches in diameter. In that case its stem is irregular and unequal, dividing very soon into branches which rise at acute angles, and only bear leaves and flowers at top. The flowers are white and very ornamental to the whole plant. Another tree, which grew in great plenty round about us, was likewise tried, and afforded a good infusion; but the resemblance it bore to the trees of the fir tribe, and a kind of resinous taste, soon convinced us that it was fitter to serve the purposes of the American spruce-tree, and that a palatable and wholesome liquor might be brewed from it, as a kind of substitute for spruce-beer. In effect, with the addition of the inspissated juice of wort, and of some molasses, we brewed a very good sort of beer, which we improved very considerably afterwards, by correcting the too great astringency of our new spruce, with an equal quantity of the new tea-tree. Its taste was pleasant, and something bitter; and the only fault we could observe in it was, that being taken on an empty stomach, it frequently caused a nausea or sickness; but in all other respects it proved a very salutary drink. The spruce of New-Zeeland is a very beautiful tree, and conspicuous on account of its pendant branches, which are loaded with numerous long thread-like leaves, of a vivid green. It frequently grows to the height of fifty or sixty, and even one hundred feet, and has above ten feet in girth. Though the spruce and the tea-trees alone afforded articles of refreshment in Dusky Bay; yet we found the woods full of trees of various kinds, very fit for the use of shipwrights, joiners, and other mechanics; and Capt. Cook was of opinion that, except in the river Thames on the northern island, he had not observed a finer growth of timber on all New-Zeeland.

We had not been above two days in this bay, before we found that our opinion of its being uninhabited was premature. On the 28th in the morning several of our officers went a shooting in a small boat, and on entering a cove two or three miles from the ship, perceived several natives upon a beach, who were about to launch their canoe. The New Zeelanders halloo'd at their approach, and seeming by this means more numerous than they really were, the officers thought proper to return and acquaint the captain with their discovery; a step which they found the more necessary, as the weather was very rainy, and might, in case of danger, have prevented their pieces from going off. They were scarcely returned on board, when a canoe appeared off a point, at about a mile's distance from the sloop; there were seven or eight people in it, who looked at us for some time, but notwithstanding all the signs of friendship which we could make, such as calling to them to come to us, waving a white cloth, and promising beads, they did not care to come nearer, and paddled back again the same way they came. They appeared to be dressed in mats, and had broad paddles with which they managed their canoe, like the inhabitants in the northern parts of New Zeeland. Captain Cook resolved to visit them in the afternoon, in order to quiet the apprehension which they seemed to have entertained. We went in two boats, accompanying him and several of the officers into the cove, where the natives had been first seen. Here we found a double canoe hauled upon the shore, near some old, low huts, about which we saw vestiges of fire places, some fishing-nets, and a few scattered fish. The canoe which appeared to be old and in bad order, consisted of two troughs or boats joined together with sticks, tied across the gunwales with strings of the New Zeeland flax-plant. Each part consisted of planks sowed together with ropes made of the flax-plant, and had a carved head coarsely representing a human face, with eyes made of round pieces of ear-shell, which somewhat resembled mother of pearl. This canoe contained two paddles, a basket full of berries of the *coriaria ruscifolia* Lin. and some fishes; but the natives were not to be seen or heard, which gave us reason to believe that they had retired into the woods. To conciliate their good will, we left some medals, looking-glasses, beads, &c. in the canoe, and embarked again after a short stay. We then rowed to the head of the cove, in order to survey it, where we found a fine brook of fresh water coming down on a flat beach, from whence the water continued shallow to a considerable extent, so that our boat ran aground several times. Ducks, shags, black oyster-catchers, and some sorts of plovers were very numerous here. At our return we visited the canoe again, added a hatchet to the other presents which we had left before, and to shew the use of it, we cut several chips out of a tree, and left it sticking there. No natives appeared this second time, though we imagined they could not be far off, as we thought we could smell the smoke of a fire. However, captain Cook desisted at present from searching in the woods, since they purposely avoided us, and choosing to leave it to time and their own free will to cultivate an intercourse with us . . .

Early on the 6th, several of the officers went into the cove, which the captain had discovered on the 2d; and the latter, accompanied by Mr. Hodges, Dr. Sparrman, my father, and myself proceeded in another boat, to continue the survey of the bay, to copy views from nature, and to search for the natural productions of the country. We directed our course to the north side, where we found a fine spacious cove, from which we had not the least prospect of the sea. Along its steep shores we observed several small but beautiful cascades, which fell from vast heights, and greatly improved the scene; they gushed out through the midst of the woods, and at last fell in a clear column, to which a ship might lie so near, as to fill her casks on board with the greatest safety, by means of a leather tube, which the sailors call a hose. At the bottom there was a shallow muddy part, with a little beach of shell-sand, and a brook, as in all the greater coves of the bay. In this fine place we found a number of wild fowl, and particularly wild ducks of which we shot fourteen, from whence we gave it the name of Duck Cove. As we were returning home, we heard a loud hallooing on the rocky point of an island, which on this occasion obtained the name of Indian Island; and standing in to the shore, we perceived one of the natives, from whom this noise proceeded. He stood with a club or battle-axe in his hand, on a projecting point, and behind him, on the skirts of the wood we saw two women, each of them having a long spear. When our boat came to the foot of the rock, we called to him, in the language of Taheitee, *tayo, harre maï,* "friend, come hither;" he did not, however, stir from his post, but held a long speech, at certain intervals pronouncing it with great earnestness and vehemence, and swinging round his club, on which he leaned at other times. Captain Cook went to the head of the boat, called to him in a friendly manner, and threw him his own and some other handkerchiefs, which he would not pick up. The captain then taking some sheets of white paper in his hand, landed on the rock unarmed, and held the paper out to the native. The man now trembled very visibly, and having exhibited strong marks of fear in his countenance, took the paper: upon which Captain Cook coming up to him, took hold of his hand, and embraced him, touching the man's nose with his own, which is their mode of salutation. His apprehension was by this means dissipated, and he called to the two women, who came and joined him, while several of us landed to keep the captain company. A short conversation ensued, of which very little was understood on both sides, for want of a competent knowledge of the language. Mr. Hodges immediately took sketches of their countenances, and their gestures shewed that they clearly understood what he was doing; on which they called him *tóä-tóä,* that term being probably applicable to the imitative arts. The man's countenance was very pleasing and open; one of the women, which we afterwards believed to be his daughter, was not wholly so disagreeable as one might have expected in New Zeeland, but the other was remarkably ugly, and had a prodigious excrescence on her upper lip. They were all of a dark brown or olive complexion; their hair was

A coastal saltwater lake at the Bay of Fires in northeast Tasmania. The second voyage reached this spot on March 17, 1773, and so named the spot for fires spotted along the coast.

black, and curling, and smeared with oil and ruddle; the man wore his tied upon the crown of the head, but the women had it cut short. Their bodies were tolerably well proportioned in the upper part; but they had remarkable slender, ill-made, and bandy legs. Their dress consisted of mats made of the New Zeeland flax-plant, interwoven with feathers; and in their ears they wore small pieces of white albatross skins stained with ruddle or ochre. We offered them some fishes and wild fowl, but they threw them back to us, intimating that they did not want provisions. The approaching night obliged us to retire, not without promising our new friends a visit the next morning. The man remained silent, and looked after us with composure and great attention, which seemed to speak a profound meditation; but the youngest of the two women, whose vociferous volubility of tongue exceeded every thing we had met with, began to dance at our departure, and continued to be as loud as ever. Our seamen passed several coarse jests on this occasion, but nothing was more obvious to us than the general drift of nature, which not only provided man with a partner to alleviate his cares and sweeten his labours, but endowed that partner likewise with a desire of pleasing by a superior degree of vivacity and affability.

QUEEN CHARLOTTE'S SOUND

The second voyage importantly featured repeat visits to harbors and islands previously called at during the first expedition. Cook's familiarity with Pacific environments and people grew, as did his appreciation of the complexity of cross-cultural encounter, and the confusions and mistakes that it could give rise to.

IT WAS . . . said that some of [the Maori] offered their children to sale. I however found that this was a mistake. The report first took its rise on board the *Adventure* where they were utter strangers to their language and customs. It was very common for these people to bring their children with them, and present them to us, in expectation that we would make them presents; this happened to me the preceding morning. A man brought his son, a boy about nine or ten years of age, and presented him to me. As the report of selling their children was then current, I thought, at first, that he wanted me to buy the boy. But at last I found that he wanted me to give him a white shirt, which I accordingly did. The boy was so fond of his new dress, that he went all over the ship, presenting himself before every one that came in his way. This freedom used by him offended Old Will, the ram goat, who gave him a butt with his horns, and knocked him backward on the deck. Will would have repeated his blow, had not some of the people come to the boy's assistance. The misfortune, however, seemed to him irreparable. The shirt was dirtied, and he was afraid to appear in the cabin before his father, until brought in by Mr Forster; when he told a very lamentable story against goury the great dog (for so they call all the quadrupeds we had aboard), nor could he be reconciled, till his shirt was washed and dried. This story, though extremely trifling in itself, will shew how liable we are to mistake these people's meaning, and to ascribe to them customs they never knew even in thought.

OPPOSITE: Maori warrior men, with their facial tattoos, ornaments, and, in the case of this man, fine flax cloaks, were impressive—even daunting.

About nine o'clock, a large double canoe, in which were twenty or thirty people, appeared in sight. Our friends on board seemed much alarmed, telling us that these were their enemies. Two of them, the one with a spear, and the other with a stone-hatchet in his hand, mounted the arm-chests on the poop, and there, in a kind of bravado, bid those enemies defiance; while the others, who were on board, took to their canoe and went ashore, probably to secure the women and children.

All I could do, I could not prevail on the two that remained to call these strangers along-side; on the contrary, they were displeased at my doing it, and wanted me to fire upon them. The people in the canoe seemed to pay very little regard to those on board, but kept advancing slowly towards the ship, and after performing the usual ceremonies, put along-side. After this the chief was easily prevailed upon to come on board, followed by many others, and peace was immediately established on all sides. Indeed, it did not appear to me that these people had any intention to make war upon their brethren. At least, if they had, they were sensible enough to know, that this was neither the time nor place for them to commit hostilities.

One of the first questions these strangers asked, was for Tupia; and when I told them he was dead, one or two expressed their sorrow by a kind of lamentation, which to me appeared more formal than real. A trade soon commenced between our people and them. It was not possible to hinder the former from selling the clothes from off their backs for the merest trifles, things that were neither useful nor curious. This caused me to dismiss the strangers sooner than I would have done. When they departed, they went to Motuara, where, by the help of our glasses, we discovered four or five canoes, and several people on the shore. This induced me to go over in my boat, accompanied by Mr Forster and one of the officers. We were well received by the chief and the whole tribe, which consisted of between

Waterspouts are frequent around what are now known as the Marlborough Sounds. Concerned that the ship might be damaged, Cook and his companions fired cannons into the phenomenon, which dispersed harmlessly.

Georg Forster produced many fine botanical studies. This is the New Zealand forest vine *Metrosideros fulgens*.

ninety and a hundred persons, men, women, and children, having with them six canoes, and all their utensils; which made it probable that they were come to reside in this sound. But this is only conjecture; for it is very common for them, when they go but a little way, to carry their whole property with them; every place being alike, if it affords them the necessary subsistence; so that it can hardly be said they are ever from home. Thus we may easily account for the emigration of those few families we found in Dusky Bay.

Living thus dispersed in small parties, knowing no head but the chief of the family or tribe, whose authority may be very little, they feel many inconveniences, to which well-regulated societies, united under one head or any other form of government, are not subject. These form laws and regulations for their general good; they are not alarmed at the appearance of every stranger; and, if attacked or invaded by a public enemy, have strong-holds to retire to, where they can with advantage defend themselves, their property, and their country. This seems to be the state of most of the inhabitants of Eahei-nomauwe; whereas those of Tavai-poenammoo, by living a wandering life in small parties, are destitute of most of these advantages, which subjects them to perpetual alarms. We generally found them upon their guard, travelling and working, as it were with their arms in their hands. Even the women are not exempted from bearing arms, as appeared by the first interview I had with the family in Dusky Bay; where each of the two women was armed with a spear, not less than 18 feet in length.

I was led into these reflections, by not being able to recollect the face of any one person I had seen here three years ago: Nor did it once appear, that any one of them had the least knowledge of me, or of any person with me that was here at that time. It is therefore highly probable that the greatest part of the people which inhabited this sound in the beginning of the year 1770, have been since driven out of it, or have, of their own accord, removed somewhere else. Certain it is, that not one third of the inhabitants were here now, that were then. Their stronghold on the point of Motuara hath been long deserted; and we found many forsaken habitations in all parts of the sound. We are not, however, wholly to infer from this, that this place hath been once very populous; for each family may, for their own convenience, when they move from place to place, have more huts than one or two.

It may be asked, if these people had never seen the *Endeavour*, nor any of her crew, how could they become acquainted with the name of Tupia, or have in their possession (which many of them had) such articles, as they could only have got from that ship? To this it may be answered, that the name of Tupia was so popular among them when the *Endeavour* was here, that it would be no wonder if, at this time, it was known over great part of New Zealand, and as familiar to those who never saw him, as to those who did. Had ships, of any other nation whatever, arrived here, they would have equally enquired of them for Tupia. By the same way of reasoning, many of the articles left here by the *Endeavour*, may be now in possession of those who never saw her. I got from one of the people, now present, an ear ornament, made of glass very well formed and polished. The glass they must have got from the *Endeavour*.

After passing about an hour on Motuara with these people, and having distributed among them some presents, and shewed to the chief the gardens we had made, I returned on board, and spent the remainder of our royal master's birth-day in festivity; having the company of Captain Furneaux and all his officers. Double allowance enabled the seamen to share in the general joy.

Both ships being now ready for sea, I gave Captain Furneaux an account in writing of the route I intended to take; which was to proceed to the east, between the latitudes of 41° and 46° S., until I arrived in the longitude of 140° or 135° W., then, provided no land was discovered; to proceed to Otaheite; from thence back to this place, by the shortest route; and after taking in wood and water, to proceed to the south, and explore all the unknown parts of the sea between the meridian of New Zealand and Cape Horn. Therefore, in case of separation before we reached Otaheite, I appointed that island for the place of rendezvous, where he was to wait till the 20th of August: If not joined by me before that time, he was then to make the best of his way back to Queen Charlotte's Sound, where he was to wait until the 20th of November: After which (if not joined by me,) he was to put to sea, and carry into execution their lordships' instructions.

Some may think it an extraordinary step in me to proceed on discoveries as far south at 46° degrees of latitude, in the very depth of winter. But though it most be owned, that winter is by no means favourable for discoveries, it nevertheless appeared to me necessary that something should be done in it, in order to lessen the work I was upon; lest I should not be able to finish the discovery of the southern part of the South Pacific Ocean the ensuing summer. Besides, if I should discover any land in my route to the east, I should be ready to begin, with the summer, to explore it. Setting aside all these considerations, I had little to fear; having two good ships well provided; and healthy crews. Where then could I spend my time better? If I did nothing more, I was at least in hopes of being able to point out to posterity, that these seas may be navigated, and that it is practicable to go on discoveries; even in the very depth of winter.

During our stay in the sound, I had observed that this second visit made to this country, had not mended the morals of the natives of either sex. I had always looked upon the females of New Zealand to be more chaste than the generality of Indian women. Whatever favours a few of them might have granted to the people in the *Endeavour*, it was generally done in a private manner, and the men did not seem to interest themselves much in it. But now, I was told, they were the chief promoters of a shameful traffic, and that for a spike-nail, or any other thing they value, they would oblige the women to prostitute themselves, whether they would or no; and even without any regard to that privacy which decency required.

TAHITI

The return to Tahiti gave the ordinary sailors and Cook the opportunity to revisit friends made during the Endeavour's *visit. There was much gift exchange, and Cook became aware that Tahitian society was no utopia or ideal order, but one marked by rivalries between aristocrats and ongoing conflict around ritual and political status.*

1773 AUGUST

Before we got to an anchor, our decks were crowded with the natives; many of whom I knew, and almost all of them knew me. A great crowd were gotten together upon the shore; amongst whom was Otoo their king. I was just going to pay him a visit, when I was told he was mataow'd, and gone to Oparree. I could not conceive the reason of his going off in a fright, as every one seemed pleased to see me. A chief, whose name was Maritata, was at this time on board, and advised me to put off my visit till the next morning, when he would accompany me; which I accordingly did.

After having given directions to pitch tents for the reception of the sick, coopers, sail-makers, and the guard, I set out on the 26th for Oparree; accompanied by Captain Furneaux, Mr Forster, and others, Maritata and his wife. As soon as we landed, we were conducted to Otoo, whom we found seated on the ground, under the shade of a tree, with an immense crowd around him. After the first compliments were over, I presented him with such articles as I guessed were most valuable in his eyes; well knowing that it was my interest to gain the friendship of this man. I also made presents to several of his attendants; and, in return, they offered me cloth, which I refused to accept; telling them that what I had given was for *tiyo* (friendship). The king enquired for Tupia, and all the gentlemen that were with me in my former voyage, by name; although I do not remember that he was personally acquainted with any of us. He promised that I should have some hogs the next day; but I had much ado to obtain a promise from him to visit me on board. He said he was, *mataou no to poupoue,* that is, afraid of the guns. Indeed all his actions shewed him to be a timorous prince. He was about thirty years of age, six feet high, and a fine, personable, well-made man as one can see. All his subjects appeared uncovered before him, his father not excepted. What is meant by uncovering, is the making bare the head and shoulders, or wearing no sort of clothing above the breast.

William Hodges made several views of Matavai Bay, with and without Cook's ships. This one, affirming the civilizing presence of the British, was for the Admiralty and is now in the collection of the Royal Museums in Greenwich. Hodges' finest paintings were made in Tahiti, where he found techniques to convey the distinctive tropical light.

When I returned from Oparree, I found the tents, and the astronomer's observatories, set up on the same spot where we observed the transit of Venus in 1769. In the afternoon, I had the sick landed; twenty from the *Adventure*, all ill of the scurvy; and one from the *Resolution*. I also landed some marines for a guard, and left the command to Lieutenant Edgecumbe of the marines.

On the 27th, early in the morning, Otoo, attended by a numerous train, paid me a visit. He first sent into the ship a large quantity of cloth, fruits, a hog, and two large fish; and, after some persuasion, came aboard himself, with his sister, a younger brother, and several more of his attendants. To all of them I made presents; and, after breakfast, took the king, his sister, and as many more as I had room for, into my boat, and carried them home to Oparree. I had no sooner landed than I was met by a venerable old lady, the mother of the late Toutaha. She seized me by both hands, and burst into a flood of tears, saying, *Toutaha Tiyo no Toutee matty Toutaha*—(Toutaha, your friend, or the friend of Cook, is dead.) I was so much affected with her behaviour, that it

would have been impossible for me to have refrained min-
gling my tears with hers, had not Otoo come and taken me
from her. I, with some difficulty, prevailed on him to let
me see her again, when I gave her an axe and some other
things. Captain Furneaux, who was with me, presented
the king with two fine goats, male and female, which if
taken care of, or rather if no care at all is taken of them will
no doubt multiply. After a short stay, we look leave and
returned on board.

Very early in the morning on the 28th, I sent Mr
Pickersgill, with the cutter, as far as Ottahourou, to procure hogs. A little after sun-rise, I had another visit from
Otoo, who brought me more cloth, a pig, and some fruit.
His sister, who was with him, and some of his attendants,
came on board; but he and others went to the *Adventure*
with the like present to Captain Furneaux. It was not
long before he returned with Captain Furneaux on board
the *Resolution*, when I made him a handsome return for the
present he had brought me, and dressed his sister out in
the best manner I could. She, the king's brother, and one
or two more, were covered before him to-day. When Otoo
came into the cabin, Ereti and some of his friends were
sitting there. The moment they saw the king enter, they
stripped themselves in great haste, being covered before.
Seeing I took notice of it, they said *Earee, Earee*; giving me
to understand that it was on account of Otoo being present. This was all the respect they paid him; for they never
rose from their seats, nor made him any other obeisance.
When the king thought proper to depart, I carried him
again to Oparree in my boat; where I entertained him and
his people with the bagpipes (of which music they are very
fond) and dancing by the seamen. He then ordered some
of his people to dance also, which consisted chiefly of con-
tortions. There were some, however, who could imitate the

The opulence of the Polynesian environment, and the
voluptuousness of Polynesian women, became a powerful theme
in European images of Tahiti. One of the earliest and most
evocative expressions of the motif is this view made by Hodges
inland from Vaitepiha Bay. The work also gives prominence to
expressions of indigenous religion, notably the sculpted wooden
ti'i (god images).

In Tahiti, Cook and his men witnessed many *heiva* or festivals. While customary life was disrupted by French colonization, *heiva* has become an annual festival.

seamen pretty well, both in country-dances and hornpipes. While we were here, I had a present of cloth from the late Toutaha's mother. This good old lady could not look upon me without shedding tears; however, she was far more composed than before. When we took leave, the king promised to visit me again the next day; but said that I must first come to him. In the evening Mr Pickersgill came back empty, but with a promise of having some hogs, if he would return in a few days.

Next morning after breakfast, I took a trip to Oparree, to visit Otoo as he had requested, accompanied by Captain Furneaux and some of the officers. We made him up a present of such things as he had not seen before. One article was a broad-sword; at the sight of which he was so intimidated, that I had much ado to persuade him to accept of it, and to have it buckled upon him; where it remained but a short time, before he desired leave to take it off, and send it out of his sight.

Soon after we were conducted to the theatre; where we were entertained with a dramatic *heuva*, or *play*, in which were both dancing and comedy. The performers were five men, and one woman, who was no less a person than the king's sister. The music consisted of three drums only; it lasted about an hour and a half, or two hours; and, upon the whole, was well conducted. It was not possible for us to find out the meaning of the play. Some part seemed adapted to the present time, as my name was frequently mentioned. Other parts were certainly wholly unconnected with us. It apparently differed in nothing, that is, in the manner of acting it, from those we saw at Ulielea in my former voyage. The dancing-dress of the lady was more elegant than any I saw there, by being decorated with long tassels, made of feathers, hanging from the waist downward. As soon as all was over, the king himself desired me to depart; and sent into the boat different kinds of fruit and fish, ready dressed. With this we returned on board; and the next morning he sent me more fruit, and several small parcels of fish.

Nothing farther remarkable happened till ten o'clock in the evening, when we were alarmed with the cry of murder, and a great noise, on shore, near the bottom of the bay, at some distance from our encampment. I suspected that it was occasioned by some of our own people; and immediately armed a boat, and sent on shore, to know the occasion of this disturbance, and to bring off such of our people as should be found there. I also sent to the *Adventure*, and to the post on shore, to know who were missing; for none were absent from the *Resolution* but those who were upon duty. The boat soon returned with three marines and a seaman. Some others belonging to the *Adventure* were also taken; and, being all put under confinement, the next morning I ordered them to be punished according to their deserts. I did not find that any mischief was done, and our people would confess nothing. I believe this disturbance was occasioned by their making too free with the women. Be this as it will, the natives were so much alarmed, that they fled from their habitations in the dead of the night, and the alarm spread many miles along the coast. For when I went to visit Otoo, in the morning, by appointment, I found him removed, or rather fled, many miles from the place of his abode. Even there I was obliged to wait some hours, before I could see him at all; and when I did, he complained of the last night's riot.

"King" Pomare, also known as Tu, was one of the most prominent and canny of the high chiefs Cook dealt with.

As this was intended to be my last visit, I had taken with me a present suitable to the occasion. Among other things were three Cape sheep, which he had seen before and asked for; for these people never lose a thing by not asking for it. He was much pleased with them; though he could be but little benefited, as they were all weathers; a thing he was made acquainted with. The presents he got at this interview entirely removed his fears, and opened his heart so much, that he sent for three hogs; one for me, one for Captain Furneaux, and one for Mr Forster. This last was small, of which we complained, calling it *ete, ete*. Presently after a man came into the circle, and spoke to the king with some warmth, and in a very peremptory manner; saying something or other about hogs. We at first thought he was angry with the king for giving us so many, especially as he took the little pig away with him. The contrary, however, appeared to be the true cause of his displeasure; for, presently after he was gone, a hog, larger than either of the other two, was brought us in lieu of the little one. When we took leave, I acquainted him that I should sail from the island the next day; at which he seemed much moved, and embraced me several times. We embarked to return on board, and he, with his numerous train, directed his march back to Oparree.

Chapter 6

FARTHEST SOUTH

Cook's plan required that the ship venture into far southern waters to definitively establish whether or not any southern continent existed. The epic foray of January 1774 brought humanity into contact with the edge of the Antarctic ice sheet for the first time and prompted Cook to articulate his own ambition, to go as far as it was possible for man to go. The cruise demonstrated that, if there might be land beyond the ice, there was no temperate or inhabitable southern land mass in this part of the ocean, demolishing the speculations of generations of geographers, who had insisted that a southern continent was required to balance the world.

OUR COURSE WAS NOW MORE SOUTHERLY, till the evening of the 13th, when we were in the latitude of 53° 0' S., longitude 118° 3' W. The wind being then at N.W. a strong gale with a thick fog and rain, which made it unsafe to steer large, I hauled up S.W., and continued this course till noon the next day, when our latitude was 56° 4' S., longitude 122° 1' W. The wind having veered to the north, and the fog continuing, I hauled to the east, under courses and close-reefed top-sails. But this sail we could not carry long; for before eight o'clock in the evening, the wind increased to a perfect storm, and obliged us to lie-to, under the mizen-stay-sail, till the morning of the 16th, when the wind having a good deal abated, and veered to west, we set the courses, reefed top-sails, and stood to the south. Soon after, the weather cleared up, and, in the evening, we found the latitude to be 56° 48' S., longitude 119° 8' W. We continued to steer to the south, inclining to the east, till the 18th, when we stood to the S.W., with the wind at S.E., being at this time in the latitude of 61° 9' S., longitude 116° 7' W. At ten o'clock in the evening, it fell calm, which continued till two the next morning, when a breeze sprung up at north, which soon after increased to a fresh gale, and fixed at N.E. With this we steered south till noon on the 20th, when, being now in the latitude of 62° 34' S., longitude 116° 24' W., we were again becalmed.

In this situation we had two ice islands in sight, one of which seemed to be as large as any we had seen. It could not be less than two hundred feet in height, and terminated in a peak not unlike the cupola of St Paul's church. At this time we had a great westerly swell, which made it improbable that any land should lie between us and the meridian of 133° ½, which was our longitude, under the latitude we were now in, when we stood to the north. In all this route we had not seen the least thing that could induce us to think we were ever in the neighbourhood of any land. We had, indeed, frequently seen pieces of sea-weed; but this, I am well assured, is no sign of the vicinity of land; for weed is seen in every part of the ocean. After a few hours calm, we got a wind from S.E.; but it was very unsettled, and attended with thick snow-showers; at length it fixed at S. by E., and we stretched to the east. The wind blew fresh, was piercing cold, and attended with snow and sleet. On the 22d, being in the latitude of 62° 5' S., longitude 112° 24' W., we saw an ice island, an antarctic peterel, several blue peterels, and some other known birds; but no one thing that gave us the least hopes of finding land.

On the 23d, at noon, we were in the latitude of 62° 22' S., longitude 110° 24'. In the afternoon, we passed an ice island. The wind, which blew fresh, continued to veer to the west; and at eight o'clock the next morning it was to the north of west, when I steered S. by W. and S.S.W. At this time we were in the latitude of 63° 20' S., longitude 108° 7' W., and had a great sea from S.W. We continued this course till noon the next day, the 25th, when we steered due south. Our latitude, at this time, was 65° 24' S., longitude 109° 31' W.; the wind was at north; the weather mild and not unpleasant; and not a bit of ice in view. This we thought a little extraordinary, as it was but a month before, and not quite two hundred leagues to the east, that we were in a manner blocked up with large islands of ice in this very latitude. Saw a single pintadoe peterel, some blue peterels, and a few brown albatrosses. In the evening, being under the same meridian, and in the latitude of 65° 44' S., the variation was 19° 27' E.; but the next morning, in the latitude of 66° 20' S., longitude the same as before, it was only 18° 20' E.; probably the mean between the two is the nearest the truth. At this time, we had nine small islands in sight; and soon after we came, the third time, within the antarctic polar circle, in the longitude of 109° 31' W. About noon, seeing the appearance of land to the S.E., we immediately trimmed our sails and stood towards it. Soon after it disappeared, but we did not give it up till eight o'clock the next morning, when we were well assured that it was nothing but clouds, or a fog bank; and then we resumed our course to the south, with a gentle breeze at N.E., attended with a thick fog, snow, and sleet.

We now began to meet with ice islands more frequently than before; and, in the latitude of 69° 38' S., longitude 108° 12' W., we fell in with a field of loose ice. As we began to be in want of water, I hoisted out two boats and took up as much as yielded about ten tons. This was cold work, but it was now familiar to us. As soon as we had done, we hoisted in the boats, and afterwards made short boards over that part of the sea we had in some measure made ourselves acquainted with. For we had now so thick a fog, that we could not see two hundred yards round us; and as we knew not the extent of the loose ice, I durst not steer to the south till we had clear weather. Thus we spent the night, or rather that part of twenty-four hours which answered to night; for we had no darkness but what was occasioned by fogs.

At four o'clock in the morning of the 29th, the fog began to clear away; and the day becoming clear and serene, we again steered to the south with a gentle gale at N.E. and N.N.E. The variation was found to be 22° 41' E. This was in the latitude of 69° 45' S., longitude 108° 5' W.; and, in the afternoon, being in the same longitude, and in the latitude of 70° 23' S., it was 24° 31' E. Soon

The ice-choked Southern Ocean near the Antarctic Peninsula.

after, the sky became clouded, and the air very cold. We continued our course to the south, and passed a piece of weed covered with barnacles, which a brown albatross was picking off. At ten o'clock, we passed a very large ice island; it was not less than three or four miles in circuit. Several more being seen a-head, and the weather becoming foggy, we hauled the wind to the northward; but in less than two hours, the weather cleared up, and we again stood south.

On the 30th, at four o'clock in the morning, we perceived the clouds, over the horizon to the south, to be of an unusual snow-white brightness, which we knew denounced our approach to field-ice. Soon after, it was seen from the top-mast-head; and at eight o'clock, we were close to its edge. It extended east and west, far beyond the reach of our sight. In the situation we were in, just the southern half of our horizon was illuminated, by the rays of light reflected from the ice, to a considerable height. Ninety-seven ice hills were distinctly seen within the field, besides those on the outside; many of them very large, and looking like a ridge of mountains, rising one above another till they were lost in the clouds. The outer or northern edge of this immense field, was composed of loose or broken ice close packed together, so that it was not possible for any thing to enter it. This was about a mile broad, within which, was solid ice in one continued compact body. It was rather low and flat (except the hills), but seemed to increase in height, as you traced it to the south; in which direction it extended beyond our sight. Such mountains of ice as these, I believe, were never seen in the Greenland seas, at least, not that I ever heard or read of, so that we cannot draw a comparison between the ice here and there.

It must be allowed, that these prodigious ice mountains must add such additional weight to the ice fields which inclose them, as cannot but make a great difference between the navigating this icy sea and that of Greenland.

I will not say it was impossible any where to get farther to the south; but the attempting it would have been a dangerous and rash enterprise, and what, I believe, no man in my

situation would have thought of. It was, indeed, *my* opinion, as well as the opinion of most on board, that this ice extended quite to the pole, or perhaps joined on some land, to which it had been fixed from the earliest time; and that it is here, that is to the south of this parallel, where all the ice we find scattered up and down to the north, is first formed, and afterwards broken off by gales of wind, or other causes, and brought to the north by the currents, which we always found to set in that direction in the high latitudes. As we drew near this ice some penguins were heard, but none seen; and but few other birds or any other thing that could induce us to think any land was near. And yet I think, there must be some to the south behind this ice; but if there is, it can afford no better retreat for birds, or any other animals, than the ice itself, with which it must be wholly covered. I, who had ambition not only to go farther than any one had been before, but as far as it was possible for man to go, was not sorry at meeting with this interruption, as it in some measure relieved us, at least shortened the dangers and hardships inseparable from the navigation of the southern polar regions. Since, therefore, we could not proceed one inch farther to the south, no other reason need be assigned for my tacking and standing back to the north; being at this time in the latitude of 71° 10' S., longitude 106° 54' W.

It was happy for us that the weather was clear when we fell in with this ice, and that we discovered it so soon as we did; for we had no sooner tacked than we were involved in a thick fog. The wind was at east, and blew a fresh breeze, so that we were enabled to return back over that space we had already made ourselves acquainted with. At noon, the mercury in the thermometer stood at 32-½, and we found the air exceedingly cold. The thick fog continuing with showers of snow, gave a coat of ice to our rigging of near an inch thick. In the afternoon of the next day the fog cleared away at intervals; but the weather was cloudy and gloomy, and the air excessively cold; however, the sea within our horizon was clear of ice.

Chapter 7

RAPANUI

Cook's next landfall in Polynesia would be Easter Island. Though struck by what he considered the poverty of the island's provisions and resources, he was intrigued to realize that the inhabitants were related to Maori—that is, they were another branch of the Polynesian peoples who, despite their lack of iron tools and western-style navigational knowledge, had the capacity to cross thousands of miles of open ocean to settle these widely dispersed islands.

1774 MARCH

At eight o'clock in the morning, on the 11th, land was seen, from the mast-head, bearing west, and at noon from the deck, extending from W. ¾ N. to W. by S., about twelve leagues distant. I made no doubt that this was Davis's Land, or Easter Island… we stretched in for the land; and by the help of our glass, discovered people, and some of those Colossean statues or idols mentioned in the account of Roggewein's voyage. At four o'clock p.m. we were half a league S.S.E. and N.N.W. of the N.E. point of the island; and, on sounding, found thirty-five fathoms, a dark sandy bottom. I now tacked, and endeavoured to get into what appeared to be a bay, on the west side of the point or S.E. side of the island; but before this could be accomplished, night came upon us, and we stood on and off, under the land, till the next morning; having sounding from seventy-five to an hundred and ten fathoms, the same bottom as before.

On the 13th, about eight o'clock in the morning, the wind, which had been variable most part of the night, fixed at S.E., and blew in squalls, accompanied with rain; but it was not long before the weather became fair. As the wind now blew right to the S.E. shore, which does not afford that shelter I at first thought, I resolved to look for anchorage on the west and N.W. sides of the island. With this view I bore up round the south point, off which lie two small islets, the one nearest the point high and peaked, and the other low and flattish. After getting round the point, and coming before a sandy beach,

we found soundings thirty and forty fathoms, sandy ground, and about one mile from the shore. Here a canoe, conducted by two men, came off to us. They brought with them a bunch of plantains, which they sent into the ship by a rope, and then they returned ashore. This gave us a good opinion of the islanders, and inspired us with hopes of getting some refreshments, which we were in great want of.

I continued to range along the coast, till we opened the northern point of the isle, without seeing a better anchoring-place than the one we had passed. We therefore tacked, and plied back to it; and, in the mean time, sent away the master in a boat to sound the coast. He returned about five o'clock in the evening; and soon after we came to an anchor in thirty-six fathoms water, before the sandy beach above mentioned. As the master drew near the shore with the boat, one of the natives swam off to her, and insisted on coming a-board the ship, where he remained two nights and a day. The first thing he did after coming a-board, was to measure the length of the ship, by fathoming her from the tafferel to the stern, and as he counted the fathoms, we observed that he called the numbers by the same names that they do at Otaheite; nevertheless his language was in a manner wholly unintelligible to all of us.

Having anchored too near the edge of a bank, a fresh breeze from the land, about three o'clock the next morning, drove us off it; on which the anchor was heaved up, and sail made to regain the bank again. While the ship was plying in, I went ashore, accompanied by some of the gentlemen, to see what the island was likely to afford us. We landed at the sandy beach, where some hundreds of the natives were assembled, and who were so impatient to see us, that many of them swam off to meet the boats. Not one of them had so much as a stick or weapon of any sort in their hands. After distributing a few trinkets amongst them, we made signs for something to eat, on which they brought down a few potatoes, plantains, and sugar canes, and exchanged them for nails, looking-glasses, and pieces of cloth.

We presently discovered that they were as expert thieves and as tricking in their exchanges, as any people we had yet met with. It was with some difficulty we could keep the hats on our heads; but hardly possible to keep any thing in our pockets, not even what themselves had sold us; for they would watch every opportunity to snatch it from us, so that we sometimes bought the same thing two or three times over, and after all did not get it.

Before I sailed from England, I was informed that a Spanish ship had visited this isle in 1769. Some signs of it were seen among the people now about us; one man had a pretty good broad-brimmed European hat on, another had a grego jacket, and another a red silk handkerchief. They also seemed to know the use of a musquet, and to stand in much awe of it; but this they probably learnt from Roggewein, who, if we are to believe the authors of that voyage, left them sufficient tokens.

* * *

OPPOSITE: The Rapanui environment was impoverished, Cook thought, but he was also astonished that the Islanders were related to other Polynesians and had reached their home by voyaging across thousands of miles of open ocean.

I SHALL NOW give some farther account of this island, which is undoubtedly the same that Admiral Roggewein touched at in April 1722; although the description given of it by the authors of that voyage does by no means agree with it now. It may also be the same that was seen by Captain Davis in 1686; for, when seen from the east, it answers very well to Wafer's description, as I have before observed. In short, if this is not the land, his discovery cannot lie far from the coast of America, as this latitude has been well explored from the meridian of 80° to 110°. Captain Carteret carried it much farther; but his track seems to have been a little too far south. Had I found fresh water, I intended spending some days in looking for the low sandy isle Davis fell in with, which would have determined the point. But as I did not find water, and had a long run to make before I was assured of getting any, and being in want of refreshments, I declined the search; as a small delay might have been attended with bad consequences to the crew, many of them beginning to be more or less affected with the scurvy.

No nation need contend for the honour of the discovery of this island, as there can be few places which afford less convenience for shipping than it does. Here is no safe anchorage, no wood for fuel, nor any fresh water worth taking on board. Nature has been exceedingly sparing of her favours to this spot. As every thing must be raised by dint of labour, it cannot be supposed that the inhabitants plant much more than is sufficient for themselves; and as they are but few in number, they cannot have much to spare to supply the wants of visitant strangers. The produce is sweet potatoes, yams, tara or eddy root, plantains, and sugar-canes, all pretty good, the potatoes especially, which are the best of the kind I ever tasted. Gourds they have also, but so very few, that a cocoa-nut shell was the most valuable thing we could give them. They have a few tame fowls, such as cocks and hens, small but well tasted. They have also rats, which it seems they eat; for I saw a man with some dead ones in his hand, and he seemed unwilling to part with them, giving me to understand they were for food. Of land-birds there were hardly any, and sea-birds but few; these were men-of-war, tropic, and egg-birds, noddies, tern, &c. The coast seemed not to abound with fish, at least we could catch none with hook and line, and it was but very little we saw among the natives.

Such is the produce of Easter Island, or Davis's Land, which is situated in latitude 27° 5' 30" S., longitude 109° 46' 20" W. It is about ten or twelve leagues in circuit, hath a hilly and stony surface, and an iron-bound shore. The hills are of such a height as to be seen fifteen or sixteen leagues. Off the south end, are two rocky islets, lying near the shore. The north and east points

Europeans knew of the famous statues of Rapanui (Easter Island) from the voyage narrative of Jacob Roggeveen, but the accounts from Cook's second voyage include the first detailed discussions of them. Made after field sketches, this vibrant Hodges painting is the first European visual image of the *ahu moai*.

of the island rise directly from the sea to a considerable height; between them and the S.E. side, the shore forms an open bay, in which I believe the Dutch anchored. We anchored, as hath been already mentioned, on the west side of the island, three miles to the north of the south point, with the sandy beach bearing E.S.S. This is a very good road with easterly winds, but a dangerous one with westerly; as the other on the S.E. side must be with easterly winds. . . .

The inhabitants of this island do not seem to exceed six or seven hundred souls, and above two-thirds of those we saw were males. They either have but few females amongst them, or else

From Rapanui, the *Resolution* made its way to the Marquesas where the people were clearly also Polynesian, speaking languages cognate with Tahitian, and bearing the tattoos recognized as a hallmark of Oceanic culture.

many were restrained from making their appearance during our stay, for though we saw nothing to induce us to believe the men were of a jealous disposition, or the women afraid to appear in public, something of this kind was probably the case.

In colour, features, and language, they bear such an affinity to the people of the more western isles, that no one will doubt they have had the same origin. It is extraordinary that the same nation should have spread themselves over all the isles in this vast ocean, from New Zealand to this island, which is almost one-fourth part of the circumference of the globe. Many of them have now no other knowledge of each other, than what is preserved by antiquated tradition; and they have, by length of time, become, as it were, different nations, each having adopted some peculiar custom or habit, &c. Nevertheless, a careful observer will soon see the affinity each has to the other. In general, the people of this isle are a slender race. I did not see a man that would measure six feet; so far are they from being giants, as one of the authors of Roggewein's voyage asserts. They are brisk and active, have good features, and not disagreeable countenances; are friendly and hospitable to strangers, but as much addicted to pilfering as any of their neighbours.

Tattowing, or puncturing the skin, is much used here. The men are marked from head to foot, with figures all nearly alike; only some give them one direction, and some another, as fancy leads. The women are but little punctured; red and white paint is an ornament with *them*, as also with the men; the former is made of turmeric, but what composes the latter I know not.

Their clothing is a piece or two of quilted cloth, about six feet by four, or a mat. One piece wrapped round their loins, and another over their shoulders, make a complete dress. But the men, for the most part, are in a manner naked, wearing nothing but a slip of cloth betwixt their legs, each end of which is fastened to a cord or belt they wear round the waist. Their cloth is made of the same materials as at Otaheite, viz. of the bark of the cloth-plant; but, as they have but little of it, our Otaheitean cloth, or indeed any sort of it, came here to a good market.

Their hair in general is black; the women wear it long, and sometimes tied up on the crown of the head; but the men wear it, and their beards, cropped short. Their headdress is a round fillet adorned with feathers, and a straw bonnet something like a Scotch one; the former, I believe, being

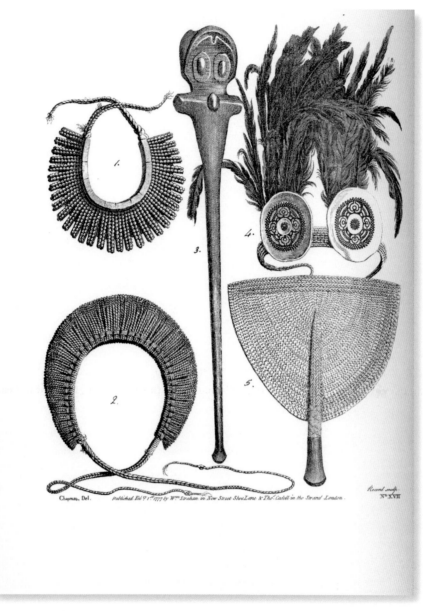

Marquesan art forms collected during the voyage included spectacular war clubs, intricately woven fans, and varied head and chest ornaments.

chiefly worn by the men, and the latter by the women. Both men and women have very large holes, or rather slits, in their ears, extending to near three inches in length. They sometimes turn this slit over the upper part, and then the ear looks as if the flap was cut off. The chief ear-ornaments are the white down of feathers, and rings, which they wear in the inside of the hole, made of some elastic substance, rolled up like a watch-spring. I judged this was to keep the hole at its utmost extension. I do not remember seeing them wear any other ornaments, excepting amulets made of bone or shells.

As harmless and friendly as these people seemed to be, they are not without offensive weapons, such as short wooden clubs and spears; the latter of which are crooked sticks about six feet long, armed at one end with pieces of flint. They have also a weapon made of wood, like the *Patoo patoo* of New Zealand.

Their houses are low miserable huts, constructed by setting sticks upright in the ground, at six or eight feet distance, then bending them towards each other, and tying them together at the top, forming thereby a kind of Gothic arch. The longest sticks are placed in the middle, and shorter ones each way, and a less distance asunder, by which means the building is highest and broadest in the middle, and lower and narrower towards each end. To these are tied others horizontally, and the whole is thatched over with leaves of sugar-cane. The door-way is in the middle of one side, formed like a porch, and so low and narrow, as just to admit a man to enter upon all fours. The largest house I saw was about sixty feet long, eight or nine feet high in the middle, and three or four at each end; its breadth, at these parts, was nearly equal to its height. Some have a kind of vaulted houses built with stone, and partly under ground; but I never was in one of these.

* * *

THE GIGANTIC STATUES, so often mentioned, are not, in my opinion, looked upon as idols by the present inhabitants, whatever they might have been in the days of the Dutch; at least I saw nothing that could induce me to think so. On the contrary, I rather suppose that they are burying-places for certain tribes or families. I, as well as some others, saw a human skeleton lying in one of the platforms, just covered with stones. Some of these platforms of masonry are thirty or forty feet long, twelve or sixteen broad, and from three to twelve in height; which last in some measure depends on the nature of the ground; for they are generally at the brink of the bank facing the sea, so that this face may be ten or twelve feet or more high, and the other may not be above three or four. They are built, or rather faced, with hewn stones, of a very large size; and the workmanship is not inferior to the best plain piece of masonry we have in England. They use no sort of cement, yet the joints are exceedingly close, and the stones morticed and tenanted one into another, in a very artful manner. The side-walls are not perpendicular, but inclining a little inwards, in the same manner that breast-works, &c. are built in Europe; yet had not all this care, pains, and sagacity, been able to preserve these curious structures from the ravages of all-devouring time.

The statues, or at least many of them, are erected on these platforms, which serve as foundations. They are, as near as we could judge, about half length, ending in a sort of stump at the bottom, on which they stand. The workmanship is rude, but not bad; nor are the features of the face ill formed, the nose and chin in particular; but the ears are long beyond proportion; and, as to the bodies, there is hardly any thing like a human figure about them.

A woven fiber and pearlshell head ornament from the Marquesas.

I had an opportunity of examining only two or three of these statues, which are near the landing-place; and they were of a grey stone, seemingly of the same sort as that with which the platforms were built. But some of the gentlemen, who travelled over the island, and examined many of them, were of opinion that the stone of which they were made, was different from any they saw on the island, and had much the appearance of being factitious. We could hardly conceive how these islanders, wholly unacquainted with any mechanical power, could raise such stupendous figures, and afterwards place the large cylindric stones before mentioned upon their heads. The only method I can conceive, is by raising the upper end by little and little, supporting it by stones as it is raised, and building about it till they got it erect; thus a sort of mount or scaffolding would be made, upon which they might roll the cylinder, and place it upon the head of the statue, and then the stones might be removed

A *haka'iki* or chief of the island of Tahuata in the southern part of the Marquesas archipelago.

from about it. But if the stones are factitious, the statues might have been put together on the place, in their present position, and the cylinder put on by building a mount round them, as above mentioned. But, let them have been made and set up by this or any other method, they must have been a work of immense time, and sufficiently shew the ingenuity and perseverance of these islanders in the age in which they were built; for the present inhabitants have most certainly had no hand in them, as they do not even repair the foundations of those which are going to decay. They give different names to them, such as Gotomoara, Marapate, Kanaro, Goway-too-goo, Matta Matta, &c. &c. to which they sometimes prefix the word Moi, and sometimes annex Areeke. The latter signifies chief, and the former burying, or sleeping-place, as well as we could understand.

Besides the monuments of antiquity, which were pretty numerous, and no where but on or near the sea-coast, there were many little heaps of stones, piled up in different places along the coast. Two or three of the uppermost stones in each pile were generally white, perhaps always so, when the pile is complete. It will hardly be doubted that these piles of stone had a meaning; probably they might mark the place where people had been buried, and serve instead of the large statues.

The working-tools of these people are but very mean, and, like those of all the other islanders we have visited in this ocean, made of stone, bone, shells, &c. They set but little value on iron or iron tools, which is the more extraordinary, as they know their use; but the reason may be, their having but little occasion for them.

TAHITIAN "NAVIES"

Cook had not anticipated returning to the Society Islands but considered it necessary to extend the voyage, in order to undertake further cruises through far southern waters. In preparation, the southern winter of 1774 would be dedicated to further investigations of the Pacific tropics. A further period in Tahiti gave the mariners the opportunity to witness spectacular gatherings of war canoes, indigenous seacraft which deeply impressed Cook and which were beautifully documented by the voyage artist, William Hodges.

ON THE 23D, SHOWERY WEATHER. Our very good friends the natives supplied us with fruit and fish sufficient for the whole crew.

On the 24th, Otoo the king, and several other chiefs, with a train of attendants, paid us a visit, and brought as presents ten or a dozen large hogs, besides fruits, which made them exceedingly welcome. I was advertised of the king's coming, and looked upon it as a good omen. Knowing how much it was my interest to make this man my friend, I met him at the tents, and conducted him and his friends on board, in my boat, where they staid dinner; after which they were dismissed with suitable presents, and highly pleased with the reception they had met with.

Next day we had much thunder, lightning, and rain. This did not hinder the king from making me another visit, and a present of a large quantity of refreshments. It hath been already mentioned, that when we were at the island of Amsterdam we had collected, amongst other curiosities, some red parrot feathers. When this was known here, all the principal people of both sexes endeavoured to ingratiate themselves into our favour by bringing us hogs, fruit, and every other thing the island afforded, in order to obtain these valuable jewels. Our having these feathers was a fortunate circumstance, for as they were valuable to the natives, they became so to us; but more especially as my stock of trade was by this time greatly exhausted; so that, if it had not been for the feathers, I should have found it difficult to have supplied the ship with the necessary refreshments.

When I put in at this island, I intended to stay no longer than till Mr Wales had made the necessary observations for the purposes already mentioned, thinking we should meet with no

ABOVE: Cook and his companions were treated to an extraordinary "review" of the "war galleys" of Tahiti. The elaborately sculpted and decorated canoes marshaled in support of the chief Pomare are depicted here.

OVERLEAF: The mariners were naturally interested in the construction and navigation of seagoing canoes, but Hodges also went to considerable trouble to detail the sculptural representations of gods and ancestors mounted on their prows. Hodges' works are among the first studies of any indigenous Oceanic art form.

better success than we did the last time we were here. But the reception we had already met with, and the few excursions we had made, which did not exceed the plains of Matavai and Oparree, convinced us of our error. We found at these two places, built and building, a great number of large canoes, and houses of every kind; people living in spacious habitations who had not a place to shelter themselves in eight months before; several large hogs about every house; and every other sign of a rising state.

Judging from these favourable circumstances that we should not mend ourselves by removing to another island, I resolved to make a longer stay, and to begin with the repairs of the ship and stores, &c. Accordingly I ordered the empty casks and sails to be got ashore to be repaired; the ship to be caulked, and the rigging to be overhauled; all of which the high southern latitudes had made indispensably necessary.

In the morning of the 26th, I went down to Oparree, accompanied by some of the officers and gentlemen, to pay Otoo a visit by appointment. As we drew near, we observed a number of large canoes in motion; but we were surprised, when we arrived, to see upwards of three hundred ranged in order, for some distance, along the shore, all completely equipped and manned,

besides a vast number of armed men upon the shore. So unexpected an armament collected together in our neighbourhood, in the space of one night, gave rise to various conjectures. We landed, however, in the midst of them, and were received by a vast multitude, many of them under arms, and many not. The cry of the latter was *Tiyo no Otoo*, and that of the former *Tiyo no Towha*. This chief, we afterwards learnt, was admiral or commander of the fleet and troops present. The moment we landed I was met by a chief whose name was Tee, uncle to the king, and one of his prime ministers, of whom I enquired for Otoo. Presently after we were met by Towha, who received me with great courtesy. He took me by the one hand, and Tee by the other; and, without my knowing where they intended to carry me, dragged me, as it were, through the crowd that was divided into two parties, both of which professed themselves my friends, by crying out *Tiyo no Tootee*. One party wanted me to go to Otoo, and the other to remain with Towha. Coming to the visual place of audience, a mat was spread for me to sit down upon, and Tee left me to go and bring the king. Towha was unwilling I should sit down, partly insisting on my going with him; but, as I knew nothing of this chief, I refused to comply. Presently Tee returned, and wanted to conduct me to the king, taking hold of my hand for that purpose. This Towha opposed; so that, between the one party and the other, I was like to have been torn in pieces; and was obliged to desire Tee to desist, and to leave me to the admiral and his party, who conducted me down to the fleet. As soon as we came before the admiral's vessel, we found two lines of armed men drawn up before her, to keep off the crowd, as I supposed, and to clear the way for me to go in. But, as I was determined not to go, I made the water, which was between me and her, an excuse. This did not answer; for a man immediately squatted himself down at my feet, offering to carry me; and then I declared I would not go. That very moment Towha quitted me, without my seeing which way he went, nor would any one inform me. Turning myself round I saw Tee, who, I believe, had never lost sight of me. Enquiring of him for the king, he told me he was gone into the country Mataou, and advised me to go to my boat; which we accordingly did, as soon as we could get collected together; for Mr Edgcumbe was the only person that could keep with me, the others being jostled about in the crowd, in the same manner we had been.

When we got into our boat, we took our time to view this grand fleet. The vessels of war consisted of an hundred and sixty large double canoes, very well equipped, manned, and armed. But I am not sure that they had their full complement of men or rowers; I rather think not. The chiefs, and all those on the fighting stages, were dressed in their war habits; that is, in a vast quantity of cloth, turbans, breast-plates, and helmets. Some of the latter were of such a length as greatly to encumber the wearer. Indeed, their whole dress seemed to be ill calculated for the day of battle, and to be designed more for shew than use. Be this as it may, it certainly added grandeur to the prospect, as they were so complaisant as to shew themselves to the best advantage. The vessels were decorated with flags, streamers, &c.; so that the whole made a grand and noble appearance, such as we had never seen before in this sea, and what no one would have expected. Their instruments of war were clubs, spears, and stones. The vessels were ranged close along-side of each other with their heads ashore, and their stern to the sea; the admiral's vessel being nearly in the centre. Besides the vessels of war, there were an hundred and seventy sail of smaller double canoes, all with a little house upon them, and rigged with mast and sail, which the war canoes had not. These, we judged, were designed for transports, victuallers, &c.; for in the war-canoes was no sort of provisions what-ever. In these three hundred and thirty vessels, I guessed there were no less than seven thousand seven hundred and sixty men; a number which appears incredible, especially as we were told they all belonged to the districts of Attahourou and Ahopatea. In this computation I allow to each war canoe forty men, troops and rowers, and to each of the small canoes eight. Most of the gentlemen who were with me, thought the number of men belonging to the war canoes exceeded this. It is certain that the most of them were fitted to row with more paddles than I have allowed them men; but, at this time, I think they were not complete. Tupia informed us, when I was first here, that the whole island raised only between six and seven thousand men; but we now saw two districts only raise that number; so that he must have taken his account from some old establishment; or else he only meant *Tatatous*, that is warriors, or men trained from their infancy to arms, and did not include the rowers, and those necessary to navigate the other vessels. I should think he only spoke of this number as the standing troops or militia of the island, and not their whole force. . .

After we had well viewed this fleet, I wanted much to have seen the admiral, to have gone with him on board the war-canoes. We enquired for him as we rowed past the fleet to no purpose. We put ashore and enquired; but the noise and crowd was so great that no one attended to what we said. At last Tee came and whispered us in the ear, that Otoo was gone to Matavai, advising us to return thither, and not to land where we were. We accordingly proceeded for the ship; and this intelligence and advice received from Tee, gave rise to new conjectures. In short, we concluded that this Towha was some powerful disaffected chief, who was upon the point of making war against his sovereign; for we could not imagine Otoo had any other reason for leaving Oparree in the manner he did.

We had not been long gone from Oparree, before the whole fleet was in motion to the westward, from whence it came. When we got to Matavai, our friends there told us, that this fleet was part of the armament intended to go against Eimea, whose chief had thrown off the yoke of Otaheite, and assumed an independency. We were likewise informed that Otoo neither was nor had been at Matavai; so that we were still at a loss to know why he fled from Oparree. This occasioned another trip thither in the afternoon, where we found him, and now understood that the reason of his not seeing me in the morning was, that some of his people having stolen a quantity of my clothes which were on shore washing, he was afraid I should demand restitution. He repeatedly asked me if I was not angry; and when I assured him that I was not, and that they might keep what they had got, he was satisfied. Towha was alarmed, partly on the same account. He thought I was displeased when I refused to go aboard his vessel; and I was jealous of seeing such a force in our neighbourhood without being able to know any thing of its design. Thus, by mistaking one another, I lost the opportunity of examining more narrowly into part of the naval force of this isle, and making myself better acquainted with its manoeuvres. Such another opportunity may never occur; as it was commanded by a brave, sensible, and intelligent chief, who would have satisfied us in all the questions we had thought proper to ask; and as the objects were before us, we could not well have misunderstood each other. It happened unluckily that Oedidee was not with us in the morning; for Tee, who was the only man we could depend on, served only to perplex us. Matters being thus cleared up, and mutual presents having passed between Otoo and me, we took leave and returned on board.

Chapter 9

NIUE

The small Polynesian island was first encountered by Europeans on this occasion, when Islanders resisted Cook's landing, prompting the navigator's much-resented naming of the place, "Savage Island."

[W]E SAW LAND FROM THE MAST-HEAD . . . and, as we drew nearer, found it to be an island, which, at five o'clock, bore west, distant five leagues. Here we spent the night plying under the topsails; and at day-break next morning, bore away, steering to the northern point, and ranging the west coast at the distance of one mile, till near noon. Then perceiving some people on the shore, and landing seeming to be easy, we brought-to, and hoisted out two boats, with which I put off to the land, accompanied by some of the officers and gentlemen. As we drew near the shore, some of the inhabitants, who were on the rocks, retired to the woods, to meet us, as we supposed; and we afterwards found our conjectures right. We landed with ease in a small creek, and took post on a high rock to prevent a surprise. Here we displayed our colours, and Mr Forster and his party began to collect plants, etc. The coast was so over-run with woods, bushes, plants, stones, etc. that we could not see forty yards round us. I took two men, and with them entered a kind of chasm, which opened a way into the woods. We had not gone far before we heard the natives approaching; upon which I called to Mr Forster to retire to the party, as I did likewise. We had no sooner joined than the islanders appeared at the entrance of a chasm not a stone's throw from us. We began to speak, and make all the friendly signs we could think of, to them, which they answered by menaces; and one of two men, who were advanced before the rest, threw a stone, which struck Mr Sparrman on the arm. Upon this two muskets were fired, without order, which made them all retire under cover of the woods; and we saw them no more.

After waiting for some little time, and till we were satisfied nothing was to be done here, the country being so overrun with bushes, that it was hardly possible to come to parley with them, we embarked and proceeded down along shore, in hopes of meeting with better success in another place. After ranging the coast for some miles, without seeing a living soul, or any convenient land-ing-place, we at length came before a small beach, on which lay four canoes. Here we landed by

Life on the water, Upolu, Samoa, 1982, as photographed by Glenn Jowitt. A boat returns from a fishing trip. Cook probably encountered some Samoans in Tonga, but the archipelago was one that he never reached.

means of a little creek, formed by the flat rocks before it, with a view of just looking at the canoes, and to leave some medals, nails, etc. in them; for not a soul was to be seen. The situation of this place was to us worse than the former. A flat rock lay next the sea; behind it a narrow stone beach; this was bounded by a perpendicular rocky cliff of unequal height, whose top was covered with shrubs; two deep and narrow chasms in the cliff seemed to open a communication into the country. In or before one of these lay the four canoes which we were going to look at; but in the doing of this, I saw we should be exposed to an attack from the natives, if there were any, without being in a situation proper for defence. To prevent this, as much as could be, and to secure a retreat in case of an attack, I ordered the men to be drawn up upon the rock, from whence they had a view of the heights; and only myself, and four of the gentlemen, went up to the canoes. We had been there but a few minutes, before the natives, I cannot say how many, rushed down the chasm out of the wood upon us. The endeavours we used to bring them to a parley, were to no purpose; for they came with the ferocity of wild boars, and threw their darts. Two or three muskets, discharged in the air did not hinder one of them from advancing still farther, and throwing another dart, or rather a spear, which passed close over my shoulder. His courage would have cost him his life, had not my musket missed fire; for I was not five paces from him when he threw his spear, and had resolved to shoot him to save myself. I was glad afterwards that it happened as it did. At this instant, our men on the rock began to fire at others who appeared on the heights, which abated the ardour of the party we were engaged with, and gave us time to join our people, when I caused the firing to cease. The last discharge sent all the islanders to the woods, from whence they did not return so long as we remained. We did not know that any were hurt. It was remarkable, that when I joined our party, I tried my musket in the air, and it went off as well as a piece could do. Seeing no good was to be got with these people, or at the isle, as having no port, we returned on board, and having hoisted in the boats, made sail to the W.S.W. I had forgot to mention in its proper order, that having put ashore a little before we came to this last place, three or four of us went upon the cliffs, where we found the country, as before, nothing but coral rocks, all over-run with bushes, so that it was hardly possible to penetrate into it; and we embarked again with intent to return directly on board, till we saw the canoes; being directed to the place by the opinion of some of us, who thought they heard some people.

The conduct and aspect of these islanders occasioned my naming it Savage Island. It is situated in the latitude 19° 1' S. longitude 169° 37' W. It is about eleven leagues in circuit; of a round form, and good height; and hath deep waters close to its shores. All the sea-coast, and as far inland as we could see, is wholly covered with trees, shrubs, etc.; amongst which were some cocoa-nut trees; but what the interior parts may produce we know not. To judge of the whole garment by the skirts, it cannot produce much; for so much as we saw of it consisted wholly of coral rocks, all over-run with woods and bushes. Not a bit of soil was to be seen; the rocks alone supplying the trees with humidity. If these coral rocks were first formed in the sea by animals, how came they thrown up to such an height? Has this island been raised by an earthquake? Or has the sea receded from it? Some philosophers have attempted to account for the formation of low isles, such as are in the sea; but I do not know that any thing has been said of high islands, or such as I have been speaking of. In this island, not only the loose rocks which cover the surface, but the cliffs which bound the shores, are of coral stone, which the continual beating of the sea has formed into a variety of curious caverns, some of them very large: The roof or rock over them being supported by pillars, which the foaming waves have formed into a multitude of shapes,

LEFT: A spear and staff from Niue. The former is possibly among those thrown at the Europeans during their attempted landing on "Savage Island."

OPPOSITE: Georg Forster painted this specimen of *Zapornia tabuensis*, the spotless crake, a type of rail found on Niue and elsewhere in western Oceania.

Rallus minutus
—— Sabuennes J. N. XIII: 717 h. ?

This young woman is decorated to perform in a customary Niuean dance. Niueans have been Christians since the late nineteenth century, but missionaries failed to dampen their interest in costume and performance.

LEFT: The deep waters off Niue continue to be fished by men in both customary-style canoes and small aluminum boats.

RIGHT: Late photographer Glenn Jowitt, whose images appear on this spread, went to great lengths to document Oceanic cultures and traditions. This image depicts a Niuean performer at the 2013 Polyfest in Auckland.

and made more curious than the caverns themselves. In one we saw light was admitted through a hole at the top; in another place, we observed that the whole roof of one of these caverns had sunk in, and formed a kind of valley above, which lay considerably below the circumjacent rocks.

I can say but little of the inhabitants, who, I believe, are not numerous. They seemed to be stout well-made men, were naked except round the waists, and some of them had their faces, breasts, and thighs painted black. The canoes were precisely like those of Amsterdam; with the addition of a little rising like a gunwale on each side of the open part; and had some carving about them, which shewed that these people are full as ingenious. Both these islanders and their canoes agree very well with the description M. de Bougainville has given of those he saw off the Isle of Navigators, which lies nearly under the same meridian.

Chapter 10

IN THE TONGAN ARCHIPELAGO

In the Tongan islands, the Europeans encountered complex, stratified chiefdoms like those of the Society Islands, and were impressed by an ordered landscape of gardens and settlements, and by rituals associated with status and political authority. Yet misunderstandings and moments of tension were inevitable here too.

1774 JUNE

Before we had well got to an anchor, the natives came off from all parts in canoes, bringing with them yams and shaddocks, which they exchanged for small nails and old rags. One man taking a vast liking to our lead and line, got hold of it, and, in spite of all the threats I could make use of, cut the line with a stone; but a discharge of small shot made him return it. Early in the morning, I went ashore with Mr Gilbert to look for fresh water. We landed in the cove above-mentioned, and were received with great courtesy by the natives. After I had distributed some presents amongst them, I asked for water, and was conducted to a pond of it that was brackish, about three-fourths of a mile from the landing-place, which I supposed to be the same that Tasman watered at. In the mean time, the people in the boat had laden her with fruit and roots, which the natives had brought down, and exchanged for nails and beads. On our return to the ship, I found the same sort of traffic carrying on there. After breakfast, I went ashore with two boats to trade with the people, accompanied by several of the gentlemen, and ordered the launch to follow with casks to be filled with water. The natives assisted us to roll them to and from the pond; and a nail or a bead was the expence of their labour. Fruits and roots, especially shaddocks and yams, were brought down in such plenty, that the two boats were laden, sent off, cleared, and laden a second time, before noon; by which time also the launch had got a full supply of water, and the botanical and shooting parties had all come in, except the surgeon, for whom we could not wait, as the tide was ebbing fast out of the cove; consequently he was left behind. As there is no getting into the cove with a boat, from between half-ebb to half-flood, we could get off no water in the afternoon. However, there is a very good landing-place, without it, near the southern point, where boats can get ashore at all times of the tide. Here some of the officers landed after dinner, where they found the surgeon, who had been robbed of his gun. Having come down to the shore some time after the boats had put off, he got a canoe to bring him on board; but, as he was getting into her, a fellow snatched hold of the gun, and ran off with it. After that no one would carry him to the ship, and they would have stripped him, as he imagined, had he not presented a tooth-pick case, which they, no doubt, thought was a little gun. As soon as I heard of this, I landed at the place above-mentioned, and the few natives who were there fled at my approach. After landing I went in search of the officers, whom I found in the cove, where we had been in the morning, with a good many of the natives about them. No step had been taken to recover the gun, nor did I think proper to take any; but in this I was wrong. The easy manner of obtaining this gun, which they now, no doubt, thought secure in their possession, encouraged them to proceed in these tricks, as will soon appear. The alarm the natives had caught being soon over, they carried fruit, etc. to the boats, which got pretty well laden before night, when we all returned on board.

Early in the morning of the 28th, Lieutenant Clerke, with the master and fourteen or fifteen men, went on shore in the launch for water. I did intend to have followed in another boat myself, but rather unluckily deferred it till after breakfast. The launch was no sooner landed than the natives gathered about her, behaving in so rude a manner, that the officers were in some doubt if they should land their casks; but, as they expected me on shore soon, they ventured, and with difficulty got them filled, and into the boat again. In the doing of this Mr Clerke's gun was snatched from him, and carried off; as were also some of the cooper's tools; and several of the people were stripped of one thing or another. All this was done, as it were, by stealth; for they laid hold of nothing by main force. I landed just as the

RIGHT: This beautiful war club, featuring fine, primarily geometric incised decoration, was collected during Cook's second or third voyage, and is now in the Museum of Archaeology and Anthropology in Cambridge.

OVERLEAF: After the voyage, William Hodges produced a series of views depicting "landings," the initial meetings between the mariners and Islanders at a number of places. These conformed to conventions, representing the encounters as major historical meetings—which they were.

LEFT: This finely carved and polished food pounder was used to prepare vegetable pastes, which formed part of virtually every meal. Vegetable pastes are still commonly eaten across the Pacific.

RIGHT: Tongan shell necklaces were highly valued.

launch was ready to put off; and the natives, who were pretty numerous on the beach, as soon as they saw me, fled; so that I suspected something had happened. However, I prevailed on many to stay, and Mr Clerke came, and informed me of all the preceding circumstances. I quickly came to a resolution to oblige them to make restitution; and, for this purpose, ordered all the marines to be armed and sent on shore. Mr Forster and his party being gone into the country, I ordered two or three guns to be fired from the ship, in order to alarm him; not knowing how the natives might act on this occasion. These orders being given, I sent all the boats off but one, with which I staid, having a good many of the natives about me, who behaved with their usual courtesy. I made them so sensible of my intention, that long before the marines came, Mr Clerke's musket was brought; but they used many excuses to divert me from insisting on the other. At length Mr Edgcumbe

The Europeans were impressed by many aspects of Tongan
culture, including elegant wood-carved headrests.

arriving with the marines, this alarmed them so much, that some fled. The first step I took was to
seize on two large double sailing canoes, which were in the cove. One fellow making resistance,
I fired some small shot at him, and sent him limping off. The natives being now convinced that I
was in earnest, all fled; but on my calling to them, many returned; and, presently after, the other
musket was brought, and laid down at my feet. That moment, I ordered the canoes to be restored,
to shew them on what account they were detained. The other things we had lost being of less
value, I was the more indifferent about them. By this time the launch was ashore for another turn
of water, and we were permitted to fill the casks without any one daring to come near us; except
one man, who had befriended us during the whole affair, and seemed to disapprove of the conduct
of his countrymen.

On my returning from the pond to the cove, I found a good many people collected together,
from whom we understood that the man I had fired at was dead. This story I treated as improbable, and addressed a man, who seemed of some consequence, for the restitution of a cooper's
adze we had lost in the morning. He immediately sent away two men, as I thought, for it; but
I soon found that we had greatly mistaken each other; for instead of the adze, they brought the
wounded man, stretched out on a board, and laid him down by me, to all appearance dead. I was
much moved at the sight; but soon saw my mistake, and that he was only wounded in the hand
and thigh. I, therefore, desired he might be carried out of the sun, and sent for the surgeon to
dress his wounds. In the mean time, I addressed several people for the adze; for as I had now
nothing else to do, I determined to have it. The one I applied the most to, was an elderly woman,
who had always a great deal to say to me, from my first landing; but, on this occasion, she gave
her tongue full scope. I understood but little of her eloquence; and all I could gather from her
arguments was, that it was mean in me to insist on the return of so trifling a thing. But when she
found I was determined, she and three or four more women went away; and soon after the adze

was brought me, but I saw her no more. This I was sorry for, as I wanted to make her a present, in return for the part she had taken in all our transactions, private as well as public. For I was no sooner returned from the pond, the first time I landed, than this old lady presented to me a girl, giving me to understand she was at my service. Miss, who probably had received her instructions, wanted, as a preliminary article, a spike-nail or a shirt, neither of which I had to give her, and soon made them sensible of my poverty. I thought, by that means, to have come off with flying colours; but I was mistaken; for they gave me to understand I might retire with her on credit. On my declining this proposal, the old lady began to argue with me; and then abuse me. Though I comprehended little of what she said, her actions were expressive enough, and shewed that her words were to this effect, sneering in my face, saying, What sort of a man are you, thus to refuse the embraces of so fine a young woman? For the girl certainly did not want beauty; which, however, I could better withstand, than the abuses of this worthy matron, and therefore hastened into the boat. They wanted me to take the young lady aboard; but this could not be done, as I had given strict orders, before I went ashore, to suffer no woman, on any pretence whatever, to come into the ship, for reasons which I shall mention in another place.

As soon as the surgeon got ashore, he dressed the man's wounds, and bled him; and was of opinion that he was in no sort of danger, as the shot had done little more than penetrate the skin. In the operation, some poultice being wanting, the surgeon asked for ripe plantains; but they brought sugar-cane, and having chewed it to a pulp, gave it him to apply to the wound. This being of a more balsamic nature than the other; proves that these people have some knowledge of simples. As soon as the man's wounds were dressed, I made him a present, which his master, or at least the man who owned the canoe, took, most probably to himself. Matters being thus settled apparently to the satisfaction of all parties, we repaired on

Hodges produced this informal study of a Tongan settlement, part of the chiefly compound, during the voyage. A pair of "fishing pigs," famous to this day on Tonga, is visible in the foreground.

Descendants of the fishing pigs of Tonga seen in Hodges' painting on the previous pages.

board to dinner, where I found a good supply of fruit and roots, and, therefore, gave orders to get every thing in readiness to sail.

I now was informed of a circumstance which was observed on board; several canoes being at the ship, when the great guns were fired in the morning, they all retired, but one man, who was bailing the water out of his canoe, which lay alongside directly under the guns. When the first was fired, he just looked up, and then, quite unconcerned, continued his work. Nor had the second gun any other effect upon him. He did not stir till the water was all out of his canoe, when he paddled leisurely off. This man had, several times, been observed to take fruit and roots out of other canoes, and sell them to us. If the owners did not willingly part with them, he took them by force; by which he obtained the appellation of custom-house officer.

Cook remarked upon sea caves found in the South Pacific, such as these on Tonga.

One time, after he had been collecting tribute, he happened to be lying alongside of a sailing canoe which was on board. One of her people seeing him look another way, and his attention otherwise engaged, took the opportunity of stealing somewhat out of his canoe; they then put off, and set their sail. But the man, perceiving the trick they had played him, darted after them, and having soon got on board their canoe, beat him who had taken his things, and not only brought back his own, but many other articles which he took from them. This man had likewise been observed making collections on shore at the trading-place. I remembered to have seen him there; and, on account of his gathering tribute, took him to be a man of consequence, and was going to make him a present; but some of their people would not let me, saying he was no *Areeke* (that is, chief). He had his hair always powdered with some kind of white dust.

Chapter 11

INTO MELANESIA

Sailing south and west, the mariners reached islands first visited by the Spanish, the archipelagos that now constitute the nation of Vanuatu. Here, groups were more localized, languages diverse, and people very cautious in their dealings with Europeans.

WE HAD NO SOONER ANCHORED than several of the natives came off in canoes. They were very cautious at first; but, at last, trusted themselves alongside, and exchanged, for pieces of cloth, arrows; some of which were pointed with bone, and dipped in some green gummy substance, which we naturally supposed was poisonous. Two men having ventured on board, after a short stay, I sent them away with presents. Others, probably induced by this, came off by moon-light; but I gave orders to permit none to come alongside, by which means we got clear of them for the night.

Next morning early, a good many came round us, some in canoes, and others swimming. I soon prevailed on one to come on board, which be no sooner did, than he was followed by more than I desired; so that not only our deck, but rigging, was presently filled with them. I took four into the cabin, and gave them various articles, which they shewed to those in the canoes, and seemed much pleased with their reception. While I was thus making friends with those in the cabin, an accident happened that threw all into confusion, but in the end, I believe, proved advantageous to us. A fellow in a canoe having been refused admittance into one of our boats that lay alongside, bent his bow to shoot a poisoned arrow at the boat-keeper. Some of his countrymen prevented his doing it that instant, and gave time to acquaint me with it. I ran instantly on deck, and saw another man struggling with him; one of those who had been in the cabin, and had leaped out of the window for this purpose. The other seemed resolved, shook him off, and directed his bow again to the boat-keeper; but, on my calling to him, pointed it at me. Having a musquet in my hand loaded with small shot, I gave him the contents. This staggered him for a moment, but did not prevent him from holding his bow still in the attitude of shooting. Another discharge of the same nature made him drop it, and the others, who were in the canoe, to paddle off with all speed. At this time, some began to shoot arrows on the other side. A musquet discharged in the air had no effect; but a four-pound shot over their heads sent them off in the utmost confusion. Many quitted their canoes and swam on shore; those in the

great cabin leaped out of the windows; and those who were on the deck, and on different parts of the rigging, all leaped overboard. After this we took no farther notice of them, but suffered them to come off and pick up their canoes; and some of them even ventured alongside of the ship. Immediately after the great gun was fired, we heard the beating of drums on shore; which was, probably, the signal for the country to assemble in arms. We now got every thing in readiness to land, to cut some wood, which we were in want of, and to try to get some refreshments, nothing of this kind having been seen in any of the canoes.

About nine o'clock, we put off in two boats, and landed in the face of four or five hundred people, who were assembled on the shore. Though they were all armed with bows and arrows, clubs and spears, they made not the least opposition. On the contrary, seeing me advance alone, with nothing but a green branch in my hand, one of them, who seemed to be a chief, giving his bow and arrows to another, met me in the water, bearing also a green branch, which having exchanged for the one I held, he then took me by the hand, and led me up to the crowd. I immediately distributed presents to them, and, in the mean time, the marines were drawn up upon the beach. I then made signs (for we understood not a word of their language) that we wanted wood; and they made signs to us to cut down the trees. By this time, a small pig being brought down and presented to me, I gave the bearer a piece of cloth, with which he seemed well pleased. This made us hope that we should soon have some more; but we were mistaken. The pig was not brought to be exchanged for what we had, but on some other account, probably as a peace-offering. For, all we could say or do, did not prevail on them to bring down, after this, above half a dozen cocoa-nuts, and a small quantity of fresh water. They set no value on nails, or any sort of iron tools; nor indeed on any thing we had. They would, now and then, exchange an arrow for a piece of cloth; but very seldom would part with a bow. They were unwilling we should go off the beach, and very desirous we should return on board. At length, about noon, after sending what wood we had cut on board, we embarked ourselves; and they all retired, some one way and some another. Before we had dined, the afternoon was too far spent to do any thing on shore; and all hands were employed, setting up the rigging, and repairing some defects in it. But seeing a man bring along the strand a buoy, which they had taken in the night from the kedge-anchor, I went on shore for it, accompanied by some of the gentlemen. The moment we landed, it was put into

ABOVE: This war club, now at Cambridge, was among the objects received by Cook and his companions in barter at Malakula.

OVERLEAF: At Malakula, Islanders were far more cautious in their response to the Europeans than were most Polynesians. The mariners may well have been regarded as returning ghosts.

the boat, by a man who walked off again without speaking one word. It ought to be observed, that this was the only thing they took, or even attempted to take from us, by any means whatever. Being landed near one of their plantations and houses, which were just within the skirts of the wood, I prevailed on the man to conduct me to them; but, though they suffered Mr Forster to go with me, they were unwilling any more should follow. These houses were something like those of the other isles; rather low, and covered with palm thatch. Some were enclosed, or walled round with boards; and the entrance to those was by a square hole at one end, which at this time was shut up, and they were unwilling to open it for us to look in. There were here about six houses, and some small plantations of roots, etc., fenced round with reeds as at the Friendly Isles. There were, likewise, some bread-fruit, cocoa-nut, and plaintain trees; but very little fruit on any of them. A good many fine yams were piled up upon sticks, or a kind of raised platform; and about twenty pigs, and a few fowls, were running about loose. After making these observations, having embarked, we proceeded to the S.E. point of the harbour, where we again landed and walked along the bench till we could see the islands to the S.E. already mentioned. The names of these we now obtained, as well as the name of that on which we were. This they called Mallicollo; the island that first appeared over the south end of Ambrym is called Apee; and the other with the hill upon it Paoom. We found on the beach a fruit like an orange, called by them Abbimora; but whether it be fit for eating, I cannot say, as this was decayed.

Proceeding next to the other side of the harbour, we there landed, near a few houses, at the invitation of some people who came down to the shore; but we had not been there five minutes before they wanted us to be gone. We complied, and proceeded up the harbour in order to sound it, and look for fresh water, of which, as yet, we had seen none, but the very little that the natives brought, which we knew not where they got. Nor was our search now attended with success; but this is no proof that there is not any. The day was too far spent to examine the place well enough to determine this point. Night having brought us on board, I was informed that no soul had been off to the ship; so soon was the curiosity of these people satisfied. As we were coming on board, we heard the sound of a drum, and, I think, of some other instruments, and saw people dancing; but us soon as they heard the noise of the oars, or saw us, all was silent.

Being unwilling to lose the benefit of the moon-light nights, which now happened, at seven a.m. on the 23d, we weighed; and, with a light air of wind, and the assistance of our boats, proceeded out of the harbour, the south end of which, at noon, bore W.S.W., distant about two miles.

When the natives saw us under sail, they came off in canoes, making exchanges with more confidence than before, and giving such extraordinary proofs of their honesty as surprised us. As the ship, at first, had fresh way through the water, several of them dropped astern after they had received our goods, and before they had time to deliver theirs in return. Instead of taking advantage of this, as our friends at the Society Isles would have done, they used their utmost efforts to get up with us, and to deliver what they had already been paid for. One man, in particular, followed us a considerable time, and did not reach us till it was calm, and the thing was forgotten. As soon as he came alongside he held up the thing which several were ready to buy; but he refused to part with it, till he saw the person to whom he had before sold it, and to him he gave it. The person, not knowing him again, offered him something in return, which he refused, and shewed him what he had given him before. Pieces of cloth, and marble paper, were in most esteem with them; but edge-tools, nails, and beads, they seemed to disregard. The greatest number of canoes we had alongside at once did not exceed eight, and not more than four or five people in each, who would frequently retire to the shore all on a sudden, before they had disposed of half their things, and then others would come off.

At the time we came out of the harbour, it was about low water, and great numbers of people were then on the shoals or reefs which lie along the shore, looking, as we supposed., for shell and other fish. Thus our being on their coast, and in one of their ports, did not hinder them from following the necessary employments. By this time they might be satisfied we meant them no harm; so that, had we made a longer stay, we might soon have been upon good terms with this ape-like nation. For, in general, they are the most ugly, ill-proportioned people I ever saw, and in every respect different from any we had met with in this sea. They are a very dark-coloured and rather diminutive race; with long heads, flat faces, and monkey countenances. Their hair mostly black or brown, is short and curly; but not quite so soft and woolly as that of a negroe. Their beards are very strong, crisp, and bushy, and generally black and short. But what most adds to their deformity, is a belt or cord which they wear round the waist, and tie so tight over the belly, that the shape of their bodies is not unlike that of an overgrown pismire. The men go quite naked, except a piece of cloth or leaf used as a wrapper.

We saw but few women, and they were not less ugly than the men; their heads, faces, and shoulders, are painted red; they wear a kind of petticoat; and some of them had something over their shoulders like a bag, in which they carry their children. None of them came off to the ship, and they generally kept at a distance when we were on shore. Their ornaments are ear-rings, made of tortoise-shell and bracelets. A curious one of the latter, four or five inches broad, wrought with thread or cord, and studded with shells, is worn by them just above the elbow. Round the right wrist they wear hogs' tusks, bent circular, and rings made of shells; and round their left, a round piece of wood, which we judged was to ward off the bow-string. The bridge of the nose is pierced, in which they wear a piece of white stone, about an inch and a half long. As signs of friendship they present a green branch, and sprinkle water with the hand over the head.

Their weapons are clubs, spears, and bows and arrows. The two former are made of hard or iron-wood. Their bows are about four feet long, made of a stick split down the middle, and are not circular. The arrows, which are a sort of reeds, are sometimes armed with a long and sharp point, made of the hard wood, and sometimes with a very hard point made of bone; and these points are all covered with a substance which we took for poison. Indeed the people themselves confirmed our suspicions, by making signs to us not to touch the point, and giving us to understand that if we were prickled by them we should die. They are very careful of them themselves, and keep them, always wrapped up in a quiver. Some of these arrows are formed with two or three points, each with small prickles on the edges, to prevent the arrow being drawn out of the wound.

The people of Mallicollo seemed to be a quite different nation from any we had yet met with, and speak a different language. Of about eighty words, which Mr Forster collected, hardly one bears any affinity to the language spoken at any other island or place I had ever been at. The letter R is used in many of their words; and frequently two or three being joined together, such words we found difficult to pronounce. I observed that they could pronounce most of our words with great ease. They express their admiration by hissing like a goose.

Chapter 12

ENCOUNTERS AT ERRAMANGA AND TANNA

In southern Vanuatu, Islanders at Erramanga tried to seize Cook's boat; relationships were more effectively established on Tanna, where natural historians and others ventured inland.

1774 AUGUST

On the 4th, at day-break, I went with two boats to examine the coast, to look for a proper landing-place, wood, and water. At this time, the natives began to assemble on the shore, and by signs invited us to land. I went first to a small beach, which is towards the head, where I found no good landing, on account of some rocks which every where lined the coast. I, however, put the boat's bow to the shore, and gave cloth, medals, etc. to some people who were there. For this treatment they offered to haul the boats over the breakers to the sandy beach, which I thought a friendly offer, but had reason afterwards to alter my opinion. When they found I would not do as they desired, they made signs for us to go down into the bay, which we accordingly did, and they ran along shore abreast of us, their number increasing prodigiously. I put in to the shore in two or three places, but, not liking the situation, did not land. By this time, I believe, the natives conceived what I wanted, as they directed me round a rocky point, where, on a fine sandy beach, I stepped out of the boat without wetting a foot, in the face of a vast multitude, with only a green branch in my hand, which I had before got from one of them. I took but one man out of the boat with me, and ordered the other boat to lie-to at a little distance off. They received me with great courtesy and politeness; and would retire back from the boat on my making the least motion with my hand. A man, whom I took to be a chief, seeing this, made them form a semicircle round the boat's bow, and beat such as attempted to break through this order. This man I loaded with presents, giving likewise to others, and asked by signs for fresh water, in hopes of seeing where they got it. The chief immediately sent a man for some, who ran to a house, and presently returned with a little in a bamboo; so that I gained

A MAN *of the* ISLAND *of* TANNA.   A WOMAN *of the* ISLAND *of* TANNA.

The European public of the period was fascinated by the peoples encountered in the South Pacific, and engraved prints based on Hodges' portraits were widely published, often in crude forms lacking the nuance of the original, carefully observed field studies.

but little information by this. I next asked, by the same means, for something to eat, and they as readily brought me a yam, and some cocoa-nuts. In short, I was charmed with their behaviour; and the only thing which could give the least suspicion was, that most of them were armed with clubs, spears, darts, and bows and arrows. For this reason I kept my eye continually upon the chief, and watched his looks as well as his actions. He made many signs to me to haul the boat up upon the shore, and at last slipped into the crowd, where I observed him speak to several people, and then return to me, repeating signs to haul the boat up, and hesitating a good deal before he would receive some spike-nails, which I then offered him. This made me suspect something was intended, and immediately I stepped into the boat, telling them by signs that I should soon return. But they were not for parting so soon, and now attempted by force, what they could not obtain by gentler means. The gang-board happened unluckily to be laid out for me to come into the boat, I say unluckily, for if it had not been out, and if the crew had been a little quicker in getting the boat off, the natives might not have had time to put their design in execution, nor would the following disagreeable scene have happened. As we were putting off the boat, they laid hold of the gang-board, and unhooked it off the boat's stern. But as they did not take it away, I thought this had been done by accident, and ordered the boat in again to take it up. Then they themselves hooked it over the boat's stern, and attempted to haul her ashore; others, at the same time, snatched the oars out of the people's hands. On my pointing a musket at them, they in some measure desisted, but returned in an instant, seemingly determined to haul the boat ashore.

Along with Niue, Erramanga was one of the few islands at which Cook's attempt to land was so violently resisted that it had to be abandoned. Hodges dramatized the conflict in this painting made after the ships returned to England.

At the head of this party was the chief; the others, who could not come at the boat, stood behind with darts, stones, and bows and arrows in hand, ready to support them. Signs and threats having no effect, our own safety became the only consideration; and yet I was unwilling to fire on the multitude, and resolved to make the chief alone fall a victim to his own treachery; but my musket at this critical moment missed fire. Whatever idea they might have formed of the arms we held in our hands, they must now have looked upon them as childish weapons, and began

to let us see how much better theirs were, by throwing stones and darts, and by shooting arrows. This made it absolutely necessary for me to give orders to fire. The first discharge threw them into confusion; but a second was hardly sufficient to drive them off the beach; and after all, they continued to throw stones from behind the trees and bushes, and, every now and then, to pop out and throw a dart. Four lay, to all appearance, dead on the shore; but two of them afterwards crawled into the bushes. Happy it was for these people, that not half our muskets would go off, otherwise many more must have fallen. We had one man wounded in the cheek with a dart, the point of which was as thick as my finger, and yet it entered above two inches, which shews that it must have come with great force, though indeed we were very near them. An arrow struck Mr Gilbert's naked breast, who was about thirty yards off; but probably it had struck something before; for it hardly penetrated the skin. The arrows were pointed with hard wood.

As soon as we got on board, I ordered the anchor to be weighed, with a view of anchoring near the landing-place. While this was doing, several people appeared on the low rock point, displaying two oars we had lost in the scuffle. I looked on this as a sign of submission, and of their wanting to give us the oars. I was, nevertheless, prevailed on to fire a four-pound shot at them, to let them see the effect of our great guns. The ball fell short, but frightened them so much, that none were seen afterwards; and they left the oars standing up against the bushes.

It was now calm; but the anchor was hardly at the bow before a breeze sprung up at north, of which we took the advantage, set our sails, and plyed out of the bay, as it did not seem capable of supplying our wants with that conveniency I wished to have. Besides, I always had it in my power to return to this place, in case I should find none more convenient farther south.

These islanders seemed to be a different race from those of Mallicollo; and spoke a different language. They are of the middle size, have a good shape, and tolerable features. Their colour is very dark, and they paint their faces, some with black, and others with red pigment. Their hair is very

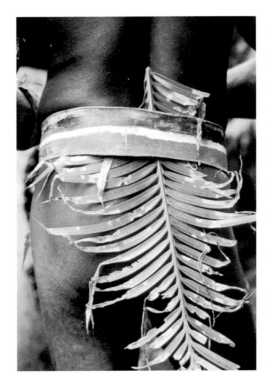

Melanesia is renowned for complex architecture and sculpture, but this Glenn Jowitt photo shows how the body was often rendered aesthetically striking with the simplest decorations.

curly and crisp, and somewhat woolly. I saw a few women, and I thought them ugly; they wore a kind of petticoat made of palm-leaves, or some plant like it. But the men, like those of Mallicollo, were in a manner naked; having only the belt about the waist, and the piece of cloth, or leaf, used as a wrapper. I saw no canoes with these people, nor were any seen in any part of this island. They live in houses covered with thatch, and their plantations are laid out by a line, and fenced round.

At two o'clock in the afternoon, we were clear of the bay, bore up round the head, and steered S.S.E. for the south end of the island, having a fine breeze at N.W. On the S.W. side of the head is a pretty deep bay, which seemed to run in behind the one on the N.W. side. Its shores are low, and the adjacent lands appeared very fertile. It is exposed to the S.E. winds; for which reason, until it be better known, the N.W. bay is preferable, because it is sheltered from the reigning winds; and the winds to which it is open, viz. from N.W. by N. to E. by N., seldom blow strong. The promontory, or peninsula, which disjoins these two bays, I named Traitor's Head, from the treacherous behaviour of its inhabitants. It is the N.E. point of the island, situated in the latitude 18° 43' S. longitude 169° 28' E., and terminates in a saddle-hill which is of height sufficient to be seen sixteen or eighteen leagues. As we advanced to S.S.E., the new island, we had before discovered, began to appear over the S.E. point of the one near us, bearing S. ½ E., distant ten or twelve leagues. After leaving this one, we steered for the east end of the other, being directed by a great light we saw upon it.

At one o'clock the next morning, drawing near the shore, we tacked and spent the remainder of the night making short boards. At sun-rise we discovered a high table land (an island) bearing E. by S., and a small low isle in the direction of N.N.E., which we had passed in the night without seeing it. Traitor's Head was still in sight, bearing N. 20° W. distant fifteen leagues, and the island to the south extended from S. 7° W. to S. 87° W. distant three or four miles. We then found that the light we had seen in the night was occasioned by a volcano, which we observed to throw up vast quantities of fire and smoke, with a rumbling noise heard at a great distance. We now made sail for the island; and, presently after, discovered a small inlet which had the appearance of being a good harbour. In order to be better informed, I sent away two armed boats, under the command of Lieutenant Cooper, to sound it; and, in the meanwhile, we stood on and off with the ship, to be ready to follow, or give them any assistance they might want. On the east point of the entrance, we observed a number of people, and several houses and canoes; and when our boats entered the harbour, they launched some, and followed them, but came not near. It was not long before Mr Cooper made the signal for anchorage; and we stood in with the ship. The wind being at west, and our course S.S.W., we borrowed close to the west point, and passed over some sunken rocks, which might have been avoided, by keeping a little more to the east, or about one-third channel over. The wind left us as soon as we were within the entrance, and obliged us to drop an anchor in four fathoms water. After this, the boats were sent again to sound; and, in the meantime, the launch was hoisted out, in order to carry out anchors to warp in by, as soon as we should be acquainted with the channel.

While we were thus employed, many of the natives got together in parties, on several parts of the shore, all armed with bows, spears, etc. Some swam off to us, others came in canoes. At first they were shy, and kept at the distance of a stone's throw; they grew insensibly bolder; and, at last, came under our stern, and made some exchanges. The people in one of the first canoes, after coming as near as they durst, threw towards us some cocoa-nuts. I went into a boat and picked them up, giving them in return some cloth and other articles. This induced others to come under the stern, and alongside, where their behaviour was insolent and daring. They wanted to carry off every thing within their reach; they got hold of the fly of the ensign, and would have torn it from the staff; others attempted to knock the rings off the rudder; but the greatest trouble they gave us was to look after the buoys of our anchors, which were no sooner thrown out of our boats, or let go from the ship, than they got hold of them. A few muskets fired in the air had no effect; but a four-pounder frightened them so much, that they quitted their canoes that instant, and took to the water. But as soon as they found themselves unhurt, they got again into their canoes, gave us some halloos, flourished their weapons, and returned once more to the buoys. This put us to the expence of a few musquetoon shot, which had the desired effect. Although none were hurt, they were afterwards afraid to come near the buoys; very soon all retired on shore, and we were permitted to sit down to dinner undisturbed.

During these transactions, a friendly old man in a small canoe made several trips between us and the shore, bringing off each time a few cocoa-nuts, or a yam, and taking in exchange whatever we gave him. Another was on the gangway when the great gun was fired, but I could not prevail on him to stay there long. Towards the evening, after the ship was moored, I landed at the head of the harbour, in the S.E. corner, with a strong party of men, without any opposition being made by a great number of the natives who were assembled in two parties, the one on our right and the other on the left, armed with clubs, darts, spears, slings, and stones, bows, and arrows, etc. After distributing to the old people (for we could distinguish no chief), and some others, presents of cloth, medals, etc. I ordered two casks to be filled with water out of a pond about twenty paces behind the landing-place; giving the natives to understand, that this was one of the articles we wanted. Besides water, we got from them a few cocoa-nuts, which seemed to be in plenty on the trees; but they could not be prevailed upon to part with any of their weapons. These they held in constant readiness, and in the proper attitudes of offence and defence; so that little was wanting to make them attack us; at least we thought so, by their pressing so much upon us, and in spite of our endeavours to keep them off. Our early re-embarking probably disconcerted their scheme; and after that, they all retired. The friendly old man before mentioned, was in one of these parties; and we judged, from his conduct, that his temper was pacific.

Chapter 13

THE DISCOVERY OF NEW CALEDONIA

Like ni-Vanuatu, the Kanak of New Caledonia were Melanesians. Contacts here were generally peaceful, and the mariners were impressed by the elaborate irrigation and agricultural systems, but the lack of the kind of linguistic understanding the explorers benefited from among Tahitians and Maori meant that understanding was limited.

1774 SEPTEMBER

The boats having made a signal for a channel, and one of them being placed on the point of the reef on the weather side of it, we stood in with the ship, and took up the other boat in our way, when the officer informed me, that where we were to pass, was sixteen and fourteen fathoms water, a fine sandy bottom, and that having put alongside two canoes, he found the people very obliging and civil. They gave him some fish; and, in return, he presented them with medals, etc. In one was a stout robust young man, whom, they understood to be a chief. After getting within the reef, we hauled up S. ½ E., for a small low sandy isle that we observed lying under the shore, being followed by all the canoes. Our sounding in standing in, was from fifteen to twelve fathoms (a pretty even fine sandy bottom,) for about two miles; then we had six, five, and four fathoms. This was on the tail of a shoal which lies a little without the small isle to the N.E. Being over it, we found seven and eight fathoms water, which shallowed gradually as we approached the shore, to three fathoms, when we tacked and stood off a little, and then anchored in five fathoms, the bottom a fine sand mixed with mud. The little sandy isle bore E. by S., three-quarters of a mile distant; and we were one mile from the shore of the main, which

OPPOSITE: Kanak men wore distinctive woven hats resembling the North African fez.

extended from S.E. by E., round to the south, to W.N.W. The island of Balabea bore
N.W. by N., and the channel, through which we came, north, four miles distant. In this
situation we were extremely well sheltered from the reigning winds, by the sandy isle and
its shoals, and by the shoal without them.

We had hardly got to an anchor, before we were surrounded by a great number
of the natives, in sixteen or eighteen canoes, the most of whom were without any sort of
weapons. At first they were shy in coming near the ship; but in a short time we prevailed
on the people in one boat to get close enough to receive some presents. These we lowered
down to them by a rope, to which, in return, they tied two fish that stunk intolerably, as
did those they gave us in the morning. These mutual exchanges bringing on a kind of
confidence, two ventured on board the ship; and presently after, she was filled with them,
and we had the company of several at dinner in the cabin. Our pease-soup, salt-beef and
pork, they had no curiosity to taste; but they eat of some yams, which we happened to
have yet left, calling them *Oobee*. This name is not unlike *Oofee*, as they are called at most
of the islands, except Mallicollo; nevertheless, we found these people spoke a language
new to us. Like all the nations we had lately seen, the men were almost naked; having
hardly any other covering but such a wrapper as is used at Mallicollo. They were curious
in examining every part of the ship, which they viewed with uncommon attention. They
had not the least knowledge of goats, hogs, dogs, or cats, and had not even a name for
one of them. They seemed fond of large spike-nails, and pieces of red cloth, or indeed of
any other colour, but red was their favourite.

After dinner, I went on shore with two armed boats, having with us one of the
natives who had attached himself to me. We landed on a sandy beach before a vast
number of people, who had got together with no other intent than to see us; for many of
them had not a stick in their hands; consequently we were received with great courtesy,
and with the surprise natural for people to express, at seeing men and things so new to
them as we must be. I made presents to all those my friend pointed out, who were either
old men, or such as seemed to be of some note; but he took not the least notice of some
women who stood behind the crowd, folding my hand when I was going to give them
some beads and medals. Here we found the same chief, who had been seen in one of the
canoes in the morning. His name, we now learnt, was Teabooma; and we had not been
on shore above ten minutes, before he called for silence. Being instantly obeyed by every
individual present, he made a short speech; and soon after another chief having called for
silence, made a speech also. It was pleasing to see with what attention they were heard.
Their speeches were composed of short sentences; to each of which two or three old men
answered, by nodding their heads, and giving a kind of grunt, significant, as I thought, of
approbation. It was impossible for us to know the purport of these speeches; but we had
reason to think they were favourable to us, on whose account they doubtless were made.

I kept my eyes fixed on the people all the time, and saw nothing to induce me to
think otherwise. While we were with them, having enquired, by signs, for fresh water,
some pointed to the east and others to the west. My friend undertook to conduct us to
it, and embarked with us for that purpose. We rowed about two miles up the coast to the

east, where the shore was mostly covered with mangrove-trees; and entering amongst them, by a narrow creek or river, which brought us to a little straggling village, above all the mangroves, there we landed and were shewn fresh water. The ground near this village was finely cultivated, being laid out in plantations of sugar-canes, plantains, yams, and other roots, and watered by little rills, conducted by art from the main stream, whose source was in the hills. Here were some cocoa-nut trees, which did not seem burdened with fruit. We heard the crowing of cocks, but saw none. Some roots were baking on a fire in an earthen jar, which would have held six or eight gallons; nor did

This war club collected during Cook's visit to New Caledonia is among the first artifacts from the island to enter European hands.

we doubt its being their own manufacture. As we proceeded up the creek, Mr Forster having shot a duck flying over our heads, which was the first use these people saw made of our fire-arms, my friend begged to have it; and when he landed, told his countrymen in what manner it was killed. The day being far spent, and the tide not permitting us to stay longer in the creek, we took leave of the people and got on board a little after sunset. From this little excursion, I found that we were to expect nothing from these people but the privilege of visiting their country undisturbed. For it was easy to see they had little else than good-nature to bestow. In this they exceeded all the nations we had yet met with; and, although it did not satisfy the demands of nature, it at once pleased and left our minds at ease.

Next morning we were visited by some hundreds of the natives; some coming in canoes, and others swimming off; so that, before ten o'clock, our decks, and all other parts of the ship, were quite full with them. My friend, who was of the number, brought me a few roots, but all the others came empty in respect to eatables. Some few had with them their arms, such as clubs and darts, which they exchanged for nails, pieces of cloth, etc. After breakfast, I sent Lieutenant Pickersgill with two armed boats to look for fresh water; for what we found the day before was by no means convenient for us to get on board. At the same time Mr Wales, accompanied by lieutenant Clerke, went to the little isle to make preparations for observing the eclipse of the sun, which was to be in the afternoon. Mr Pickersgill soon returning, informed me that he had found a stream of fresh water, pretty convenient to come at. I therefore ordered the launch to be hoisted out to complete our water, and then went to the isle to assist in the observation.

* * *

EARLY IN THE MORNING of the 7th, the watering-party, and a guard, under the command of an officer, were sent ashore; and soon after a party of us went to take a view of the country. As soon as we landed we made known our design to the natives, and two of them undertaking to be our guides, conducted us up the hills by a tolerably good path. In our route, we met several people, most of whom turned back with us; so that at last our train was numerous. Some we met who wanted us to return; but we paid no regard to their signs, nor did they seem uneasy when we proceeded. At length we reached the summit of one of the hills, from which we saw the sea in two places, between some advanced hills, on the opposite or S.W. side of the land. This was an useful discovery, as it enabled us to judge of the breadth of the land, which, in this part, did not exceed ten leagues.

Between those advanced hills, and the ridge we were upon, was a large valley, through which ran a serpentine river. On the banks of this were several plantations, and some villages, whose inhabitants we had met on the road, and found more on the top of the hill gazing at the ship, as might be supposed. The plain, or flat land, which lies along the shore we were upon, appeared from the hills to great advantage; the winding streams which ran through out, the plantations, the little straggling villages, the variety in the woods, and the shoals on the coast, so variegating the scene, that the whole might afford a picture for romance. Indeed, if it were not for those fertile spots on the plains, and some few on the sides of the mountains, the whole country might be called a dreary waste. The mountains, and other high places, are, for the most part, incapable of cultivation, consisting chiefly of rocks, many of which are full of mundicks. The little soil that is upon them is scorched and burnt up with the sun; it is, nevertheless, coated with coarse grass and other plants, and here and there trees and shrubs. The country, in general, bore great resemblance to some parts of New Holland under the same parallel of latitude, several of its natural productions seeming to be the same, and the woods being without underwood, as in that country. The reefs on the coast and several other similarities, were obvious to every one who had seen both countries. We observed all the N.E. coast to be covered with shoals and breakers, extending to the northward, beyond the Isle of Balabea, till they were lost in the horizon. Having made these observations, and our guides not chusing to go farther, we descended the mountains by a road different from that by which we ascended. This brought us down through some of their plantations in the plains, which I observed were laid out with great judgment, and cultivated with much labour. Some of them were lying in fallow, some seemingly lately laid down, and others of longer date, pieces of which they were again beginning to dig up. The first thing I observed they did, was to set fire to the grass, etc. which had over-run the surface. Recruiting the land by letting it lie some years untouched, is observed by all the nations in this sea; but they seem to have no notion of manuring it, at least I have no where seen it done. Our excursion was finished by noon, when we returned on board to dinner; and one of our guides having left us, we brought the other with us, whose fidelity was rewarded at a small expence.

In the afternoon I made a little excursion along-shore to the westward, in company with Mr Wales. Besides making observations on such things as we met, we got the names of several places, which I then thought were islands; but upon farther enquiry, I found they were districts upon the same land. This afternoon a fish being struck by one of the natives near the watering-place, my clerk purchased it, and sent it to me after my return on board.

It was of a new species, something like a sun-fish, with a large long ugly head. Having no suspicion of its being of a poisonous nature, we ordered it to be dressed for supper; but, very luckily, the operation of drawing and describing took up so much time, that it was too late, so that only the liver and row were dressed, of which the two Mr Forsters and myself did but taste. About three o'clock in the morning, we found ourselves seized with an extraordinary weakness and numbness all over our limbs. I had almost lost the sense of feeling; nor could I distinguish between light and heavy bodies, of such as I had strength to move; a quart-pot, full of water, and a feather, being the same in my hand. We each of us took an emetic, and after that a sweat, which gave us much relief. In the morning, one of the pigs, which had eaten the entrails, was found dead. When the natives came on board and saw the fish hanging up, they immediately gave us to understand it was not wholesome food, and expressed the utmost abhorrence of it; though no one was observed to do this when the fish was to be sold, or even after it was purchased.

On the 8th, the guard and a party of men were on shore as usual. In the afternoon, I received a message from the officer, acquainting me that Teabooma the chief was come with a present consisting of a few yams and sugar-canes. In return, I sent him, amongst other articles, a dog and a bitch, both young, but nearly full grown. The dog was red and white, but the bitch was all red, or the colour of an English fox. I mention this, because they may prove the Adam and Eve of their species in that country. When the officer returned on board in the evening, he informed me that the chief came, attended by about twenty men, so that it looked like a visit of ceremony. It was some time before he would believe the dog and bitch were intended for him; but as soon as he was convinced, he seemed lost in an excess of joy, and sent them away immediately.

Next morning early, I dispatched Lieutenant Pickersgill and Mr Gilbert with the launch and cutter to explore the coast to the west; judging this would be better effected in the boats than in the ship, as the reef would force the latter several leagues from land. After breakfast, a party of men was sent on shore, to make brooms; but myself and the two Mr Forsters were confined on board, though much better, a good sweat having had an happy effect. In the afternoon a man was seen, both ashore and alongside the ship, said to be as white as an European. From the account I had of him (for I did not see him,) his whiteness did not proceed from hereditary descent, but from chance or some disease; and such have been seen at Otaheite and the Society Isles. A fresh easterly wind, and the ship lying a mile from the shore, did not hinder those good-natured people from swimming off to us in shoals of twenty or thirty, and returning the same way.

On the 10th, a party was on shore as usual; and Mr Forster so well recovered as to go out botanizing.

In the evening of the 11th, the boats returned, when I was informed of the following circumstances. From an elevation which they reached the morning they set out, they had a view of the coast. Mr Gilbert was of opinion that they saw the termination of it to the west, but Mr Pickersgill thought not; though both agreed that there was no passage for the ship that way. From this place, accompanied by two of the natives, they went to Balabea, which they did not reach till after sunset, and left again next morning before sun-rise; consequently this was a fruitless expedition, and the two following days were spent in getting up to the ship. As they went down to the isle, they saw abundance of turtle; but the violence of the wind and sea made it impossible to strike any. The cutter was near being lost, by suddenly filling with water, which obliged them to throw several things overboard, before they could free her, and stop the leak she had sprung. From a fishing canoe, which they met coming in from the reefs, they got as much fish as they could eat; and they were received by Teabi, the chief of the isle of Balabea, and the people, who came in numbers to see them, with great courtesy. In order not to be too much crowded, our people drew a line on the ground, and gave the others to understand they were not to come within it. This restriction they

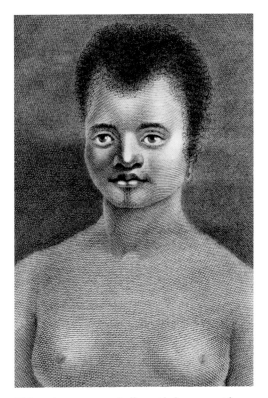

Melanesian women typically avoided contact with Europeans, but Hodges was able to produce this portrait of a Kanak woman at Balade.

observed, and one of them, soon after, turned to his own advantage. For happening to have a few cocoa-nuts, which one of our people wanted to buy, and he was unwilling to part with, he walked off, and was followed by the man who wanted them. On seeing this, he sat down on the sand, made a circle round him, as he had seen our people do, and signified that the other was not to come within it; which was accordingly observed. As this story was well attested, I thought it not unworthy of a place in this journal.

Early in the morning of the 12th, I ordered the carpenter to work, to repair the cutter, and the water to be re-placed, which we had expended the three preceding days. As Tea Booma the chief had not been seen since he got the dogs, and I wanted to lay a foundation for stocking the country with hogs also, I took a young boar and a sow with me in the boat, and went up to the mangrove creek to look for my friend, in order to give them to him.

But when we arrived there, we were told that he lived at some distance, and that they would send for him. Whether they did or no I cannot say; but he not coming, I resolved to give them to the first man of note I met with. The guide we had to the hills happening to be there, I made him understand that I intended to leave the two pigs on shore, and ordered them out of the boat for that purpose. I offered them to a grave old man, thinking he was a proper person to entrust them with; but he shook his head, and he and all present, made signs to take them into the boat again. When they saw I did not comply, they seemed to consult with one another what was to be done; and then our guide told me to carry them to the Alekee (chief). Accordingly I ordered them to be taken up, and we were conducted by him to a house, wherein were seated, in a circle, eight or ten middle-aged persons. To them I and my pigs being introduced, with great courtesy they desired me to sit down; and then I began to expatiate on the merits of the two pigs, explaining to them how many young ones the female would have at one time, and how soon these would multiply to some hundreds. My only motive was to enhance their value, that they might take the more care of them; and I had reason to think I in some measure succeeded. In the mean time, two men having left the company, soon returned with six yams, which were presented to me; and then I took my leave and went on board.

I have already observed, that here was a little village; I now found it much larger than I expected; and about it, a good deal of cultivated land, regularly laid out, planted and planting with taro or eddy root, yams, sugar-canes, and plantains. The taro plantations were prettily watered by little rills, continually supplied from the main channel at the foot of the mountains, from whence these streams were conducted in artful meanders. They have two methods of planting these roots, some are in square or oblong patches, which lie perfectly horizontal, and sink below the common level of the adjacent land, so that they can let in on them as much water as they think necessary. I have generally seen them covered two or three inches deep; but I do not know that this is always necessary. Others are planted in ridges about three or four feet broad, and two, or two and a half high. On the middle or top of the ridge, is a narrow gutter, in and along which is conveyed, as above described, a little rill that waters the roots, planted in the ridge on each side of it; and these plantations are so judiciously laid out, that the same stream waters several ridges. These ridges are sometimes the divisions to the horizontal plantations; and when this method is used, which is for the most part observed where a pathway, or something of that sort, is requisite, not an inch of ground is lost. Perhaps there may be some difference in the roots, which may make these two methods of raising them necessary. Some are better tasted than others, and they are not all of a colour; but be this as it may, they are very wholesome food, and the tops make good greens, and are eaten as such by the natives. On these plantations men, women, and children were employed.

In the afternoon I went on shore, and, on a large tree, which stood close to the shore, near the watering-place, had an inscription cut, setting forth the ship's name, date, etc. as a testimony of our being the first discoverers of this country, as I had done at all others, at which we had touched, where this ceremony was necessary. This being done, we took leave of our friends, and returned on board; when I ordered all the boats to be hoisted in, in order to be ready to put to sea in the morning.

. . . the country bears great resemblance to New South Wales, or New Holland, and that some of its natural productions are the same. In particular, we found here, the tree which is covered with a soft white ragged bark, easily peeled off, and is, as I have been told, the same that, in the East Indies, is used for caulking of ships. The wood is very hard, the leaves are long and narrow, of a pale dead green, and a fine aromatic; so that it may properly be said to belong to that continent. Nevertheless, here are several plants, etc. common to the eastern and northern islands, and even a species of the passionflower, which, I am told, has never before been known to grow wild any where but in America. Our botanists did not complain for want of employment at this place; every day bringing something new in botany or other branches of natural history. Land-birds, indeed, are not numerous, but several are new. One of these is a kind of crow, at least so we called it, though it is not half so big, and its feathers are tinged with blue. They also have some very beautiful turtle-doves, and other small birds, such as I never saw before.

All our endeavours to get the name of the whole island proved ineffectual. Probably it is too large for them to know by one name. Whenever we made this enquiry, they always gave us the name of some district or place, which we pointed to; and, as before observed, I got the names of several, with the name of the king or chief of each. Hence I conclude, that the country is divided into several districts, each governed by a chief; but we know nothing of the extent of his power. Balade was the name of the district we were at, and Tea Booma the chief. He lived on the other side of the ridge of hills, so that we had but little of his company, and therefore could not see much of his power. *Tea* seems a title prefixed to the names of all, or most, of their chiefs or great men. My friend honoured me by calling me *Tea* Cook.

Chapter 14

RETURN TO SHIP COVE

Before venturing again into far southern waters, Cook revisited Ship Cove for supplies. Confusing reports of a shipwreck and of violence were troubling, but he was unable to determine whether some misadventure had befallen the crew of the Adventure.

AFTER LEAVING NORFOLK ISLE, I steered for New Zealand, my intention being to touch at Queen Charlotte's Sound, to refresh my crew, and put the ship in a condition to encounter the southern latitudes.

On the 17th, at day-break, we saw Mount Egmont, which was covered with everlasting snow, bearing S.E. ½ E. Our distance from the shore was about eight leagues, and, on sounding, we found seventy fathoms water, a muddy bottom. The wind soon fixed in the western board, and blew a fresh gale, with which we steered S.S.E. for Queen Charlotte's Sound, with a view of falling in with Cape Stephens. At noon Cape Egmont bore E.N.E. distant three or four leagues; and though the mount was hid in the clouds, we judged it to be in the same direction as the Cape; latitude observed 39° 24'. The wind increased in such a manner as to oblige us to close-reef our top-sails, and strike top-gallant yards. At last we could bear no more sail than the two courses, and two close-reefed top-sails; and under them we stretched for Cape Stephens, which we made at eleven o'clock at night.

At midnight we tacked and made a trip to the north till three o'clock next morning, when we bore away for the sound. At nine we hauled round Point Jackson through a sea which looked terrible, occasioned by a rapid tide, and a high wind; but as we knew the coast, it did not alarm us. At eleven o'clock we anchored before Ship Cove; the strong flurries from off the land not permitting us to get in.

* * *

Nothing remarkable happened till the 24th, when, in the morning, two canoes were seen coming down the sound; but as soon as they perceived the ship, they retired behind a point on the west side. After breakfast I went in a boat to look for them; and as we proceeded along the shore, we shot several birds. The report of the muskets gave notice of our approach, and the natives discovered themselves in Shag Cove by hallooing to us; but as we drew near to their habitations, they all fled to the woods, except two or three men, who stood on a rising ground near the shore, with their arms in their hands. The moment we landed, they knew us. Joy then took place of fear; and the rest of the natives hurried out of the woods, and embraced us over and over again; leaping and skipping about like madmen, but I observed that they would not suffer some women, whom we saw at a distance, to come near us. After we had made them presents of hatchets, knives, and what else we had with us, they gave us in return a large quantity of fish, which they had just caught. There were only a few amongst them whose faces we could recognise, and on our asking why they were afraid of us, and enquiring for some of our old acquaintances by name, they talked much about killing, which was so variously understood by us, that we could gather nothing from it, so that, after a short stay, we took leave, and went on board.

Next morning early, our friends, according to a promise they had made us the preceding evening, paying us a visit, brought with them a quantity of fine fish, which they exchanged for Otaheitean cloth, etc. and then returned to their habitations.

On the 26th, we got into the after-hold four boat-load of shingle ballast, and struck down six guns, keeping only six on deck. Our good friends the natives, having brought us a plentiful supply of fish, afterwards went on shore to the tents, and informed our people there, that a ship like ours had been lately lost in the strait; that some of the people got on shore; and that the natives stole their clothes, etc. for which several were shot; and afterwards, when they could fire no longer, the natives having got the better, killed them with their patapatoos, and eat them, but that they themselves had no hand in the affair, which, they said, happened at Vanna Aroa, near Terrawhitte, on the other side of the strait. One man said it was two moons ago: But another contradicted him, and counted on his fingers about twenty or thirty days. They described by actions how the ship was beat to pieces by going up and down against the rocks, till at last it was all scattered abroad.

The next day some others told the same story, or nearly to the same purport, and pointed over the east bay, which is on the east side of the sound, as to the place where it happened. These stories making me very uneasy about the *Adventure*, I desired Mr Wales, and those on shore, to let me know if any of the natives should mention it again, or to send them to me; for I had not heard any thing from them myself. When Mr Wales came on board to dinner he found the very people who had told him the story on shore, and pointed them out to me. I enquired about the affair, and endeavoured to come at the truth by every method I could think of. All I could get from them was, "Caurey," (no); and they not only denied every syllable of what they had said on shore, but seemed wholly ignorant of the matter; so that I began to think our people had misunderstood them, and that the story referred to some of their own people and boats.

On the 28th, fresh gales westerly, and fair weather. We rigged and fitted the top-masts. Having gone on a shooting-party to West Bay, we went to the place where I left the hogs and fowls; but saw no vestiges of them, nor of any body having been there since. In our return, having visited the natives, we got some fish in exchange for trifles which we gave them. As we were coming away, Mr Forster thought be heard the squeaking of a pig in the woods, close by their habitations; probably they may have those I left with them when last here. In the evening we got on board, with about a dozen and a half of wild fowl, shags, and sea-pies. The sportsmen who had been out in the woods near the ship were more successful among the small birds.

* * *

Though the Maori of Queen Charlotte's Sound were
seminomadic, settlements of this kind also existed.
Cook met different groups on his visits to the area.

EARLY IN THE MORNING of the 5th, our old friends made us a visit, and brought a seasonable supply of fish. At the same time I embarked in the pinnace, with Messrs Forsters and Sparrman, in order to proceed up the sound. I was desirous of finding the termination of it; or rather of seeing if I could find any passage out to sea by the S.E., as I suspected from some discoveries I had made when first here. In our way up, we met with some fishers, of whom we made the necessary enquiry; and they all agreed that there was no passage to the sea by the head of the sound. As we proceeded, we, some time after, met a canoe conducted by four men coming down the sound. These confirmed what the others had said, in regard to there being no passage to the sea the way we were going; but gave us to understand that there was one to the east, in the very place where I expected to find it. I now laid aside the scheme of going to the head of the sound, and proceeded to this arm, which is on the S.E. side, about four or five leagues above the isle of Motuara.

A little within the entrance on the S.E. side, at a place called Kotieghenooee, we found a large settlement of the natives., The chief, whose name was Tringo-boohee, and his people, whom we found to be some of those who had lately been on board the ship, received us with great courtesy. They seemed to be pretty numerous both here and in the neighbourhood. Our stay with them was short, as the information they gave us encouraged us to pursue the object we had in view. Accordingly, we proceeded down the arm E.N.E. and E. by N., leaving several fine coves on both sides, and at last found it to open into the strait by a channel about a mile wide, in which ran out a strong tide; having also observed one setting down the arm, all the time we had been in it. It was now about four o'clock in the afternoon, and in less than an hour after, this tide ceased, and was succeeded by the flood, which came in with equal strength.

The outlet lies S.E. by E. and N.W. by W. and nearly in the direction of E.S.E. and W.N.W. from Cape Terrawhitte. We found thirteen fathoms water a little within the entrance, clear ground. It seemed to me that a leading wind was necessary to go in and out of this passage, on account of the rapidity of the tides. I, however, had but little time to make observations of this nature, as night was at hand, and I had resolved to return on board. On that account I omitted visiting a large *hippa*, or strong-hold, built on an elevation on the north side, and about a mile or two within the entrance, the inhabitants of it, by signs, invited us to go to them; but, without paying any regard to them, we proceeded directly for the ship, which we reached by ten o'clock, bringing with us some fish we had got from the natives, and a few birds we had shot. Amongst the latter were some of the same kinds of ducks we found in Dusky Bay, and we have reason to believe that they are all to be met with here. For the natives knew them all by the drawings, and had a particular name for each.

On the 6th, wind at N.E., gloomy weather with rain. Our old friends having taken up their abode near us, one of them, whose name was Pedero, (a man of some note,) made me a present of a staff of honour, such as the chiefs generally carry. In return, I dressed him in a suit of old clothes, of which he was not a little proud. He had a fine person, and a good presence, and nothing but his colour distinguished him from an European. Having got him, and another, into a communicative mood, we began to enquire of them if the *Adventure* had been there during my absence; and they gave us to understand, in a manner which admitted of no doubt, that, soon after we were gone, she arrived; that she staid between ten and twenty days, and had been gone ten months. They likewise asserted that neither she, nor any other ship, had been stranded on the coast, as had been reported. This assertion, and the manner in which they related the coming and going of the *Adventure*, made me easy about her; but did not wholly set aside our suspicions of a disaster having happened to some other strangers. Besides what has been already related, we had been told that a ship had lately been here, and was gone to a place called Terato, which is on the north side of the strait. Whether this story related to the former or no, I cannot say. Whenever I questioned the natives about it, they always denied all knowledge of it, and for some time past, had avoided mentioning it. It was but a few days before, that one man received a box on the ear for naming it to some of our people.

After breakfast I took a number of hands over to Long Island, in order to catch the sow, to put her to the boar and remove her to some other place; but we returned without seeing her. Some of the natives had been there not long before us, as their fires were yet burning; and they had undoubtedly taken her away. Pedero dined with us, eat of every thing at table, and drank more wine than any one of us, without being in the least affected by it.

The 7th, fresh gales at N.E. with continual rain.

The 8th, fore-part rain, remainder fair weather. We put two pigs, a boar, and a sow, on shore, in the cove next without Cannibal Cove; so that it is hardly possible all the methods I have taken to stock this country with these animals should fail. We had also reason to believe that some of the cocks and hens which I left here still existed, although we had not seen any of them; for an hen's egg was, some days before, found in the woods almost new laid.

On the 9th, wind westerly or N.W., squally with rain. In the morning we unmoored, and shifted our birth farther out of the cove, for the more ready getting to sea the next morning; for at present the caulkers had not finished the sides, and till this work was done we could not sail. Our friends having brought us a very large and seasonable supply of fish, I bestowed on Pedero a present of an empty oil-jar, which made him as happy as a prince. Soon after, he and his party left the cove, and retired to their proper place of abode, with all the treasure they had received from us. I believe that they gave away many of the things they, at different times, got from us, to their friends and neighbours, or else parted with them to purchase peace of their more powerful enemies; for we never saw any of our presents after they were once in their possession: And every time we visited them they were as much in want of hatchets, nails, etc. to all appearance, as if they never had had any among them.

I am satisfied that the people in this sound, who are, upon the whole, pretty numerous, are under no regular form of government, or so united as to form one body politic. The head of each tribe, or family, seems to be respected; and that respect may, on some occasions, command obedience; but I doubt if any amongst them have either a right or power to enforce it. The day we were with Tringo-boohee, the people came from all parts to see us, which he endeavoured to prevent. But though he went so far as to throw stones at some, I observed that very few paid any regard either to his words or actions; and yet this man was spoken of as a chief of some note. I have, before, made some remarks on the evils attending these people for want of union among themselves; and the more I was acquainted with them, the more I found it to be so. Notwithstanding they are cannibals, they are naturally of a good disposition, and have not a little humanity.

Chapter 15

THE SOUTHERN CIRCUMNAVIGATION COMPLETE

A third grueling and extended cruise took the Resolution *into high latitudes in southern Pacific, to Tierra del Fuego, and far southern Atlantic waters. Uninhabited and freezing islands such as South Georgia were discovered, but the passage confirmed that there was no inhabitable southern land.*

AT NINE O'CLOCK the next morning we saw an island of ice, as we then thought, but at noon were doubtful whether it was ice or land. At this time it bore E. ¾ S., distant thirteen leagues; our latitude was 53° 56' ½, longitude 39° 24' W.; several penguins, small divers, a snow-peterel, and a vast number of blue peterels about the ship. We had but little wind all the morning, and at two p.m. it fell calm. It was now no longer doubted that it was land, and not ice, which we had in sight. It was, however, in a manner wholly covered with snow. We were farther confirmed in our judgement of its being land, by finding soundings at one hundred and seventy-five fathoms, a muddy bottom. The land at this time bore E. by S., about twelve leagues distant. At six o'clock the calm was succeeded by a breeze at N.E., with which we stood to S.E. At first it blew a gentle gale; but afterwards increased so as to bring us under double-reefed top-sails, and was attended with snow and sleet.

We continued to stand to the S.E. till seven in the morning on the 15th, when the wind veering to the S.E., we tacked and stood to the north. A little before we tacked, we saw the land bearing E. by N. At noon the mercury in the thermometer was at 35° ¼. The wind blew in squalls, attended with snow and sleet, and we had a great sea to encounter. At a lee-lurch which the ship took, Mr Wales observed her to lie down 42°. At half past four p.m. we took in the top-sails, got down top-gallant yards, wore the ship, and stood to the S.W., under two courses. At midnight the storm abated, so that we could carry the top-sails double-reefed.

At four in the morning of the 16th we wore and stood to the east, with the wind at S.S.E., a moderate breeze, and fair; at eight o'clock saw the land extending from E. by N. to N.E. by N.; loosed a reef out of each top-sail, got top-gallant yards across, and set the sails. At noon observed in latitude 54° 25' ½, longitude 38° 18' W. In this situation we had one hundred and ten fathoms water; and the land extended from N. ½ W. to E., eight leagues distant. The northern extreme was the same that we first discovered, and it proved to be an island, which obtained the name of Willis's Island, after the person who first saw it.

At this time we had a great swell from the south, an indication that no land was near us in that direction; nevertheless the vast quantity of snow on that in sight induced us to think it was extensive, and I chose to begin with exploring the northern coast. With this view we bore up for Willis's Island, all sails set, having a fine gale at S.S.W. As we advanced to the north, we perceived another isle lying east of Willis's, and between it and the main. Seeing there was a clear passage between the two isles, we steered for it, and at five o'clock, being in the middle of it, we found it about two miles broad.

Willis's Isle is an high rock of no great extent, near to which are some rocky islets. It is situated in the latitude of 54° S., longitude 38° 23' W. The other isle, which obtained the name of Bird Isle, on account of the vast number that were upon it, is not so high, but of greater extent, and is close to the N.E. point of the main land, which I called Cape North.

The S.E. coast of this land, as far as we saw it, lies in the direction of S. 50° E., and N. 50° W. It seemed to form several bays or inlets; and we observed huge masses of snow, or ice, in the bottoms of them, especially in one which lies ten miles to the S.S.E. of Bird Isle.

After getting through the passage, we found the north coast trended E. by N., for about nine miles; and then east and east-southerly to Cape Buller, which is eleven miles more. We ranged the coast, at one league distance, till near ten o'clock, when we brought-to for the night, and on sounding found fifty fathoms, a muddy bottom.

At two o'clock in the morning of the 17th we made sail in for the land, with a fine breeze at S.W.; at four, Willis's Isle bore W. by S., distant thirty-two miles; Cape Buller, to the west of which lie some rocky islets, bore S.W. by W.; and the most advanced point of land to the east, S. 63° E. We now steered along shore, at the distance of four or five miles, till seven o'clock, when, seeing the appearance of an inlet, we hauled in for it. As soon as we drew near the shore, having hoisted out a boat, I embarked in it, accompanied by Mr Forster and his party, with a view of reconnoitring the bay before we ventured in with the ship. When we put off from her, which was about four miles from the shore, we had forty fathoms water. I continued to sound as I went farther in, but found no bottom with a line of thirty-four fathoms, which was the length of that I had in the boat, and which also proved too short to sound the bay, so far as I went up it. I observed it to lie in S.W. by S. about two leagues, about two miles broad, well sheltered from all winds; and I judged there might be good anchorage before some sandy beaches which are on each side, and likewise near a low flat isle, towards the head of the bay. As I had come to a resolution not to bring the ship in, I did not think it worth my while to go and examine these places; for it did not seem probable that any one would ever be benefited by the discovery. I landed at three different

places, displayed our colours, and took possession of the country in his majesty's name, under a discharge of small arms.

I judged that the tide rises about four or five feet, and that it is high water on the full and change days about eleven o'clock.

The head of the bay, as well as two places on each side, was terminated by perpendicular ice-cliffs of considerable height. Pieces were continually breaking off, and floating out to sea; and a great fall happened while we were in the bay, which made a noise like cannon.

The inner parts of the country were not less savage and horrible. The wild rocks raised their lofty summits till they were lost in the clouds, and the valleys lay covered with everlasting snow. Not a tree was to be seen, nor a shrub even big enough to make a toothpick. The only vegetation we met with was a coarse strong-bladed grass growing in tufts, wild burnet, and a plant like moss, which sprung from the rocks.

Seals, or sea-bears, were pretty numerous. They were smaller than those at Staten Land: Perhaps the most of those we saw were females, for the shores swarmed with young cubs. We saw none of that sort which we call lions; but there were some of those which the writer of Lord Anson's voyage describes under that name; at least they appeared to us to be of the same sort; and are, in my opinion, very improperly called lions, for I could not see any grounds for the comparison.

Here were several flocks of penguins, the largest I ever saw; some which we brought on board weighed from twenty-nine to thirty-eight pounds. It appears by Bougainville's account of the animals of Falkland Islands, that this penguin is there; and I think it is very well described by him under the name of first class of penguins. The oceanic birds were albatrosses, common gulls, and that sort which I call Port Egmont hens, terns, shags, divers, the new white bird, and a small bird like those of the Cape of Good Hope, called yellow birds; which, having shot two, we found most delicious food.

* * *

IT MUST NOT, however, be understood that we were in want of provisions: we had yet plenty of every kind; and since we had been on this coast, I had ordered, in addition to the common allowance, wheat to be boiled every morning for breakfast; but any kind of fresh meat was preferred by most on board to salt. For my own part, I was now, for the first time, heartily tired of salt meat of every kind; and though the flesh of the penguins could scarcely vie with bullock's liver, its being fresh was sufficient to make it go down. I called the bay we had been in, Possession Bay. It is situated in the latitude of 54° 5' S., longitude 37° 18' W., and eleven leagues to the east of Cape North. A few miles to the west of Possession Bay, between it and Cape Buller, lies the Bay of Isles, so named on account of several small isles lying in and before it.

OPPOSITE: Penguins on South Georgia Island. Cook happened upon the island late in his second voyage and during the course of a grueling cruise that proved there was no inhabitable southern land. Nearly a century and a half later, South Georgia would become inextricably linked with another great British explorer: Sir Ernest Shackleton.

As soon as the boat was hoisted in, we made sail along the coast to the east, with a fine breeze at W.S.W. From Cape Buller the direction of the coast is S. 72° 30' E., for the space of eleven or twelve leagues, to a projecting point, which obtained the name of Cape Saunders. Beyond this cape is a pretty large bay, which I named Cumberland Bay. In several parts in the bottom of it, as also in some others of less extent, lying between Cape Saunders and Possession Bay, were vast tracks of frozen snow, or ice, not yet broken loose. At eight o'clock, being just past Cumberland Bay, and falling little wind, we hauled off the coast, from which we were distant about four miles, and found one hundred and ten fathoms water.

We had variable light airs and calms till six o'clock the next morning, when the wind fixed at north, and blew a gentle breeze; but it lasted no longer than ten o'clock, when it fell almost to a calm. At noon, observed in latitude 54° 30' S., being then about two or three leagues from the coast, which extended from N. 59° W. to S. 13° W. The land in this last direction was an isle, which seemed to be the extremity of the coast to the east. The nearest land to us being a projecting point which terminated in a round hillock, was, on account of the day, named Cape Charlotte. On the west side of Cape Charlotte lies a bay which obtained the name of Royal Bay, and the west point of it was named Cape George. It is the east point of Cumberland Bay, and lies in the direction of S.E. by E. from Cape Saunders, distant seven leagues. Cape George and Cape Charlotte lie in the direction of S. 37° E. and N. 37° W., distant six leagues from each other. The isle above-mentioned, which was called Cooper's Isle, after my first lieutenant, lies in the direction of S. by E., distant eight leagues from Cape Charlotte. The coast between them forms a large bay, to which I gave the name of Sandwich. The wind being variable all the afternoon we advanced but little; in the night it fixed at S. and S.S.W., and blew a gentle gale, attended with showers of snow.

The 19th was wholly spent in plying, the wind continuing at S. and S.S.W., clear pleasant weather, but cold. At sunrise a new land was seen, bearing S.E. ½ E. It first appeared in a single hill, like a sugar-loaf; some time after other detached pieces appeared above the horizon near the hill. At noon, observed in the latitude 54° 42' 30" S., Cape Charlotte bearing N. 38° W., distant four leagues; and Cooper's Isle S. 31° W. In this situation a lurking rock, which lies off Sandwich Bay, five miles from the land, bore W. ½ N., distant one mile, and near this rock were several breakers. In the afternoon we had a prospect of a ridge of mountains behind Sandwich Bay, whose lofty and icy summits were elevated high above the clouds. The wind continued at S.S.W. till six o'clock, when it fell to a calm. At this time Cape Charlotte bore N. 31° W., and Cooper's Island W.S.W. In this situation we found the variation, by the azimuths, to be 11° 39', and by the amplitude, 11° 12' E. At ten o'clock, a light breeze springing up at north, we steered to the south till twelve, and then brought-to for the night.

At two o'clock in the morning of the 20th we made sail to S.W. round Cooper's Island. It is a rock of considerable height, about five miles in circuit, and one mile from the main. At this isle the main coast takes a S.W. direction for the space of four or five leagues to a point, which I called Cape Disappointment. Off that are three small isles, the southernmost of which is green, low, and flat, and lies one league from the cape.

As we advanced to S.W. land opened, off this point, in the direction of N. 60° W., and nine leagues beyond it. It proved an island quite detached from the main, and obtained the name of

Pickersgill Island, after my third officer. Soon after a point of the main, beyond this island, came in sight, in the direction of N. 55° W., which exactly united the coast at the very point we had seen, and taken the bearing of, the day we first came in with it, and proved to a demonstration that this land, which we had taken for part of a great continent, was no more than an island of seventy leagues in circuit.

Who would have thought that an island of no greater extent than this, situated between the latitude of 54° and 55°, should, in the very height of summer, be in a manner wholly covered, many fathoms deep, with frozen snow, but more especially the S.W. coast? The very sides and craggy summits of the lofty mountains were cased with snow and ice; but the quantity which lay in the valleys is incredible; and at the bottom of the bays the coast was terminated by a wall of ice of considerable height. It can hardly be doubted that a great deal of ice is formed here in the water, which in the spring is broken off, and dispersed over the sea; but this island cannot produce the ten-thousandth part of what we saw; so that either there must be more land, or the ice is formed without it. These reflections led me to think that the land we had seen the preceding day might belong to an extensive track, and I still had hopes of discovering a continent. I must confess the disappointment I now met with did not affect me much; for, to judge of the bulk by the sample, it would not be worth the discovery.

I called this island the isle of Georgia, in honour of his majesty. It is situated, between the latitudes of 53° 57' and 54° 57' S.; and between 38° 13' and 35° 34' west longitude. It extends S.E. by E. and N.W. by W., and is thirty-one leagues long in that direction; and its greatest breadth is about ten leagues. It seems to abound with bays and harbours, the N.E. coast especially; but the vast quantity of ice must render them inaccessible the greatest part of the year; or, at least, it must be dangerous lying in them, on account of the breaking up of the ice cliffs.

It is remarkable that we did not see a river, or stream of fresh water, on the whole coast. I think it highly probable that there are no perennial springs in the country; and that the interior parts, as being much elevated, never enjoy heat enough to melt the snow in such quantities as to produce a river, or stream, of water. The coast alone receives warmth sufficient to melt the snow, and this only on the N.E. side; for the other, besides being exposed to the cold south winds, is, in a great degree, deprived of the sun's rays, by the uncommon height of the mountains. It was from a persuasion that the sea-coast of a land situated in the latitude of 54°, could not, in the very height of summer, be wholly covered with snow, that I supposed Bouvet's discovery to be large islands of ice. But after I had seen this land, I no longer hesitated about the existence of Cape Circumcision; nor did I doubt that I should find more land than I should have time to explore. With these ideas I quitted this coast, and directed my course to the E.S.E. for the land we had seen the preceding day.

Chapter 16

THE VOYAGE'S ACHIEVEMENTS

The ship made its way to the Cape of Good Hope and then north to England. Cook distilled the voyage's findings.

I HAD NOW MADE THE CIRCUIT of the southern ocean in a high latitude, and traversed it in such a manner as to leave not the least room for the possibility of there being a continent, unless near the Pole, and out of the reach of navigation. By twice visiting the tropical sea, I had not only settled the situation of some old discoveries, but made there many new ones, and left, I conceive, very little more to be done even in that part. Thus I flatter myself, that the intention of the voyage has, in every respect, been fully answered; the southern hemisphere sufficiently explored, and a final end put to the searching after a southern continent, which has, at times, ingrossed the attention of some of the maritime powers, for near two centuries past, and been a favourite theory amongst the geographers of all ages.

That there may be a continent, or large tract of land, near the Pole, I will not deny; on the contrary I am of opinion there is; and it is probable that we have seen a part of it. The excessive cold, the many islands and vast floats of ice, all tend to prove that there must be land to the south; and for my persuasion that this southern land must lie, or extend, farthest to the north opposite to the southern Atlantic and Indian oceans, I have already assigned some reasons; to which I may add the greater degree of cold experienced by us in these seas, than in the southern Pacific ocean under the same parallels of latitude.

OPPOSITE: The Society Islander Mai, known generally as Omai, traveled back to England with Captain Furneaux in Cook's consort, the *Adventure*. The first Polynesian to visit England, he was treated as a curiosity and a sensation by polite society.

Sciæna argyrea

As on the first voyage, the natural history findings were rich and varied, despite the extended periods spent in the Antarctic. This is one of Georg Forster's many field drawings.

In this last ocean, the mercury in the thermometer seldom fell so low as the freezing point, till we were in 60° and upwards; whereas in the others, it fell as low in the latitude of 54°. This was certainly owing to there being a greater quantity of ice, and to its extending farther to the north, in these two seas than in the south Pacific; and if ice be first formed at, or near land, of which I have no doubt, it will follow that the land also extends farther north.

The formation or coagulation of ice-islands has not, to my knowledge, been thoroughly investigated. Some have supposed them to be formed by the freezing of the water at the mouths of large rivers, or great cataracts, where they accumulate till they are broken off by their own weight. My observations will not allow me to acquiesce in this opinion; because we never found any of the ice which we took up incorporated with earth, or any of its produce, as I think it must have been, had it been coagulated in land-waters. It is a doubt with me, whether there be any rivers in these countries. It is certain, that we saw not a river, or stream of water, on all the coast of Georgia, nor on any of the southern lands. Nor did we ever see a stream of water run from any of the ice-islands. How are we then to suppose that there are large rivers? The valleys are covered, many fathoms deep, with everlasting snow; and, at the sea, they terminate in icy cliffs of vast height. It is here where the ice-islands are formed; not from streams of water, but from consolidated snow and sleet, which is almost continually falling or drifting down from the mountains, especially in the winter, when the frost must be intense. During that season, the ice-cliffs must so accumulate as to fill up all the bays, be they ever so large. This is a fact which cannot be doubted, as we have seen it so in summer. These cliffs accumulate by continual falls of snow, and what drifts from the mountains, till they are no longer able to support their own weight; and then large pieces break off, which we call ice-islands. Such as have a flat even surface, must be of the ice formed in the bays, and before the flat vallies; the others, which have a tapering unequal surface, must be formed on, or under, the side of a coast composed of pointed rocks and precipices, or some such uneven surface. For we cannot suppose that snow alone, as it falls, can form, on a plain surface, such as the sea, such a variety of high peaks and hills, as we saw on many of the ice-isles. It is certainly more reasonable to believe that they are formed on a coast whose surface is something similar to theirs. I have observed that all the ice-islands of any extent, and before they begin to break to pieces, are terminated by perpendicular cliffs of clear ice or frozen snow, always on one or more sides, but most generally all round. Many, and those of the largest size, which had a hilly and spiral surface, shewed a perpendicular cliff, or side, from the summit of the highest peak down to its base. This to me was a convincing proof, that these, as well as the flat isles, must have broken off from substances like themselves, that is, from some large tract of ice.

When I consider the vast quantity of ice we saw, and the vicinity of the places to the Pole where it is formed, and where the degrees of longitude are very small, I am led to believe that these ice-cliffs extend a good way into the sea, in some parts, especially in such as are sheltered from the violence of the winds. It may even be doubted if ever the wind is violent in the very high latitudes. And that the sea will freeze over, or the snow that falls upon it, which amounts to the same thing, we have instances in the northern hemisphere. The Baltic, the Gulph of St Laurence, the Straits of Belle-Isle, and many other equally large seas, are frequently frozen over in winter. Nor is this at all extraordinary, for we have found the degree of cold at the surface of the sea, even in summer, to be two degrees below the freezing point; consequently nothing kept it from freezing but the salt it contains, and the agitation of its surface. Whenever this last ceaseth in winter, when the frost is set in, and there comes a fall of snow, it will freeze on the surface as it falls, and in a few days, or perhaps in one night, form such a sheet of ice as will not be easily broken up. Thus a foundation will be laid for it to accumulate to any thickness by falls of snow, without its being at all necessary for the sea-water to freeze. It may be by this means these vast floats of low ice we find in the spring of the year are formed, and which, after they break up, are carried by the currents to the north. For, from all the observations I have been able to make, the currents every where, in the high latitudes, set to the north, or to the N.E. or N.W.; but we have very seldom found them considerable.

If this imperfect account of the formation of these extraordinary floating islands of ice, which is written wholly from my own observations, does not convey some useful hints to an abler pen, it will, however, convey some idea of the lands where they are formed: Lands doomed by Nature to perpetual frigidness; never to feel the warmth of the sun's rays; whose horrible and savage aspect I have not words to describe. Such are the lands we have discovered; what then may we expect those to be which lie still farther to the south? For we may reasonably suppose that we have seen the best, as lying most to the north. If any one should have resolution and perseverance to clear up this point by proceeding farther than I have done, I shall not envy him the honour of the discovery; but I will be bold to say, that the world will not be benefited by it.

Chapter 17

THE GRASS COVE MASSACRE

Only after returning to England did Cook learn the shocking truth behind the rumors of violence he had heard in Queen Charlotte Sound. Lieutenant James Burney was among those who witnessed the aftermath of a massacre.

ON THE 17TH OF DECEMBER, having refitted the ship, completed our water and wood, and got every thing ready for sea, we sent our large cutter, with Mr Rowe, a midshipman, and the boat's crew, to gather wild greens for the ship's company; with orders to return that evening, as I intended to sail the next morning. But on the boat's not returning the same evening, nor the next morning, being under great uneasiness about her, I hoisted out the launch, and sent her with the second lieutenant, Mr Burney, manned with the boat's crew and ten marines, in search of her. My orders to Mr Burney were first, to look well into East Bay, and then to proceed to Grass Cove, the place to which Mr Rowe had been sent; and if he heard nothing of the boat there, to go farther up the sound, and come back along the west shore. As Mr Rowe had left the ship an hour before the time proposed, and in a great hurry, I was strongly persuaded that his curiosity had carried him into East Bay, none in our ship having ever been there; or else, that some accident had happened to the boat, either by going adrift through the boat-keeper's negligence, or by being stove among the rocks. This was almost every body's opinion; and on this supposition, the carpenter's mate was sent in the launch, with some sheets of tin. I had not the least suspicion that our people had received any injury from the natives, our boats having frequently been higher up, and worse provided. How much I was mistaken, too soon appeared; for Mr Burney having returned about eleven o'clock the same night, made his report of a horrible scene indeed, which cannot be better described than in his own words, which now follow.

"On the 18th, we left the ship; and having a light breeze in our favour, we soon got round Long Island, and within Long Point. I examined every cove, on the larboard hand, as we went along, looking well all around with a spy-glass, which I took for that purpose. At half past one, we stopped at a beach on the left-hand side going up East Bay, to boil some victuals, as we brought nothing but raw meat with us. Whilst we were cooking, I saw an Indian on the opposite shore, running along a beach to the head of the bay. Our meat being drest, we got into the boat and put off; and, in a short time, arrived at the head of this reach, where we saw an Indian settlement.

"As we drew near, some of the Indians came down on the rocks, and waved for us to be gone, but seeing we disregarded them, they altered their notes. Here we found six large canoes hauled up on the beach, most of them double ones, and a great many people; though not so many as one might expect from the number of houses and size of the canoes. Leaving the boat's crew to guard the boat, I stepped ashore with the marines (the corporal and five men), and searched a good many of their houses, but found nothing to give me any suspicion. Three or four well-beaten paths led farther into the woods, where were many more houses; but the people continuing friendly, I thought it unnecessary to continue our search. Coming down to the beach, one of the Indians had brought a bundle of *Hepatoos* (long spears), but seeing I looked very earnestly at him, he put them on the ground, and walked about with seeming unconcern. Some of the people appearing to be frightened, I gave a looking-glass to one, and a large nail to another. From this place the bay ran, as nearly as I could guess, N.N.W. a good mile, where it ended in a long sandy beach. I looked all around with the glass, but saw no boat, canoe, or sign of inhabitant. I therefore contented myself with firing some guns, which I had done in every cove as I went along.

"I now kept close to the east shore, and came to another settlement, where the Indians invited us ashore. I enquired of them about the boat, but they pretended ignorance. They appeared very friendly here, and sold us some fish. Within an hour after we left this place, in a small beach adjoining to Grass Cove, we saw a very large double canoe just hauled up, with two men and a dog. The men, on seeing us, left their canoe, and ran up into the woods. This gave me reason to suspect I should here get tidings of the cutter. We went ashore, and searched the canoe, where we found one of the rullock-ports of the cutter, and some shoes, one of which was known to belong to Mr Woodhouse, one of our midshipmen. One of the people, at the same time, brought me a piece of meat, which he took to be some of the salt meat belonging to the cutter's crew. On examining this, and smelling to it, I found it was fresh. Mr Fannin (the master) who was with me, supposed it was dog's flesh, and I was of the same opinion; for I still doubted their being cannibals. But we were soon convinced by most horrid and undeniable proof.

"A great many baskets (about twenty) lying on the beach, tied up, we cut them open. Some were full of roasted flesh, and some of fern-root, which serves them for bread. On, farther search, we found more shoes, and a hand, which we immediately knew to have belonged to Thomas Hill, one of our fore-castle men, it being marked T.H. with an Otaheite tattow-instrument. I went with some of the people a little way up the woods, but saw nothing else. Coming down again, there was a round spot covered with fresh earth, about four feet diameter, where something had

OVERLEAF: This drawing—a later reconstruction, not a sketch made of the spot—evokes the shock and trauma of the Europeans who discovered that their shipmates had been not only massacred by the Maori at Grass Cove, but cooked and partially consumed.

been buried. Having no spade, we began to dig with a cutlass; and in the mean time I launched the canoe with intent to destroy her; but seeing a great smoke ascending over the nearest hill, I got all the people into the boat, and made what haste I could to be with them before sun-set.

"On opening the next bay, which was Grass Cove, we saw four canoes, one single and three double ones, and a great many people on the beach, who, on our approach; retreated to a small hill, within a ship's length of the water side, where they stood talking to us. A large fire was on the top of the high land, beyond the woods, from whence, all the way down the hill, the place was thronged like a fair. As we came in, I ordered a musquetoon to be fired at one of the canoes, suspecting they might be full of men lying down in the bottom; for they were all afloat, but nobody was seen in them. The savages on the little hill still kept hallooing, and making signs for us to land. However, as soon as we got close in, we all fired. The first volley did not seem to affect them much; but on the second, they began to scramble away as fast as they could, some of them howling. We continued firing as long as we could see the glimpse of any of them through the bushes. Amongst the Indians were two very stout men, who never offered to move till they found themselves forsaken by their companions; and then they marched away with great composure and deliberation; their pride not suffering them to run. One of them, however, got a fall, and either lay there, or crawled off on all-fours. The other got clear, without any apparent hurt. I then landed with the marines, and Mr Fannin staid to guard the boat.

"On the beach were two bundles of celery, which had been gathered for loading the cutter. A broken oar was stuck upright in the ground, to which the natives had tied their canoes; a proof that the attack had been made here. I then searched all along at the back of the beach, to see if the cutter was there. We found no boat, but instead of her, such a shocking scene of carnage and bar-barity as can never be mentioned or thought of but with horror; for the heads, hearts, and lungs of several of our people were seen lying on the beach, and, at a little distance, the dogs gnawing their entrails.

"Whilst we remained almost stupified on the spot, Mr Fannin called to us that he heard the savages gathering together in the woods; on which I returned to the boat, and hauling along-side the canoes, we demolished three of them. Whilst this was transacting, the fire on the top of the hill disappeared; and we could hear the Indians in the woods at high words; I suppose quarrelling whether or no they should attack us, and try to save their canoes. It now grew dark; I therefore just stepped out, and looked once more behind the beach to see if the cutter had been hauled up in the bushes; but seeing nothing of her, returned, and put off. Our whole force would have been barely sufficient to have gone up the hill; and to have ventured with half (for half must have been left to guard the boat) would have been fool-hardiness.

"As we opened the upper part of the sound, we saw a very large fire about three or four miles higher up, which formed a complete oval, reaching from the top of the hill down almost to the water-side, the middle space being inclosed all round by the fire, like a hedge. I consulted with Mr Fannin, and we were both of opinion that we could expect to reap no other advantage than the poor satisfaction of killing some more of the savages. At leaving Grass Cove, we had fired a general volley towards where we heard the Indians talking; but, by going in and out of the boat, the arms had got wet, and four pieces missed fire. What was still worse, it began to rain; our ammunition was more than, half expended, and we left six large canoes behind us in one place. With so many disadvantages, I did not think it worth while to proceed, where nothing could be hoped for but revenge.

"Coming between two round islands, situated to the southward of East Bay, we imagined we heard somebody calling; we lay on our oars, and listened, but heard no more of it; we hallooed several times, but to little purpose; the poor souls were far enough out of hearing, and, indeed, I think it some comfort to reflect, that in all probability every man of them must have been killed on the spot."

Thus far Mr Burney's report; and to complete the account of this tragical transaction, it may not be unnecessary to mention, that the people in the cutter were Mr Rowe, Mr Woodhouse, Francis Murphy, quarter-master; William Facey, Thomas Hill, Michael Bell, and Edward Jones, fore-castle men; John Cavanaugh, and Thomas Milton, belonging to the after-guard; and James Sevilley, the captain's man, being ten in all. Most of these were of our very best seamen, the stoutest and most healthy people in the ship. Mr Burney's party brought on board two hands, one belonging to Mr Rowe, known by a hurt he had received on it; the other to Thomas Hill, as before-mentioned; and the head of the captain's servant. These, with more of the remains, were tied in a hammock, and thrown over-board, with ballast and shot sufficient to sink it. None of their arms nor cloaths were found, except part of a pair of trowsers, a frock, and six shoes, no two of them being fellows.

I am not inclined to think this was any premeditated plan of these savages; for, the morning Mr Rowe left the ship, he met two canoes, which came down and staid all the fore-noon in Ship Cove. It might probably happen from some quarrel which was decided on the spot, or the fairness of the opportunity might tempt them, our people being so incautious, and thinking themselves too secure. Another thing which encouraged the New Zealanders, was, they were sensible that a gun was not infallible, that they sometimes missed, and that, when discharged, they must be loaded before they could be used again, which time they knew how to take advantage of. After their success, I imagine there was a general meeting on the east side of the sound. The Indians of Shag Cove were there; this we knew by a cock which was in one of the canoes, and by a long single canoe, which some of our people had seen four days before in Shag Cove, where they had been with Mr Rowe in the cutter.

We were detained in the Sound by contrary winds four days after this melancholy affair happened, during which time we saw none of the inhabitants. What is very remarkable, I had been several times up in the same cove with Captain Cook, and never saw the least sign of an inhabitant, except some deserted towns, which appeared as if they had not been occupied for several years; and yet, when Mr Burney entered the cove, he was of opinion there could not be less than fifteen hundred or two thousand people. I doubt not, had they been apprized of his coming, they would have attacked him. From these considerations, I thought it imprudent to send a boat up again; as we were convinced there was not the least probability of any of our people being alive.

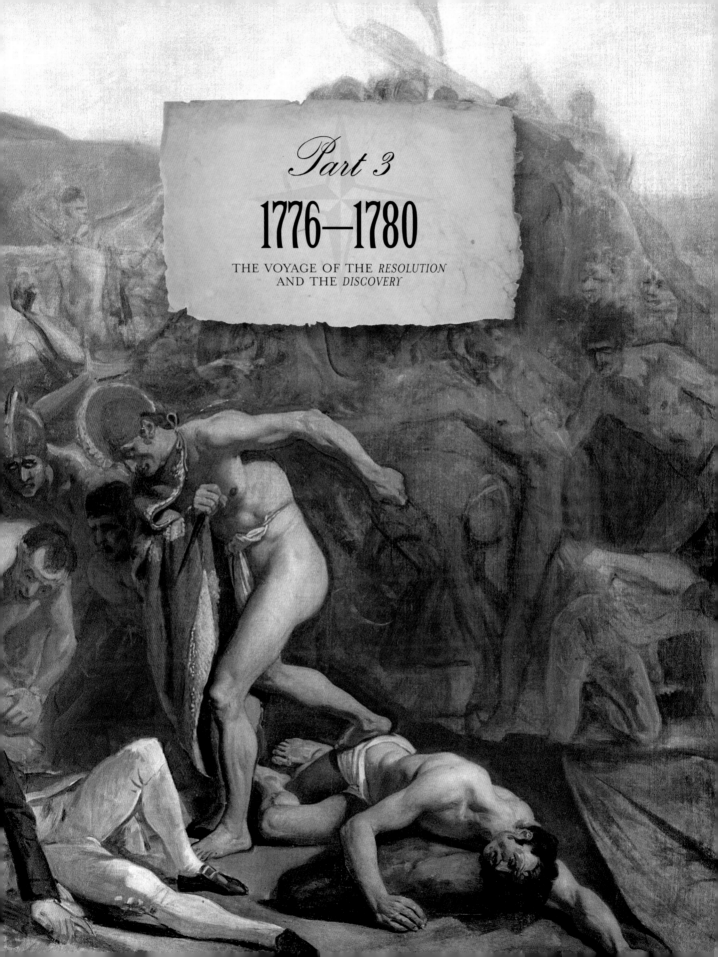

Part 3

1776—1780

THE VOYAGE OF THE *RESOLUTION*
AND THE *DISCOVERY*

IF ALL THREE OF COOK'S VOYAGES WERE EXTRAORDINARY—and extraordinarily demanding and difficult—his last expedition was especially challenging, both as a navigational project and as a human effort. As an exploratory mission, it was different from the first two voyages in a simple sense. Whereas the first and especially the second voyage were concerned with the search for land, the third was charged with finding a sea-passage through a landmass. Its question, like that of the existence of a Southern Continent, was one that had long been raised by geographers and theorists of navigation and commerce. Might there exist a Northwest Passage, that is, a navigable sea route between the North Atlantic and the North Pacific that would enable a swifter voyage between Europe and the ports of eastern Asia, which were becoming of increasing significance for trade?

In the twenty-first century, following global warming, and with ships more capable of coping with ice floes than their eighteenth-century predecessors, such a passage is now feasible, but the coastlines of the American continent in the North Pacific were poorly established on the charts that were generally available in Europe up to the 1770s, and some suggested that there might be sea passages that connected Hudson's Bay and the Pacific, around the present situation of Vancouver. It was Cook's mission to test these possibilities and, if necessary, to venture farther north to try to establish whether there might alternatively be a northeastern passage that would make it possible to reach the Pacific by following the north Asian coast.

The task would prove, in its way, as arduous as the long cruises of the second voyage through frigid Antarctic waters. When they reached it, the northwest coast featured many broad and deep openings. In some cases their investigation proved time-consuming. Yet it repeatedly became clear that each only led so far inland and that, in fact, those charts which implied that Alaska was separated by navigable channels from the rest of the continent were mystifications.

The effort was draining not least because it started late. Delays in reaching the Pacific meant that Cook had to defer these investigations by a season. The opportunity to revisit Tahiti among other Pacific islands was rewarding, but Cook was also suffering strain and increasingly alienated from his crews, who introduced venereal diseases among previously uninfected Islanders, a form of harm that Cook considered profoundly shocking—a poisonous legacy that dishonored his voyages.

PREVIOUS: German artist Johann Zoffany created this enduring oil-on-canvas depiction of Cook's death in 1779.

At the same time, the navigator became a more experienced, passionately curious, and insightful observer of the dramatic rituals he had the chance to observe, as well as an interested interpreter of more routine aspects of indigenous culture and society. In Tonga, he participated, fascinated, in a royal ritual, and in Hawaii he similarly entered into cult activities which none of the Europeans could fully understand. Considered one of the varied personifications of the god Lono by the Hawaiians, Cook was celebrated at the time of his first visit to the great island of Hawaii itself. But when the ships returned following a storm and damage, he was reappearing in the wrong season and the European presence gave rise to much tension, leading to a violent skirmish and Cook's death. The episode was controversial at the time and has been much debated since. The texts selected here record the perceptions of those present on the voyage.

Chapter 1

THE SECRET INSTRUCTIONS

The directions customarily given to the commander by the Admiralty lords might well have initially been drafted by Cook himself; certainly, they reflected his sense of the ambitions of the voyage and the particular challenges it faced.

BY THE COMMISSIONERS for executing the Office of Lord High Admiral of GREAT BRITAIN and IRELAND, &c.

SECRET INSTRUCTIONS for Captain JAMES COOK, Commander of his Majesty's Sloop the RESOLUTION.

Whereas the Earl of Sandwich has signified to us his Majesty's pleasure, that an attempt should be made to find out a northern passage by sea from the Pacific to the Atlantic Ocean; and whereas we have, in pursuance thereof, caused his Majesty's sloops *Resolution* and *Discovery* to be fitted, in all respects, proper to proceed upon a voyage for the purpose above-mentioned, and, from the experience we have had of your abilities and good conduct in your late voyages, have thought fit to intrust you with the conduct of the present intended voyage, and with that view appointed you to command the first mentioned sloop, and directed Captain Clerke, who commands the other, to follow your orders for his further proceedings; you are hereby required and directed to proceed with the said two sloops directly to the Cape of Good Hope, unless you shall judge it necessary to stop at Madeira, the Cape de Verd, or Canary Islands, to take in wine for the use of their companies; in which case you are at liberty to do so, taking care to remain there no longer than may be necessary for that purpose.

OPPOSITE: In this fine portrait by the voyage artist, John Webber, Cook is older but fully possessed of the determination of character with which he was famously associated. It is not known when the painting was made; Webber painted Cook informally during the voyage and this work was possibly developed later on the basis of those studies. It was owned by Cook's widow, Elizabeth Cook, and subsequently by other family members.

On your arrival at the Cape of Good Hope, you are to refresh the sloops companies, and to cause the sloops to be supplied with as much provisions and water as they can conveniently stow.

You are, if possible, to leave the Cape of Good Hope by the end of October, or the beginning of November next, and proceed to the Southward in search of some islands said to have been lately seen by the French, in the latitude of 48° 0' South, and about the meridian of Mauritus. In case you find those islands, you are to examine them thoroughly for a good harbor; and upon discovering one, make the necessary observations to facilitate the finding it again; as a good port, in that situation, may hereafter prove very useful, although it should afford little or nothing more than shelter, wood, and water. You are not, however, to spend too much time in looking out for those islands, or in the examination of them, if found, but proceed to Otaheite, or the Society Isles (touching at new Zealand in your way thither, if you should judge it necessary and convenient), and taking care to arrive there time enough to admit of your giving the sloops companies the refreshment they may stand in need of, before you prosecute the farthest object of these instructions.

Upon your arrival at Otaheite, of the Society Isles, you are to land Omiah at such of them as he may choose, and leave him there.

You are to distribute among the Chiefs of the islands such part of the presents with which you have been supplied, as you shall judge proper, reserving the remainder to distribute among the natives of the countries you may discover in the Northern Hemisphere: And having refreshed the people belonging to the sloops under your command, and taken on board such wood and water as they may respectively stand

in need of, you are to leave those islands in the beginning of February, or sooner if you shall judge it necessary, and then proceed in as direct a course as you can to the coast of New Albion, endeavoring to fall in with, unless you find it necessary to recruit your wood and water.

The ships called at Kerguelen Island over Christmas, 1776. The place, inhabited only by penguins, appeared barren and desolate.

THE "DISCOVERY" (COOK'S SHIP).

Lindsay, "History of Merchant Shipping;" from a drawing by E. W. Cook, R

Like the other ships of Cook's expeditions, the consort on the third voyage, HMS *Discovery*, was a Whitby-built collier. Her commander was Charles Clerke, who had sailed on HMS *Dolphin* with John Byron and on Cook's first and second voyages.

You are also, in your way thither, strictly enjoined to not touch upon any part of the Spanish dominions on the Western continent of America, unless driven thither by some unavoidable accident; in which case you are to stay no longer than shall be absolutely necessary, and to be very careful not to give any umbrage or offence to any of the inhabitants or subjects of his Catholic Majesty. And if, in your farther progress to the Northward, as hereafter directed, you find any subjects of any European Prince or State upon any part of the coast you may think proper to visit, you are not to disturb them, or give them any just cause of offence, but, on the contrary, to treat them with civility and friendship.

Upon your arrival on the coast of New Albion, you are to put into the first convenient port to recruit your wood and water, and procure refreshments, and then to proceed Northward along the coast, as far as the latitude of 65°, or farther, if you are not obstructed by lands of ice; taking care not to lose any time in exploring rivers or inlets, or upon any other account, until you get into the before-mentioned latitude of 65°, where we could wish you to arrive in the month of June next. When you get that length, you are very carefully to search for, and to explore, such rivers or inlets as may appear to be of a considerable extent, and pointing towards Hudson's or Baffin's Bays; and if, from your own observations, or from any information you may receive from the natives (who, there is reason to believe, are the same race of people, and speak the same language, of which you are furnished with a Vocabulary, as the Esquimaux), there shall appear to be a certainty, or even a probability, of a water passage into the afore-mentioned bays, or either of them, you are, in such case, to use your utmost endeavors to pass through with one or both of the sloops, unless you shall be of opinion that the passage may be effected with more certainty, or with greater probability, by smaller vessels; in which case you are to set up the frames of one or both the small vessels with which you are provided, and, when they are put together, and are properly fitted, stored, and vict-ualed, you are to dispatch one or both of them, under the care of proper officers, with a sufficient number of petty officers, men, and boats, in order to attempt the said passage; with such instruc-tions for their rejoining you, if they should fail, or for their farther proceedings, if they should succeed in the attempt, as you shall judge most proper. But, nevertheless, if you shall find it more eligible to pursue any other measures than those above pointed out, in order to make a discovery of the before-mentioned passage (if any such there be), you are at liberty, and we leave it to your discretion, to pursue such measures accordingly.

In case you shall be satisfied that there is no passage through to the above-mentioned bays, sufficient for the purposes of navigation, you are, at the proper season of the year, to repair to the port of St. Peter and St. Paul in Kamtschatka, or wherever else you shall judge more proper, in order to refresh your people and pass the winter; and, in the Spring of the ensuing year 1778, to proceed from thence to the Northward, as far as, in your prudence, you may think proper, in further search of the North East, or North West passage, from the Pacific Ocean into the Atlantic Ocean, or the North Sea: and if, from your own observation, or any information you may receive, there shall appear to be a probability of such passage, you are to proceed as above directed: and, having discovered such passage, or failed in the attempt, make the best of your way back to England, by such route as you may think best for the improvement of geography and navigation; repairing to Spithead with both sloops, where they are to remain till further order.

At whatever places you may touch in the course of your voyage, where accurate observations of the nature hereafter mentioned have not already been made, you are, as far as your time will allow, very carefully to observe the true situation of such places, both in latitude and longitude; the variation of the needle; bearings of head-lands; height, direction, and course of the tides and currents; depths and foundings of the sea; shoals, rocks, etc.; and also to survey, make charts, and take views of such bays, harbours, and different parts of the coast, and to make such notations thereon, as may be useful either to navigation or commerce. You are also carefully to observe the nature of the soil, and the produce thereof; the animals and fowls that inhabit or frequent it; the fishes that are to be round in the rivers or upon the coast, and in what plenty; and, in case there are any peculiar to such places, to describe them as minutely, and to make as accurate drawings of them, as you can: and, if you find any metals, minerals, or valuable stones, or any extraneous fossils, you are to bring home specimens of each; as also of the seeds of such trees, shrubs, plants, fruits, and grains, peculiar to those places, as you may be able to collect, and to transmit them to our Secretary, that proper examination and experiments may be made of them. You are likewise to observe the genius, temper, disposition, and number of the natives and inhabitants, where you find any; and to endeavor, by all proper means, to cultivate a friendship with them; making them presents of such trinkets as you may have on board, and they may like best; inviting them to traffic; and shewing them every kind of civility and regard; but taking care, nevertheless, not to suffer yourself to be surprized by them, but to be always on your guard against any accidents.

You are also, with the consent of the natives, to take possession, in the name of the King of Great Britain, of convenient situations in such countries as you may discover, that have not already been discovered or visited by any other European power; and to distribute among the inhabitants such things as will remain as traces and testimonies of your having been there; but if you find the countries so discovered are uninhabited, you are to take possession of them for his Majesty, by setting up proper marks and inscriptions, as first discoverers and posessors.

But forasmuch as, in undertakings of this nature, several emergencies may arise not to be foreseen, and therefore not particularly to be provided for by instructions before-hand; you are, in all such cases, to proceed as you shall judge most advantageous to the service on which you are employed.

You are, by all opportunities, to send our Secretary, for our information, accounts of your proceedings, and copies of the surveys and drawings you shall have made; and upon your arrival in England, you are immediately to repair to this office, in order to lay before us a full account of your proceedings in this whole course of your voyage; taking care, before you leave the sloop, to demand from the officers and petty officers, the log-books and journals they may have kept, and to seal them up for our inspection; and enjoining them, and the whole crew, not to divulge where they have been, until they shall have permission so to do: and you are to direct Captain Clerk to do the same, with respect to the officers, petty officers, and crew of the *Discovery*.

If any accident should happen to the *Resolution* in the course of the voyage, so as to disable her from proceeding any farther, you are, in such case, to remove yourself and her crew into the *Discovery*, and to prosecute your voyage in her; her Commander being hereby strictly required to receive you on board, and to obey your orders, the same, in every respect, as when you were actually on board the *Resolution*: And, in the case of your inability, by sickness or otherwise, to carry these Instructions into execution, you are to be careful to leave them with the next officer in command, who is hereby required to execute them in the best manner he can.

Given under our hands the 6th day of July, 1776,

SANDWICH.C. SPENCER.H. PALLISTER
By command of their Lordships,
PH. STEPHENS.

OPPOSITE: The contentious character of Johann Reinhold Forster apparently put Cook off taking a scientist on the third voyage, but he was fortunate that the surgeon's mate, William Wade Ellis, was an able zoological illustrator.

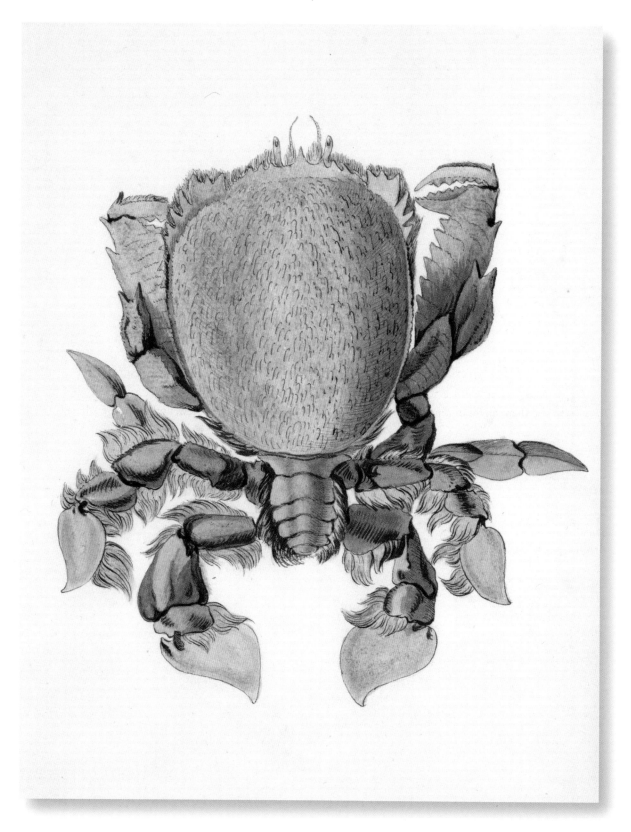

flavinuchr

Chapter 2

THE TASMANIAN ABORIGINES

Cook sailed first to the Cape of Good Hope and then across the Southern Indian Ocean to what was then called Van Dieman's Land, now Tasmania. The encounter with indigenous Australians was the first since the period in north Queensland following the Endeavour's *near-wreck in 1770; these people were similarly cautious in their dealings with the intruders.*

AS SOON AS WE HAD ANCHORED, I ordered the boats to be hoisted out. In one of them I went myself, to look for the most commodious place for furnishing ourselves with the necessary supplies; and Captain Clerke went in his boat upon the same service. Wood and water we found in plenty, and in situations convenient enough, especially the first. But grass, of which we stood most in need, was scarce, and also very coarse. Necessity, however obliged us to take such as we could get.

Next morning early, I sent Lieutenant King to the East side of the bay with two parties; one to cut wood, and the other to cut grass, under the protection of the marines, whom I judged it prudent to land as a guard. For although, as yet, none of the natives had appeared, there could be no doubt that some were in our neighbourhood, as we had seen columns of smoke, from the time of our approaching the coast; and some now was observed, at no great distance up in the woods. I also sent the launch for water; and afterwards visited all the parties myself. In the evening we drew the seine at the head of the bay, and, at one haul, caught a great quantity of fish. We should have got many more, had not the net broken in drawing it ashore. Most of them were of that sort known to seamen by the name of elephant fish. After this, every one repaired on board with what wood and grass we had cut, that we might be ready to sail whenever the wind should serve.

This not happening next morning, the people were sent on shore again, on the same duty as the day before. I also employed the carpenter with part of his crew, to cut some spars for the use of the ship; and dispatched Mr. Roberts, one of the mates, in a small boat to survey the bay.

OPPOSITE: The green rosella (*Platycercus caledonicus*) is endemic to Tasmania and would have been sighted during the visit to Adventure Bay.

In the afternoon, we were agreeably surprised, at the place where we were cutting wood, with a visit from some of the natives; eight men and a boy. They approached us from the woods, without betraying any marks of fear, or rather with the greatest confidence imaginable; for none of them had any weapons, except one, who held in his hand a stick about two feet long, and pointed at one end.

They were quite naked, and wore no ornaments; unless we consider as such, and as a proof of their love of finery, some large punctures or ridges raised on different parts of their bodies, some in straight, and others in curved lines.

They were of the common stature, but rather slender. Their skin was black, and also their hair, which was as wooly as that of any native of Guinea; but they were not distinguished by remarkably thick lips, nor flat noses. On the contrary, their features were far from being disagreeable. They had pretty good eyes; and their teeth were tolerably even, but very dirty. Most of them had their hair and beards smeared with a red ointment; and some had their faces also painted with the same composition.

They received every present we made to them, without the least appearance of satisfaction. When some bread was given, as soon as they understood that it was to be eaten, they either returned it, or threw it away, without even tasting it. They also refused some elephant fish, both raw and dressed, which we offered to them. But upon giving some birds to them, they did not return these, and easily made us comprehend that they were fond of such food. I had brought two pigs ashore, with a view to leave them in the woods. The instant these came within their reach, they seized them, as a dog would have done, by the ears, and were for carrying them off immediately; with no other intention, as we could perceive, but to kill them.

Being desirous of knowing the use of the stick which one of our visiters carried in his hand, I made signs to them to shew me; and so far succeeded, that one of them set up a piece of wood as a mark, and threw at it, at the distance of about twenty yards. But we had little reason to commend his dexterity; for, after repeated trials, he was still very wide from the object. Omai, to shew them how much superior our weapons were to theirs, then fired his musquet at it; which alarmed them so much, that notwithstanding all we could do or say, they ran instantly into the woods. One of them was so frightened, that he let drop an axe and two knives, that had been given to him. From us, however, they went to the place, where some of the *Discovery*'s people were employed in taking water into their boat. The officer of that party, not knowing that they had paid us so friendly a visit, nor what their intent might be, fired a musquet in the air, which sent them off with the greatest precipitation.

Thus ended our first interview with the natives. Immediately after their final retreat, judging that their fears would prevent their remaining near enough to observe what was passing, I ordered the two pigs, being a boar and fow, to be carried about a mile within the woods, at the head of the bay. I saw them left there, by the side of a fresh-water brook. A young bull and a cow, and some sheep and goats, were also, at first, intended to have been left by me, as an additional present to Van Diemen's Land. But I soon laid aside all thought of this, from a persuasion that the natives, incapable of entering into my views of improving their country, would destroy them. If ever they should meet with the pigs, I have no doubt this will be their fate. But as that race of animals soon becomes wild, and is fond of the thickest cover of the woods, there is great probability of their

John Webber dramatized a meeting with the Aboriginal people of Adventure Bay, Tasmania, which likely took place on January 29, 1777. The precise spot of this encounter can be located today, and there is a substantial shell midden there, reflecting coastal foraging on the site.

being preserved. An open place must have been chosen for the accommodation of the other cattle; and in such a situation, they could not possibly have remained concealed many days.

The morning of the 29th was ushered in with a dead calm, and effectually prevented our sailing. I therefore sent a party over to the East point of the bay to cut grass; having been informed that some of a superior quality grew there. Another party, to cut wood, was ordered to go to the usual place, and I accompanied them myself. We observed several of the natives, this morning, sauntering along the shore, which assured us, that though their consternation had made them leave us so abruptly the day before, they were convinced that we intended them no mischief, and were desirous of renewing the intercourse. It was natural that I should wish to be present on the occasion.

We had not been long landed, before about twenty of them, men and boys, joined us, without expressing the least sign of fear or distrust. There was one of this company conspicuously deformed; and who was not more distinguishable by the hump on his back, than by the drollery of his gestures, and the seeming humour of his speeches; which he was very fond of exhibiting, as we supposed, for our entertainment. But, unfortunately, we could not understand him; the language spoken here being wholly unintelligible to us. It appeared to me, to be different from that spoken by the inhabitants of the more northern parts of this country, whom I met with in my first voyage; which is not extraordinary, since those we now saw, and those we then visited, differ in many other respects. Nor did they seem to be such miserable wretches as the natives whom Dampier mentions to have seen on its western coast.

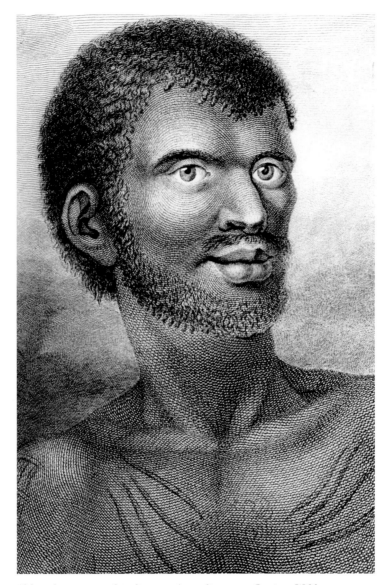

Although contacts with indigenous Australians were fleeting, Webber
produced a number of portraits including this one of a man with conspicuous
chest scarifications, probably associated with initiation or mourning.

Some of our present groupe wore, loose, round, their necks, three or four folds of small cord, made of the fur of some animal; and others of them had a narrow slip of the *kangooroo* skin tied round their ancles. I gave to each of them a string of beads, and a medal; which I thought they received with some satisfaction. They seemed to set no value on iron, or on iron tools. They were even ignorant of the use of fish-hooks, if we might judge form their manner of looking at some of ours which we shewed to them.

We cannot, however, suppose it to be possible that a people who inhabit a sea-coast, and who seem to derive no part of their sustenance from the productions of the ground, should not be acquainted with some mode of catching fish, though we did not happen to see any of them thus employed; nor observe any canoe or vessel, in which they could go upon the water. Though they absolutely rejected the sort of fish we offered to them, it was evident that shellfish, at least, made a part of their food, from the many heaps of muscle-shells we saw in different parts near the shore, and about some deserted habitations near the head of the bay. These were little sheds or hovels built of sticks, and covered with bark. We could also perceive evident signs of their sometimes taking up their abode in the trunks of large trees, which had been hollowed out by fire, most probably for this very purpose. In or near all these habitations, and wherever there was a heap of shells, there remained the marks of fire; an indubitable proof that they do not eat their food raw.

After staying about an hour with the wooding party and the natives, as I could now be pretty confident that the latter were not likely to give the former any disturbance, I left them, and went over to the grass-cutters on the East point of the bay, and found that they had met with a fine patch. Having seen the boats loaded, I left that party, and returned on board to dinner; where, some time after, Lieutenant King arrived.

From what I learnt, that I had but just left the shore, when several women and children made their appearance, and were introduced to him by some of the men who attended them. He gave presents to all of them, of such trifles as he had about him. These females wore a *kangooroo* skin (in the same shape as it came from the animal) tied over the shoulders, and round the waist. But its only use seemed to be, to support their children when carried on their backs; for it did not cover those parts which most nations conceal; being, in all other respects, as naked as the men, and as black, and their bodies marked with scars in the same manner. But in this they differed from the men, that though their hair was of the same colour and texture, some of them had their heads completely shorn or shaved; in others this operation had been performed only on one side, while rest of them had all the upper parts of the head shorn close, leaving a circle of hair all around, somewhat like the tonsure of the Romish Ecclesiastics. Many of the children had fine features, and were thought pretty; but of the persons of the women, especially those advanced in years, a less favourable report was made. However, some of the Gentlemen belonging to the *Discovery*, I was told, paid their addresses, and made liberal offers of presents, which were rejected with great disdain; whether from a sense of virtue, or the fear of displeasing their men, I shall not pretend to determine. That this gallantry was not very agreeable to the latter, is certain: for an elderly man, as soon as he observed it, ordered all the women and children to retire, which they obeyed, though some of them shewed a little reluctance.

This conduct of Europeans amongst Savages, to their women, is highly blameable; as it creates a jealousy in their men, that may be attended with consequences fatal to the success of the common enterprize, and to the whole body of adventurers, without advancing the private purpose of the individual, or enabling him to gain the object of his wishes. I believe it has been generally found amongst uncivilized people, that their women are easy of access, the men are the first to offer them to strangers; and that, where this is not the case, neither the allurements of presents, nor the opportunity of privacy, will be likely to have the desired effect. This observation, I am sure, will hold good, throughout all the parts of the South Sea where I have been. Why then should men act so absurd a part, as to risk their own safety, and that of all their companions, in pursuit of a gratification which they have no probability of attaining?

Chapter 3

RETURN TO QUEEN CHARLOTTE'S SOUND

On his return from his second voyage, the truth of what Cook had suspected became clear: there had been some terrible incident of violence. He learned that a boat's crew from the second ship, the Adventure, *had provoked Maori and been not only massacred but dismembered and consumed. The reality of cannibalism—scarcely believed by many of the Europeans up to this time—and the fact of European victims were deeply shocking. Cook would revisit not only the place but the perpetrator, against whom he perhaps surprisingly refused to exact revenge, blaming the conflict upon the carelessness or anger of the mariners.*

WE HAD NOT BEEN LONG at anchor before several canoes, filled with natives, came along-side of the ships; but very few of them would venture on board; which appeared the more extraordinary, as I was well known to them all. There was one man in particular amongst them, whom I had treated with remarkable kindness, during the whole of my stay when I was last here. Yet now, neither professions of friendship, nor presents, could prevail upon him to come into the ship. This shyness was to be accounted for only upon this supposition, that they were apprehensive we had revisited their county, in order to revenge the death of Captain Furneaux's people. Seeing Omai on board my ship now, whom they must have remembered to have seen on board the *Adventure* when the melancholy affair happened, and whole first conversation with them, as they approached, generally turned on that subject, they must be well assured that I was no longer a

OPPOSITE: This painting by English portraitist Nathaniel Dance-Holland communicates the intimate nature of the meetings between Maori and Europeans. Cook's second-in-command, Charles Clerke, is attentively examined by a tattooed Maori.

stranger to it. I thought it necessary, therefore, to use every endeavour to assure them of the continuance of my friendship, and that I should not disturb them on that account. I do not know whether this had any weight with them; but certain it is, that they very soon laid aside all manner of restraint and distrust.

On the 13th we set up two tents, one from each ship; on the same spot where we had pitched them formerly. The observatories were at the same time erected; and Messrs. King and Bayly began their operations immediately, to find the rate of the time-keeper, and to make other observations. The remainder of the empty water-casks were also sent on shore, with the cooper to trim, and a sufficient number of sailors to fill them. Two men were appointed to brew spruce beer; and the carpenter and his crew were ordered to cut wood. A boat, with a party of men, under the direction of one of the mates, was sent to collect grass for our cattle; and the people that remained on board were employed in refitting the ship, and arranging the provisions. In this matter, we were all profitably busied during our stay. For the protection of the party on shore, I appointed a guard of ten marines, and ordered arms for all the workmen; and Mr. King, and two or three petty officers, constantly remained with them. A boat was never sent to any considerable distance from the ships without being armed, and under the direction of such officers as I could depend upon, and who were well acquainted with the natives. During my former visits to this county, I had never taken some of these precautions; nor were they, I firmly believe, more necessary now than they had been formerly. But after the tragic fate of the *Adventure*'s boat's crew in this sound, and of Captain Marion du Fresne, and of some of his people, in the Bay of Islands [in 1772], it was impossible totally to divest ourselves of all apprehension of experiencing a similar calamity.

If the natives entertained any suspicion of our revenging these acts of barbarity, they very soon laid it aside. For, during the course of this day, a great number of families came from

Ship Cove was again the site of busy interaction between the mariners and local Maori. This work by James Webber highlights the authority and independence of the Maori warriors.

Cook and his men were entranced by Polynesian dance in the 1770s. The practice is no less important to Islanders across the Pacific today. Dance told stories and was an expression of competition among local and tribal groups. Today groups of migrants from various island nations compete regularly at festivals in Auckland and elsewhere. These images were captured by Glenn Jowitt.

different parts of the coast, and took up their residence close to us; so that there was not a spot in the cove where a hut could be put up, that was not occupied by them, except the place where we had fixed our little encampment. This they left us in quiet possession of; but they came and took away the ruins of some old huts that were there, as materials for their new erections.

* * *

THE ADVANTAGE WE received from the natives coming to live with us, was not inconsiderable. For, every day, when the weather would permit, some of them went out to catch fish; and we generally got, by exchanges, a good share of the produce of their labours. This supply, and what our own nets and lines afforded us, was so ample, that we seldom were in want of fish. Nor was there any deficiency of other refreshments. Celery, scurvy-grass, and portable soup were boiled with the peace and wheat, for both ships companies, every day during our whole stay; and they had spruce-beer for their drink. So that, if any of our people had contracted the seeds of the seeds of the scurvy, such a regimen soon removed them. But the truth is, when we arrived here, there were only two invalids (and these on board the *Resolution*) upon the sick lifts in both ships. Besides the natives who took up their abode close to us, we were occasionally visited by others of them, whose residence was not far off; and by some who lived more remote. Their articles of commerce were, curiosities, fish, and women. The two first always came to a good market; which the latter did not. The seamen had taken a kind of dislike to these people; and were either unwilling, or afraid, to associate with them; which produced this good effect, that I know no instance of a man's quitting his station, to go to their habitations.

A connection with women I allow, because I cannot prevent it; but never encourage, because I always dread its consequences. I know, indeed, that many men are of opinion, that such inter-course is one of our greatest securities amongst savages; and perhaps they who, either from necessity or choice, are to remain and settle with them, may find it so. But with travellers and transient visiters, such as we were, it is generally otherwise; and, in our situation, a connection with their women betrays more men than it saves. What else can be reasonably expected, since all their views are selfish, without the least mixture of regard or attachment? My own experience, at least, which hath been pretty extensive, hath not pointed out to me one instance to the contrary.

Amongst our occasional visiters, was a chief named Kahoora, who, as I was informed, headed the party that cut of Captain Furneaux's people, and himself killed Mr. Rowe, the officer who commanded. To judge of the character of Kahoora, by what I heard from many of his country-men, he seemed to be more feared than beloved amongst them. Not satisfied with telling me that he was a very bad man, some of them even importuned me to kill him: and, I believe, they were not a little surprised that I did not listen to them; for, according to their ideas of equity, this ought to have been done. But if I had followed the advice of all our pretended friends, I might have extirpated the whole race; for the people of each hamlet or village, by turns, applied to me to destroy the other. One would have almost thought it impossible, that to striking a proof of the divided state in which this miserable people live, could have been assigned. And yet I was sure that I did not misconceive the meaning of those who made these strange applications to me; for Omai, whose language was a dialect of their own, and perfectly understood all that they said, was our interpreter.

* * *

AS WE RETURNED down the sound, we visited Grass Cove, the memorable scene of the Massacre of Captain Furneaux's people. Here I met with my old friend Pedro, who was almost continually with me the last time I was in this sound, and is mentioned in my History of that Voyage. He, and another of his countrymen, received us on the beach, armed with the pa-too and spear. Whether this form of reception was a mark of their courtesy or of their fear, I cannot say; but I thought they betrayed manifest signs of the latter. However, if they had any apprehensions, a few presents soon removed them, and brought down to the beach two or three more of the family; but the greatest part of them remained out of sight.

Whilst we were at this place, our curiosity prompted us to inquire into the circumstances attending the melancholy fate of our countrymen; and Omai was made use of as our interpreter for this purpose. Pedro, and the rest of the natives present, answered all the questions that were put to them on the subject, without reserve, and like men who are under no dread of punishment for a crime of which they are not guilty. For we already knew that none of them had been concerned in the unhappy transaction. They told us, that while our people were sitting at dinner, surrounded by several of the natives, some of the latter stole, or snatched from them, some bread and fish, for which they were beat. This being resented, a quarrel ensued, and two New Zealanders were shot dead, by the only two musquets that were fired. For before our people had time to discharge a third, or to load again those that had been fired, the natives rushed in upon them, overpowered them with their numbers, and put them all to death. Pedro and his companions, besides relating the history of the massacre, made us acquainted with the very spot that was the scene of it. It is at the corner of the cove on the right-hand. They pointed to the place of the sun, to mark to us at what hour of the day it happened; and, according to this, it must have been late in the afternoon. They also shewed us the place where the boat lay; and it appeared to be about two hundred yards distant from that where the crew were seated. One of their number, a black servant of Captain Furneaux, was left in the boat to take care of her.

We were afterward told that this black was the cause of the quarrel, which was said to have happened thus: Once of the natives stealing something out of the boat, the Negro gave him a severe blow with a stick. The cries of the fellow being heard by his countrymen at a distance, they imagined he was being killed, and immediately began the attack on our people; who, before they had time to reach the boat, or to arm themselves against the unexpected impending danger, fell a sacrifice to the fury of their savage assailants.

The first of these accounts, was confirmed by the testimony of many of the natives, whom we conversed with, at different times, and who, I think, could have no interest in deceiving us. The second manner of relating the transaction, rests upon the authority of the young New Zealander, who chose to abandon his country and go away with us, and who, consequently, could have no possible view in disguising the truth. All agreeing that the quarrel happened when the boat's crew were sitting at their meal, it is highly probably that both the accounts are true, as they perfectly coincide. For we may very naturally suppose, that while some of the natives were stealing from the man who had been left in the boat, others of them might take the same liberties with the property of our people who were on shore.

Be this as it will, all agree, that the quarrel first took its rise from some thefts, in the commission of which the natives were detected. All agree, also, that there was no premeditated plan of bloodshed, and that, if these thefts had not been, unfortunately, too hastily resented, no mischief would have happened. For Kahoora's greatest enemies, those who solicited his destruction most earnestly, at the same time confessed that he had no intention to quarrel, much less to kill, till the fray had actually commenced. It also appears that the unhappy victims were under no sort of apprehension of their fate; otherwise they never would have ventured to sit down to a repast at so considerable a distance from their boat, amongst people who were the next moment to be their murderers. What became of the boat I never could learn. Some said she was pulled to pieces and burnt; others told us that she was carried, they knew not whither, by a party of strangers.

* * *

WE HAD NOT BEEN LONG at anchor near Motuara, before three or four canoes, filled with natives, came off to us from the South East side of the sound; and a brisk trade was carried no with them for the

In tropical Polynesia, the sea has been vital to maritime lives for centuries. It remains vital to Islanders' lives and environments today, a fact documented by late photographer Glenn Jowitt. This scene was captured in the Cook Islands.

curiosities of this place. In one of these canoes was Kahoora, whom I have already mentioned as the leader of the party who cut off the crew of the *Adventure*'s boat. This was the third time he had visited us, without betraying the smallest appearance of fear. I was ashore when he now arrived, but had got on board just as he was going away. Omai, who had returned with me, presently pointed him out, and solicited me to shoot him. Not satisfied with this, he addressed himself to Kahoora, threatening to be his executioner, if ever he presumed to visit us again.

The New Zealander paid so little regard to these threats that he returned, the next morning, with his whole family, men, women, and children, to the number of twenty and upwards. Omai was the first who acquainted me with his being along-side the ship, and desired to know if he should ask him to come on board. I told him he might; and accordingly he introduced the Chief into his cabin, saying, "There is Kahoora; kill him!" But, as if he had forgot his former threats, or were afraid that I should call upon him to perform them, he immediately retired. In a short time, however he returned; and seeing the Chief unhurt, he expostulated with me very

Two young boys are at home in the lagoon waters in the Tokelau Islands. As was common among mariners of the day, many of Cook's sailors were unable to swim.

earnestly, saying, "Why do you not kill him? You tell me, if a man kills another in England, that he is hanged for it. This man has killed ten, and yet you will not kill him; thought many of his countrymen desire it, and it would be very good." Omai's arguments, though specious enough, having no weight with me, I desired him to ask the Chief, why he had killed Captain Furneaux's people? At this question, Kahoora folded his arms, hung down his head, and looked like one caught in a trap: And, I firmly believe, he expected instant death. But no sooner was he assured of his safety, than he became cheerful. He did not, however, seem willing to give me an answer to the question that had been put to him, till I had, again and again, repeated my promise that he should not be hurt. Then he ventured to tell us, that one of his countrymen having brought a stone hatchet to barter, the man, to whom it was offered, took it, and would neither return it, nor give any thing for it; on which the owner of it snatched up the bread as an equivalent; and then the quarrel began.

The remainder of Kahoora's account of this unhappy affair, differed very little from what we had before learnt, from the rest of his countrymen. He mentioned the narrow escape he had, during the fray; a musquet being levelled at him, which he avoided by skulking behind the boat; and another man, who stood close to him, was shot dead. As soon as the musquet was discharged, he instantly seized the opportunity to attack Mr. Rowe, who commanded the party, and who defended himself with his hanger (with which he wounded Kahoora in the arm), till he was overpowered by numbers.

Mr. Burney, who was sent by Captain Furneaux the next day, with an armed party, to look for his missing people, upon discovering the horrid proofs of their shocking fate, had fired several vollies amongst the crowds of natives who still remained assembled on the spot, and were, probably, partaking of the detestable banquet. It was natural to suppose that he had not fired in vain; and that, therefore, some of the murderers and devourers of our unhappy countrymen had suffered under our just resentment. Upon inquiry, however, into this matter, not only from Kahoora, but from others who had opportunities of knowing, it appeared that our supposition was groundless, and that not one of the shots fired by Mr. Burney's people had taken effect, so as to kill, or even to hurt, a single person.

It was evident, that most of the natives we had met with since our arrival, as they knew I was fully acquainted with the history of the massacre, and expected I should avenge it with the death of Kahoora. And many of them seemed not only to wish it, but expressed their surprize at my forbearance. As he could not be ignorant of this, it was a matter of wonder to me, that he put himself so often in my power. When he visited us while the ships lay in the Cove, confiding in the number of his friends that accompanied him, he might think himself safe. But his two last visits had been made under such circumstances, that he could no longer rely upon this. We were then at anchor in the entrance of the Sound, and at some distance from any shore; so that he could not have any assistance from thence, nor flatter himself he could have the means of making his escape, had I determined to detain him. And yet, after his first fears, on being interrogated, were over, he was so far from entertaining any uneasy sensations, that, on seeing a portrait of one of his countrymen hanging up in the cabin, he desired to have his own portrait drawn; and sat till Mr. Webber had finished it, without marking the least impatience. I must confess, I admired his courage, and was not a little pleased to observe the extent of the confidence he put in me. For he placed his whole safety in the declarations I had uniformly made to those who solicited his death, That I had always been a friend to them all, and would continue so, unless they gave me cause to act otherwise: that as to their inhuman treatment of our people, I should think no more of it, the transaction having happened long ago, and when I was not present; but that, if ever they made a second attempt of that kind, they might rest assured of feeling the weight of my resentment.

W.W Ellis ad vivo delin:t et pinx

P euchlory Port

Chapter 4

THE TONGAN 'INASI

Cook and his companions had already been favorably impressed by the Tongan people, society, and environment: this seemed an ordered, aristocratic society, in which gardens were carefully tended and fenced, and where ceremony, and especially dance, appeared not only finely choreographed, but an expression of cultural advancement. Yet Tongans were among the most avid thieves the mariners had encountered, hence barter frequently degenerated into chaos and conflict, and often common men who were stealing desired goods for their chiefs were harshly punished. Cook never knew that some chiefs hatched a plot to kill him and seize the ships—a plan that was seriously entertained but then called off. From Cook's perspective, the high point of the visit was his opportunity to witness and participate in an extraordinary ritual, which featured the presentation of vegetable sacrifices to the high chief.

WE WERE NOW READY TO SAIL; but the wind being Easterly, we had not sufficient day light to turn through the narrows, either with the morning, or with the evening flood; the one falling out too early, and the other too late. So that, without a leading wind, we were under a necessity of waiting two or three days.

I took the opportunity of this delay, to be present at a public solemnity, to which the king had invited us, when we went last to visit him, and which, he had informed us, was to be performed on the 8th. With a view to this, he and all the people of note, quitted our neighbourhood on the 7th and repaired to Mooa, where the solemnity was to be exhibited. A party of us followed them, the next morning. We understood, form what Poulaho had said to us, that his

OPPOSITE: This blue-crowned lorikeet (*Vini australis*) was probably painted by the surgeon-artist William Ellis during the sojourn in the Tongan islands.

son and heir was now to be initiated into certain privileges; amongst which was, that of eating with his father; an honour he had not, as yet, been admitted to.

We arrived at Mooa about eight o'clock, and found the king, with a large circle of attendants sitting before him, within an inclosure so small and dirty, as to excite my wonder that any such could be found in that neighbourhood. They were intent upon their usual morning occupation, in preparing a bowl of *kava*. As this was no liquor for us, we walked out to visit some of our friends, and to observe what preparations might be making for the ceremony, which was soon to begin. About ten o'clock, the people began to assemble, in a large area, which is before the *malaee*, or great house, to which we had been conducted the first time we visited Mooa. At the end of a road, that opens into this area, stood some men with spears and clubs, who kept constantly reciting, or chanting, short sentences, in a mournful tone, which conveyed some idea of distress, and as if they called for something. This was continued about an hour; and, in the mean time, many people came down the road, each of them bringing a yam, tied to the middle of a pole, which they laid down, before the persons who continued repeating the sentences. While this was going on, the king and prince arrived, and seated themselves upon the area; and we were desired to sit down by them, but to pull off our hats, and to untie our hair. The bearers of the yams being all come in, each pole was taken up between two men, who carried it over their shoulders. After forming themselves into companies, of ten or twelve persons each, they marched across the place, with a quick pace; each company, headed by a man bearing a club or spear, and guarded, on the right, by several others, armed with different weapons. A man carrying a living pigeon on a perch, closed the rear of the procession, in which about two hundred and fifty persons walked.

Omai was desired by me, to ask the Chief, to what place the yams were to be thus carried, with so much solemnity? but, as he seemed unwilling to give us the information we wanted, two or three of us followed the procession, contrary to his inclination. We found, that they stopped before a *morai* or *siatooka* of one house standing upon a mount, which was hardly a quarter of a mile from the place where they first assembled. Here we observed them depositing the yams, and making them up into bundles; but for what purpose, we could not learn. And; as our presence seemed to give them uneasiness, we left them, and returned to Poulaho, who told us, we might amuse ourselves by walking about, as nothing would be done for some time. The fear of losing any part of the ceremony, prevented our being long absent. When we returned to the king, he desired me to order the boat's crew not to stir from the boat; for, as every thing would, very soon, be *taboo*, if any of our people, or of their own, should be found walking about, they would be knocked down with clubs; nay *mateed*, that is, killed. He also acquainted us, that we could not be present at the ceremony; but that we should be conducted to a place, where we might see everything that passed. Objections were made to our dress. We were told, that, to qualify us to be present, it was necessary that we should be naked as low as the breast, with out hats off, and our hair untied. Omai offered to conform to these requisites, and began to strip; other objections were then started; so that the exclusion was given to him equally with ourselves.

I did not much like this restriction; and, therefore, stole out, to see what might now be going forward. I found very few people stirring, except those dressed to attend the ceremony; some of whom had in their hands small poles, about four feet long, and to the under-part of these were fastened two or three other sticks, not bigger than one finger, and about six inches in length.

In May 1777, Cook was received and entertained on the island of Haʻapai, also known as Lifuka, with performances including a boxing match.

These men were going toward the *morai* just mentioned. I took the same road, and was, several times, stopped by them, all crying out *taboo*. However, I went forward, without much regarding them, till I came in sight of the *morai*, and of the people who were sitting before it. I was now urged, very strongly, to go back; and, not knowing what might be the consequence of a refusal, I complied. I had observed, that the people, who carried the poles, passed this *morai*, or what I may, as well, call temple; and guessing, from this circumstance, that something was transacting beyond it, which might be worth looking at, I had thoughts of advancing, by making a round, for this purpose; but I was so closely watched by three men, that I could not put my design in execution. In order to shake these fellows off, I returned to the *malice*, where I had left the king, and, from thence, made an elopement a second time; but I instantly met with the same three men; so that it seemed, as if they had been ordered to watch my motions. I paid no regard to what they said or did, till I came within sight of the king's principal *siatooka* or *morai*, which I have already described, before which a great number of men were sitting, being the same persons whom I had just before seen pass by the other *morai*, from which this was but a little distant. Observing, that I could watch the proceedings of this company from the king's plantation, I repaired thither, very much to the satisfaction of those who attended me.

As soon as I got in, I acquainted the gentlemen who had come with me from the ships, with what I had seen; and we took a proper station, to watch the result. The number of people, at the *siatooka*, continued to increase for some time; and, at length, we could see them quit their sitting posture, and march off in procession. They walked in pairs, one after another, every pair carrying, between them, one of the small poles above-mentioned, on their shoulders. We were told, that the small pieces of sticks, fastened to the poles, were yams; so that, probably, they were meant to represent this root emblematically. The hindmost men of each couple, for the most part, placed one of his hands to the middle of the pole, as if, without this addition support, it were not strong enough to carry the weight that hung to it, and under which they all seemed to bend, as they walked. This procession consisted of one hundred and eight pairs, and all, or most of them, men of rank. They came close by the fence behind which we stood; so that we had a full view of them.

Having waited there, till they had all passed, we then repaired to Poulaho's house, and saw him going out. We could not be allowed to follow him; but were, forthwith conducted to the place allotted to us, which was behind a fence, adjoining to the area of the *siatooka* where the yams had been deposited in the forenoon. As we were not the only people who were excluded from being publicly present at this ceremony, but allowed to peep from behind the curtain, we had a good deal of company; and I observed, that all the other inclosures, round the place, were filled with people. And yet, all imaginable care seemed to be taken, that they should see as little as possible; for the fences had not only been repaired that morning, but, in many places, raised higher than common; so that the tallest man could not look over them. To remedy this defect in our station,

Customary authority and rank remain vitally important in the kingdom of Tonga. These girls, photographed by the late Glenn Jowitt, are contributing to the public celebrations associated with King Tupou's 83rd birthday in 2001.

The elegance and choreography of Tongan dance astonished the Europeans, some of whom considered it more sophisticated than European dances of the time.

we took the liberty to cut holes in the fence, with our knives; and, by this means, we could see, pretty distinctly, every thing that was transacting on the other side.

On our arrival at our station, we found two or three hundred people, sitting on the grass, near the end of the road that opened into the area of the *morai*; and the number continually increased, by others joining them. At length, arrived a few men carrying some small poles, and branches or leaves of the cocoa-nut tree; and, upon their first appearance, an old man seated himself in the road, and, with his face toward them, pronounced a long oration in a serious tone. He then retired back, and the others advancing to the middle of the area, began to erect a small shed; employing, for that purpose, the materials above-mentioned. When they had finished their work, they all squatted down, for a moment, before it, then rose up, and retired to the rest of the company. Soon after, came Poulaho's son, preceded by four or five men, and they seated themselves a little aside from the shed, and rather behind it. After them, appeared twelve or fourteen women of the first rank, walking slowly in pairs, each pair carrying between them, a narrow piece of white cloth extended, about two or three yards in length. These marched up to the prince, squatted down before him; and, having wrapped some of the pieces of the cloth they had brought, round his body, they rose up, and retired in the same order, to some distance on his left, and there seated themselves. Poulaho himself soon made his appearance, preceded by four men, who walked two and two abreast, and sat down on his son's left hand, about twenty paces from him. The young prince, then, quitting his first position, went and sat down under the shed, with his attendants; and a considerable number more placed themselves on the grass, before this royal canopy. The prince himself sat facing the people, with his back to the *morai*. This being done, three companies,

Cook was absorbed by the *'inasi*, a complex sequence of presentations and rites which he thought implied a Tongan belief in a supreme being.

of ten or a dozen men in each, started up from amongst the large crowd, a little after each other, and running hastily to the opposite side of the area, sat down for a few seconds; after which, they returned, in the same manner, to their former stations. To them succeeded two men, each of whom held a small green branch in his hand, who got up and approached the prince, sitting down, for a few seconds, three different times, as they advanced; and then, turning their backs, retired in the same manner, inclining their branches to each other as they sat. In a little time, two more repeated this ceremony.

The grand procession, which I had seen march off from the other *morai*, now began to come in. To judge of the circuit they had made, from the time they had been absent, it must have been pretty large. As they entered the area, they marched up to the right of the shed, and, having prostrated themselves on the grass, deposited their pretended burthens (the poles above-mentioned), and faced round to the prince. They then rose up, and retired in the same order, closing their hands, which they held before them, with the most serious aspect, and seated themselves along the front of the area. During all the time that this numerous band were coming in, and depositing their poles, three men, who sat under the shed, with the prince, continued pronouncing separate sentences, in a melancholy tone. After this, a profound silence ensued, for a little time, and then a man, who sat in the front of the area, began an oration (or prayer), during which, at several different times, he went and broke one of the poles, which had been brought in by those who had walked in procession. When he had ended, the people, sitting before the shed, separated, to make a lane, through which the prince and his attendants passed, and the assembly broke up.

* * *

Cook, fascinated by what he had seen, returned the following day.

SOON AFTER, THE procession came in, each two persons bearing on their shoulders a pole, round the middle of which, a cocoa-nut leaf was plaited. These were deposited with ceremonies similar to those observed on the preceding day. The first procession was followed by the second; the men composing which, brought baskets, such as are usually employed by this people to carry provisions in, and made of palm leaves. These were followed by a third procession, in which were brought different kinds of small fish; each fixed at the end of a forked stick. The baskets were carried up to an old man, whom I took to be the Chief Priest, and who sat on the prince's right-hand, without the shed. He held each in his hand, while he made a short speech or prayer; then laid it down, and called for another, repeating the same words as before; and thus he went through the whole number of baskets. The fish were presented, one by one, on the forked sticks, as they came in, to two men, who sat on the left; and who, till now, held green branches in their hands. The first fish they laid down on their right, and the second on their left. When the third was presented, a stout looking man, who sat behind the other two, reached his arm over between them, and made a snatch at it; as also did the other two, at the very same time. Thus they seemed to contend for every fish that was presented; but as there were two hands against one, besides the advantage of situation, the man behind got nothing but pieces; for he never quitted his hold, till the fish was torn out of his hand; and what little remained in it, he shook out behind him. The others laid what they got, on the right and left alternately. At length, either by accident or by design, the man behind got possession of a whole fish, without either of the other two so much as touching it. At this, the word *mareeai*, with signifies *very good*, or *well done*, was uttered in a low voice throughout the whole crowd. It seemed, that he had performed now all that was expected from him; for he made no attempt upon the few fish that came after. These fish, as also the baskets, were all delivered, by the persons who brought them in, sitting; and, in the same order and manner, the small poles, which the first procession carried, had been laid upon the ground.

The last procession being closed, there was some speaking or praying, by different persons. Then, on some signal being given, we all started up, ran several paces to the left, and sat down with our backs to the prince, and the few who remained with him. I was desired not to look behind me. However, neither this injunction, nor the remembrance of Lot's wife, discouraged me from facing about. I now saw that the prince had turned his face to the *morai*. But this last movement had brought so many people between him and me, that I could not perceive what was doing. I was afterward assured, that, at this very time, the prince was admitted to the high honour of eating with his father; which, till now, had never been permitted to him; a piece of roasted yam being presented to each of them for this purpose. This was the more probable, as we had been told, before-hand, that this was to happen during the solemnity; and as all the people turned their backs to them, at this time, which they always do when their monarch eats.

After some little time, we all faced about, and formed a semicircle before the prince, leaving a large open space between us. Presently there appeared some men coming toward us, two and two, making a noise that might be called singing, and waving their hands as they advanced. When they had got close up to us, they made a shew of walking very fast, without proceeding a single step. Immediately after, three or four men started up from the crowd, with large sticks in their hands, who ran toward those new-comers. The latter instantly threw down the poles from their shoulders, and scampered off; and the others attacked the poles; and, having beat them most unmercifully, returned to their places. As the pole-bearers ran off, they gave the challenge that is usual here in wrestling; and, not long after, a number of stout fellows came from the same quarter, repeating the challenge as they advanced. These were opposed by a party, who came from the opposite side almost at the same instant. The two parties paraded about the area for a few minutes, and then retired, each to their own side. After this, there were wrestling and boxing-matches for about half an hour. Then two men seated themselves before the prince, and made speeches, addressed, as I thought, entirely to him. With this the solemnity ended, and the whole assembly broke up.

I now went and examined the several baskets which had been presented; a curiosity that I was not allowed before to indulge; because every thing was then *taboo*. But the solemnity being now over, they became, simply, what I found them to be, empty baskets. So that, whatever they were supposed to contain, was emblematically represented. And so, indeed, was every other thing which had been brought in procession, except the fish.

We endeavoured, in vain, to find out the meaning, not only of the ceremony in general, which is called *Natche*, but of its different parts. We seldom got any other answer to our inquiries, but *taboo*; a word, which, I have before observed, is applied to many other things. But, as the prince was, evidently, the principal person concerned in it; and as we had been told by the king, ten days before the celebration of the *Natche*, that the people would bring in yams for him and his son to eat together; and as he even described some part of the ceremony, we concluded, from what he had then said, and from what we now saw, that an oath of allegiance, if I may so express myself, or solemn promise, was, on this occasion, made to the prince, as the immediate successor to the regal dignity, to stand by him, and to furnish him with the several articles that were here emblematically represented. This seems the more probably, as all the principal people of the island, whom we had ever seen, assisted in the processions. But, be this as it may, the whole was conducted with a great deal of mysterious solemnity; and, that there was a mixture of religion in the institution; was evident, not only from the place where it was performed, but from the manner of performing it. Our dress and deportment had never been called in question, upon any former occasion whatever. Now, it was expected that we should be uncovered as low as the waist; that our hair should be loose, and flowing over our shoulders; that we should, like themselves, sit cross-legged; and, at times, in the most humble posture, with down-cast eyes, and hands locked together; all which requisites were most devoutly observed by the whole assembly. And, lastly, every one was excluded from the solemnity, but the principal people, and those who assisted in the celebration. All these circumstances were to me a sufficient testimony, that, upon this occasion, they considered themselves as acting under the immediate inspection of a Supreme Being.

The present *Natche* may be considered, from the above account of it, as merely figurative. For the small quantity of yams, which we saw the first day, could not be intended as a general contribution; and, indeed, we were given to understand, that they were a portion consecrated to the *Otooa*, or Divinity. But we were informed, on the same account, a far more important and grander solemnity; on which occasion, not only the tribute of Tongaraboo, but that of Hapaee, Vavaoo,

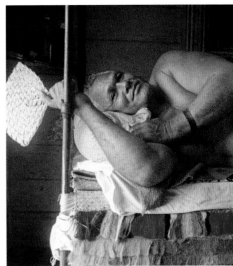

LEFT: Gifts of fabric were important in ceremonies witnessed by Cook. Such gifts remain important in Tonga today. This photo shows the presentation of barkcloth on King Tupou's birthday.

RIGHT: A quiet afternoon in a Tongan house today. Both photographs were created by Glenn Jowitt.

and of all the other islands, would be brought to the Chief, and confirmed more awfully, by sacrificing ten human victims from amongst the inferior sort of people. A horrid solemnity indeed! and which is a most significant instance of the influence of gloomy and ignorant superstition, over the minds of one of the most benevolent and humane nations upon earth. On inquiring into the reasons of so barbarous a practice, they only said, that it was a necessary part of the *Natche*; and that, if they omitted it, the Deity would certainly destroy their king.

Before the assembly broke up, the day was far spent; and as we were at some distance from the ships, and had an intricate navigation to go through, we were in haste to set out from Mooa. When I took leave of Poulaho, he pressed me much to stay till the next day, to be present at a funeral ceremony. The wife of Mareewagee, who was mother in-law to the king, had lately died; and her corpse had, on account of the *Natche*, been carried on board a canoe that lay in the *lagoon*. Poulaho told me, that, as soon as he had paid the last offices to her, he would attend me to Eooa; but, if I did not wait, there he would follow me thither. I understood, at the same time, that, if it had not been for the death of this woman, most of the Chiefs would have accompanied us to that island; where, it seems, all of them have possessions. I would gladly have waited to see this ceremony also, had not the tide been now favourable for the ships to get through the narrows. The wind, besides, which, for several days past, had been very boisterous, was not moderate and settled; and to have lost this opportunity, might have detained us a fortnight longer. But what was decisive against my waiting, we understood that the funeral ceremonies would last five days, which was too long a time, as the ships lay in such a situation, that I could not get to sea at pleasure. I, however, assured the king, that, if we did not fail, I should certainly visit him again the next day. And so we all took leave of him, and set out for the ships, where we arrived about eight o'clock in the morning.

Chapter 5

FAREWELL TO TAHITI

It was too late to attempt to reach and explore the north Pacific during the northern summer of 1777, so Cook extended his visits to the islands of the Pacific tropics. In Tahiti he saw old friends again, returned the Islander Mai (called Omai in the sources of the period), who Captain Furneaux had brought back to England, and witnessed further Polynesian rituals. Though Cook was not pious, he was Christian, and his admiration for, and curiosity about, Polynesian life were qualified by rites that he considered barbaric.

THAT THE OFFERING OF HUMAN SACRIFICES is part of the religious institutions of this island, had been mentioned by Mons. de Bougainville, on the authority of the native whom he carried with him to France. During my last visit to Otaheite, and while I had opportunities of conversing with Omai on the subject, I had satisfied myself, that there was too much reason to admit, that such a practice, however inconsistent with the general humanity of the people, was here adopted. But as this was one of those extraordinary facts, about which many are apt to retain doubts, unless the relater himself has had ocular proof to confirm what he had heard from others, I thought this a good opportunity of obtaining the highest evidence of its certainty, by being present myself at the solemnity; and, accordingly, proposed to Otoo that I might be allowed to accompany him. To this he readily consented; and we immediately set out in my boat, with my old friend Potatou, Mr. Anderson, and Mr. Webber; Omai following in a canoe.

In our way we landed upon a little island, which lies off Tettaha, where we found Towha and his retinue. After some little conversation between the two Chiefs, on the subject of the war, Towha addressed himself to me, asking my assistance. When I excused myself, he seemed angry; thinking it strange, that I, who had always declared myself to be the friend of their island, would

OPPOSITE: This young Polynesian woman was depicted by John Webber as ready to make a major gift of the barkcloth in which she was wrapped and the chest ornaments (*taumi*) attached to it.

ABOVE: This view of Huahine, in the Society Islands, was the work of John Cleveley, an accomplished marine artist who had not participated in the voyages. Cleveley drew on published accounts of the voyages in an attempt to cash in on the wide fascination of the time.

OPPOSITE: The "princess" Poetua was held hostage aboard ship in order to secure the return of seamen who had absconded. There is no indication of this context in Webber's magnificent painting, of which he produced several versions, now in London, Canberra, and Wellington.

not now go and fight against its enemies. Before we parted, he gave to Otoo two or three red feathers, tied up in a tuft; and a lean half-starved dog was put in a canoe that was to accompany us. We then embarked again, taking on board a priest who was to assist at the solemnity.

As soon as we landed at Attahooroo, which was about two o'clock in the afternoon, Otoo expressed his desire that the seamen might be ordered to remain in the boat; and that Mr. Anderson, Mr. Webber, and myself, might take off our hats, as soon as we should come to the *Morai*, to which we immediately proceeded, attended by a great many men, and some boys; but not one woman. We found four priests, and their attendants, or assistants, waiting for us. The dead body, or sacrifice, was in a small canoe that lay on the beach, and partly in the wash of the sea, fronting the *morai*. Two of the priests, with some of their attendants, were sitting by the canoe; the others at the *morai*. Our company stopped about twenty or thirty paces from the priests. Here Otoo placed himself; we, and a few others standing by him; while the bulk of the people remained at a greater distance.

The ceremonies now began. One of the priest's attendants brought a young plantain-tree, and laid it down before Otoo. Another approached with a small tuft of red feathers, twisted on some fibres of the cocoa-nut husk, with which he touched one of the king's feet, and then retired

with it to his companions. One of the priests, seated at the *morai*, facing those who were upon the beach, now began a long prayer; and, at certain times, send down young plantain trees, which were laid upon the sacrifice. During this prayer, a man, who stood by the officiating priest, held in his hands two bundles, seemingly of cloth. In one of them, as we afterward found, was the royal *maro*; and the other, if I may be allowed the expression, was the ark of the *Eatooa*. As soon as the prayer was ended, the priests at the *morai*, with their attendants, went and sat down by those upon the beach, carrying with them the two bundles. Here they renewed their prayers; during which the plantain-trees were taken, one by one, at different times, from off the sacrifice; which was partly wrapped up in cocoa leaves and small branches. It was now taken out of the canoe, and laid upon the beach, with the feet to the sea. The priests placed themselves around it, some sitting and others standing; and one, or more of them, repeated sentences for about ten minutes. The dead body was not uncovered, by removing the leaves and branches, and laid in a parallel direction with the sea-shore. One of the priests then, standing at the feet of it, pronounced a long prayer, in which he was, at times, joined by the others; each holding in his hand a tuft of red feathers. In the course of this prayer, some hair was pulled off the head of the sacrifice, and the left eye taken out; both which were presented to Otoo, wrapped up in a green leaf. He did not, however touch it; but gave, to the man who presented it, the tuft of feathers, which he had received from Towha. This, with the hair and eye, was carried back to the priests. Soon after, Otoo sent to them another piece of feathers, which he had given me in the morning to keep in my pocket. During some of this last ceremony, a king-fisher making a noise in the trees, Otoo turned to me, saying, "That is the *Eatooa*;" and seemed to look upon it as a good omen.

The body was then carried a little way, with its head toward the *morai*, and laid under a tree; near which were fixed three broad thin pieces of wood, differently, but rudely, carved. The bundles of cloth were laid on a part of the *morai*; and the tufts of red feathers were placed at the feet of the sacrifice; round which the priests took their stations; and we were now allowed to go as near as we pleased. He who seemed to be the chief priest sat at a small distance, and spoke for a quarter

A view of Opunohu Bay and Cook's Bay from a vantage point in the interior of Moorea.

of an hour, but with different tones and gestures; so that he seemed often to expostulate with the dead person, to whom he constantly addressed himself; and, sometimes, asked several questions, seemingly with respect to the propriety of his having been killed. At other times, he made several demands, as if the deceased either now had power himself, or interest with the Divinity, to engage him to comply with such requests. Amongst which, we understood, he asked him to deliver Eimeo, Maheine its chief, the hogs, women, and other things of the island, into their hands; which was, indeed, the express intention of the sacrifice. He then chanted a prayer, which lasted near half an hour, in a whining, melancholy tone, accompanied by two other priests; and in which Potatou, and some others, joined. In the course of this prayer, some more hair was plucked by a priest from the head of the corpse, and put upon one of the bundles. After this, the chief priest prayed alone, holding in his hand the feathers which came from Towha. When he had finished, he gave them to another, who prayed in like manner. Then all the tufts of feathers were laid upon the bundles of cloth; which closed the ceremony at this place.

The corpse was then carried up to the most conspicuous part of the *morai*, with the feathers, the two bundles of cloth, and the drums; the last of which beat slowly. The feathers and bundles were laid against the pile of stones, and the corpse at the foot of them. The priests having again seated themselves round it, renewed their prayers; while some of the attendants dug a hold about two feet deep, into which they threw the unhappy victim, and covered it over with earth and stones. While they were putting him into the grave, a boy squeaked aloud, and Omai said to me, that it was the *Eatooa*. During this time, a fire having been made, the dog, before mentioned, was produced, and killed, by twisting his neck, and suffocating him. The hair was singed off, and the entrails taken out, and thrown into the fire, where they were left to consume. But the heart, liver, and the kidneys were only roasted, by being laid on hot flames for a few minutes; and the body of the dog, after being besmeared with the blood, which had been collected into a cocoa-nut shell, and dried over the fire, was, with the liver, etc. carried and laid down before the priests, who sat praying, round the grave. They continued their ejaculations over the dog, for some time, while two men, at intervals, beat on two drums very loud; and a boy screamed, as before, in a loud, shrill

Webber painted this view of the exceptionally beautiful valley of Vaitepiha on northeastern Tahiti.

voice, three different times. This, as we were told, was to invite the *Eatooa* to feast on the banquet that they had prepared for him. As soon as the priests had ended their prayers, the carcase of the dog, with what belonged to it, were laid on a *whatta*, or scaffold, about six feet high, that stood close by, on which lay the remains of two other dogs, and of two pigs, which had lately been sacrificed, and, at this time, emitted an intolerable stench. This kept us at a greater distance, than would, otherwise, have been required of us. For, after the victim was removed from the sea-side toward the *morai*, we were allowed to approach as near as we pleased. Indeed, after that, neither seriousness nor attention were much observed by the spectators. When the dog was put upon the *whatta*, the priests and attendants gave a kind of shout, which closed the ceremonies for the present. The day being now also closed, we were conducted to the house belonging to Potatou, where we were entertained, and lodged for the night. We had been told, that the religious rites were to be renewed in the morning; and I would not leave the place, while any thing remained to be seen.

Being unwilling to lose any part of the solemnity, some of us repaired to the scene of action pretty early, but found nothing going forward. However, soon after, a pig was sacrificed, and laid upon the same *whatta* with the others. About eight o'clock, Otoo took us again to the *morai*, where the priests, and a great number of men, were, by this time, assembled. The two bundles occupied the place in which we had seen them deposited the preceding evening; the two drums stood in the front of the *morai*, but somewhat nearer it than before; and the priests were beyond them. Otoo placed himself between the two drums, and desired me to stand by him.

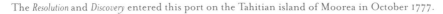

The ceremony began, as usual, with bringing a young plantain-tree, and laying it down at the king's feet. After this a prayer was repeated by the priests, who held in their hands several tufts of red feathers, and also a plume of ostrich feathers, which I had given to Otoo on my first arrival, and had been consecrated to this use. When the priests had made an end of the prayer, they changed their station, placing themselves between us and the *morai*; and one of them, the same person who had acted the principal part the day before, began another prayer, which lasted about half an hour. During the continuance of this, the tufts of feathers were, one by one, carried and laid upon the ark of the *Eatooa*.

Some little time after, four pigs were produced; one of which was immediately killed; and the others were taken to a sty, hard by, probably reserved for some future occasion of sacrifice. One of the bundles was now untied; and it was found, as I have before observed, to contain the *maro*, with which these people invest their kings; and which seems to answer, in some degree, to the European ensigns of royalty. It was carefully taken out of the cloth, in which it had been wrapped up, and spread, at full length, upon the ground before the priests. It is a girdle, about five yards long, and fifteen inches broad; and, from its name, seems to be put on in the same manner as is the common *maro*, or piece of cloth, used, by these people, to wrap around the waist. It was ornamented with red and yellow feathers; but mostly with the latter, taken from a dove found upon the island. The other end was bordered with eight pieces, each about the size and shape of a horse-shoe, having their edges fringed with black feathers. The other end was forked, and the

The *Resolution* and *Discovery* entered this port on the Tahitian island of Moorea in October 1777.

Cook and others were fascinated in the nature of Polynesian religious belief. Webber and others produced careful visual studies of shrines and the treatment of the deceased, who were wrapped in barkcloth, which was associated with sanctity.

points were of different lengths. The feathers were in square compartments, ranged in two rows, and, otherwise, so disposed as to produce a pleasing effect. They had been first pasted or fixed upon some of their own country cloth; and then sewed to the upper end of the pendant which Captain Wallis had displayed, and left flying ashore, the first time that he landed at Matavai. This was what they told us; and we had no reason to doubt it, as we could easily trace the remains of an English pendant. About six or eight inches square of the *maro* was unornamented; there being no feathers upon that space, except a few that had been sent by Waheadooa, as already mentioned. The priests made a long prayer, relative to this part of the ceremony; and, if I mistook not, they called it the prayer of the *maro*. When it was finished, the badge of royalty was carefully folded up, put into a cloth, and deposited again upon the *morai*.

The other bundle, which I have distinguished by the name of the ark, was next opened, at one end. But we were not allowed to go near enough to examine its mysterious contents. The information we received was, that the *Eatooa*, to whom they had been sacrificing, and whose name is *Oora*, was concealed in it; or rather, what is supposed to represent him. This sacred repository is made of the twisted fibres of the husk of the cocoa-nut, shaped somewhat like a large fid, or sugar loaf; that is, roundish, with one end much thicker than the other. We had, very often, got small ones from different people, but never knew their use before.

By this time, the pig, that had been killed, was cleaned, and the entrails taken out. These happened to have a considerable share of those convulsive motions, which often appear, in different parts, after an animal is killed; and this was considered by the spectators as a very favourable omen to the expedition, on account of which the sacrifices had been offered. And being exposed for some time, that those who chose, might examine their appearances, the entrails were carried to the priests, and laid down before them. While one of their number prayed, another inspected

the entrails more narrowly, and kept turning them gently with a stick. When they had been sufficiently examined, they were thrown in the fire, and left to consume. The sacrificed pig, and its
liver, etc. were now put upon the *whatta*, where the dog had been deposited the day before; and
then all the feathers, except the ostrich plume, were inclosed with the *Eatooa*, in the ark; and the
solemnity finally closed.

Four double canoes lay upon the beach, before the place of sacrifice, all the morning. On the
fore-part of each of these, was fixed a small platform, covered with palm-leaves, tied in mysterious
knots; and this also is called a *morai*. Some cocoa-nuts, plantains, pieces of bread-fruit, fish, and
other things, lay upon each of these naval *morais*. We were told, that they belonged to the *Eatooa*;
and that they were to attend the fleet designed to go against Eimeo.

The unhappy victim, offered to the object of their worship upon this occasion, seemed to
be a middle-aged man; and, as we were told, was a *towtow*; that is, one of the lowest class of the
people. But, after all my inquiries, I could not learn, that he had been pitched upon, on account of
any particular crime, committed by him, meriting death. It is certain, however, that they generally
make choice of such guilty persons for their sacrifices; or else of common, low, fellows, who stroll
about, from place to place, and from island to island, without having any fixed abode, or any visible way of getting an honest livelihood; of which description of men, enough are to be met with
at these islands. Having had an opportunity of examining the appearance of the body of the poor
sufferer, now offered up, I could observe, that it was bloody about the head and face, and a good
deal bruised upon the right temple; which marked the manner of his being killed. And we were
told, that he had been privately knocked on the head with a stone.

Those who are devoted to suffer, in order
to perform this bloody act of worship, are never
apprized of their fate, till the blow is given that
puts an end to their existence. Whenever any
one of the great Chiefs thinks a human sacrifice necessary, on any particular emergency,
he pitches upon the victim. Some of his trusty
servents are then sent, who fall upon him suddenly, and put him to death with a club, or by
stoning him. The king is next acquainted with
it, whose presence, at the solemn rites that
follow, is, as I was told, absolutely necessary;
and indeed, on the present occasion, we could
observe, that Otoo bore a principal part. The
solemnity itself is called *Poore Eree*, or Chief's
Prayer; and the victim, who is offered up,

Tattoos fascinated Cook's sailors, and some were
among the first European mariners to take on
tattoos themselves. Discouraged by missionaries for
decades, the art is undergoing a revival in parts of
the Pacific, as seen in this Glenn Jowitt photo.

Taata-taboo, or consecrated man. This is the only instance where we have heard the word *taboo* used at this island, where it seems to have the same mysterious signification as at Tonga; though it is there applied to all cafes where things are not to be touched. But at Otaheite, the word *raa* serves the same purpose, and is full as extensive in its meaning.

The *morai* (which, undoubtedly, is a place of worship, sacrifice, and burial, at the same time), where the sacrifice was now offered, is that where the supreme Chief of the whole island, is always buried, and is appropriated to his family, and some of the principal people. It differs little from the common ones, except in extent. Its principal part, is a long, oblong pile of stones, lying loosely upon each other, about twelve or fourteen feet high, contracted towards the top, with a square area, on each side, loosely paved with pebble stones, under which the bones of the Chiefs are buried. At a little distance from the end nearest the sea, is the place where the sacrifices are offered; which, for a considerable extent, is also loosely paved. There is here a very large scaffold, or *whatta*, on which the offerings of fruits, and other vegetables, are laid. But the animals are deposited on a smaller one, already mentioned, and the human sacrifices are buried under different parts of the pavement. There are several other reliques which ignorant superstition had scattered about this place; such as small stones, raised in different parts of the pavement; some with bits of cloth tied round them; others covered with it; and upon the side of the large pile, which fronts the area, are placed a great many pieces of carved wood, which are supposed to be sometimes the residence of their divinities, and, consequently, held sacred. But

one place, more particular than the rest, isa heap of stones, at one end of the large *whatta*, before which the sacrifice was offered, with a kind of platform at one side. On this are laid the sculls of all the human sacrifices, which are taken up after they have been several months under ground. Just above them, are placed a great number of the pieces of wood; and it was also here, where the *maro*, and the other bundle, supposed to contain the god *Oro* (and which I call the ark), were laid, during the ceremony; a circumstance which denotes its agreement with the altar of other nations.

It is much to be regretted, that a practice so horrid in its own nature, and so destructive of that inviolable right of self-preservation, which every one is born with, should be found still existing; and (such is the power of superstition to counteract the first principles of humanity!) existing amongst a people, in many other respects, emerged from the brutal manners of savage life. What is still worse, it is probable, that these bloody rites of worship are prevalent throughout all the wide extended islands of the Pacific Ocean. The similarity of customs and language, which our late voyages have enabled us to trace, between the most distant of these islands, makes it not unlikely, that some of the more important articles of their religious institutions should agree. And, indeed, we had the most authentic information, that human sacrifices continue to be offered at the Friendly

Tahitians occasionally practiced human sacrifice in order to ensure divine support for a project such as a military expedition. Those sacrificed were criminals, hence the system was no more arbitrary or brutal than the capital punishment of England at the time. On publication this image inflamed the imagination of evangelicals, helping to marshal support for the first Christian missions to Tahiti, which reached the islands just under twenty years later.

Islands. When I described the *Natchei* at *Tonga-taboo*, I mentioned that, on the approaching sequel of that festival, we had been told, that ten men were to be sacrificed. This may give us an idea of the extent of this religious massacre, in that island. And though we should suppose, that never more than one person is sacrificed, on any single occasion, at Otaheite, it is more than probable, that these occasions happen so frequently, as to make a shocking waste of the human race; for I counted no less than forty-nine skulls, of former victims, lying before the *morai*, where we saw one more added to the number. And as none of those skulls had, as yet, suffered any considerable change from the weather, it may hence be inferred, that no great length of time had elapsed, since, at least, this considerable number of unhappy wretches had been offered upon this altar of blood.

Ellis ad viv. del. et pinx. 1779.

Chapter 6

THE HAWAIIAN ISLANDS

In January 1778, Cook departed the uninhabited Christmas Island and sailed toward America. The mariners were surprised and excited to encounter new islands, which it soon became apparent formed part of another great Polynesian archipelago thus far unknown to Europeans. Again, the visit raised moral problems that troubled Cook deeply.

ON THE 19TH, AT SUN-RISE, the island first seen, bore East, several leagues distant. This being directly to windward, which prevented our getting near it, I stood for the other, which we could reach; and, not long after, discovered a third island in the direction of West North West, as far distant as land could be seen. We had now a fine breeze at East by North; and I steered for the East end of the second island; which, at noon, extended form North, half East, to West North West, a quarter West, and the nearest part being about two leagues distant. At this time, we were in some doubt whether or no the land before us was inhabited; but this doubt was soon cleared up, by seeing some canoes coming off from shore, toward the ships. I immediately brought to, to give them time to join us. They had from three to six men each; and, on their approach, we were agreeably surprized to find, that they spoke the language of Otaheite, and of the other islands we had lately visited. It required but very little address, to get them to come along-side; but not intreaties could prevail upon any of them to come on board. I tied some brass medals to a rope, and gave them to those in one of the canoes, who, in return, tied some small mackerel to the rope, as an equivalent. This was repeated; and some small nails, or bits of iron, which they valued more than any other article, were given them. For these they exchanged more fish, and a sweet potatoe; a sure sign that they had some notion of bartering; or, at least, of returning one present for another. They had nothing else in the their canoes, except some large gourd shells, and a kind of fishing-net; but one of them offered for sale the piece of stuff that he wore round his waist, after the manner of the other islands. These people were of a brown colour; and, though of the common size, were

OPPOSITE: The *'o'u* is a Hawaiian honeycreeper that is now critically endangered, or possibly even extinct.

stoutly made. There was little difference in the casts of their colour, but a considerable variation in their features; some of their visages not being very unlike those of Europeans. The hair of most of them was crop pretty short; others had it flowing loose; and, with a few, it was tied in a bunch on the crown of the head. In all, it seemed to be naturally black; but most of them had stained it, as is the practice of the Friendly Islanders, with some stuff which gave it a brown or burnt colour. In general, they wore their beards. They had no ornaments about their persons, nor did we observe that their ears were perforated; but some were punctured on the hands, or near the groin, though in a small degree; and the bits of cloth, which they wore, were curiously stained with red, black, and white colours. They seemed very mild; and had no arms of any kind, if we except some small stones, which they had evidently brought for their own defence; and these they threw overboard when they found that they were not wanted.

Seeing no sign of an anchoring-place at this Eastern extreme of the island, I bore away to leeward, and ranged along the South East side, at the distance of half a league from the shore. As soon as we made sail, the canoes left us; but others came off, as we proceeded along the coast, bringing with them roasting-pigs, and some very fine potatoes, which they exchanged, as the others had done, for whatever was offered to them. Several small pigs were purchased for a sixpenny nail; so that we again found ourselves in a land of plenty; and just at the time when the turtle, which we had so fortunately procured at Christmas Island, were nearly expended. We passed several villages; some seated near the sea, and others farther up the country. The inhabitants of all of them crowded to the shore, and collected themselves on the elevated places to view the ships. The land upon this side of the island rises, in a gentle slope, from the sea to the foot of the mountains, which occupy the centre of the country, except at one place near the East end, where they rise directly from the sea, and seemed to be formed of nothing but stone, or rocks lying in horizontal *strata*. We saw no wood, but what was up in the interior part of the island, except a few trees about the villages; near which, also, we could observe several plantations of plantains and sugar-canes, and spots that seemed cultivated for roots.

We continued to sound, without striking ground with a line of fifty fathoms, till we came abreast of a low point, which is about the middle of this side of the island, or rather nearer the North West end. Here we met with twelve and fourteen fathoms, over a rocky bottom. Being past this point, from which the coast trended more Northerly, we had twenty, then sixteen, twelve, and, at last, five fathoms over a sandy bottom. The last soundings were about a mile from the shore. Night now put a stop to any farther researches; and we spent it standing off and on. The next morning, we stood in for the land, and were met with several canoes full of people; some of whom took courage, and ventured on board.

ABOVE: This drum, made of wood, sharkskin, and fiber, was collected during Cook's third voyage.

OPPOSITE: In the Hawaiian Islands, Cook encountered another great Polynesian civilization. The islands' kingdoms were on a still grander scale than those of Tahiti and Tonga.

In the course of my several voyages, I never before met with the natives of any place so much astonished, as these people were, upon entering a ship. Their eyes were continually flying from object to object; the wildness of their looks and gestures fully expressing their entire ignorance about every thing they saw, and strongly marking to us, that, till now, they had never been visited by Europeans, nor been acquainted with any of our commodities, except iron; which, however, it was plain, they had only heard of, or had known it in some small quantity, brought to them at some distant period. They seemed only to understand, that it was a substance, much better adapted to the purposes of cutting, or of boring of holes, than any thing their own country produced. They asked for by the name of *hamaite*, probably referring to some instrument, in the making of which iron could be usefully employed; for they applied that name to the blade of a knife, though we could be certain that they had no idea of that particular instrument; nor could they, at all, handle it properly. For the same reason, they frequently called iron by the name of *toe*, which, in their language, signifies a hatchet, or rather a kind of adze. On asking them what iron was, they immediately answered, "We do not know; you know what it is, and we only understand it as *toe*, or *hamaite*." When we shewed them some beads, they asked first, "What they were; and then, whether they should eat them." But on their being told, that they were to be hung in their ears, they returned them as useless. They were equally indifferent to a looking-glass, which was offered them, and returned it, for the same reason; but sufficiently expressed their desire for *hamaite* and *toe*, which they wished might be very large. Plates of earthen-ware, china-cups, and other such things, were so new to them, that they asked if they were made out of wood; but wished to have some, that they might carry them to be looked at on shore. They were, in some respects, naturally well bred; or, at least, fearful of giving offence, asking, where they should sit down, whether they might spit upon the deck, and the like. Some of them repeated a long prayer before they came on board; and others, afterward, sung and made motions with their hands, such as we had been accustomed to see in the dances of the islands we had lately visited. There was another circumstance, in which they also perfectly resembled those other islanders. At first, on their encountering the ship, they endeavoured to steal every thing they came near; or rather to take it openly, as what we either should not resent, or not hinder. We soon convinced them of their mistake; and if they, after some time, became less active in appropriating to themselves whatever they took a fancy to, it was because they found that we kept a watchful eye over them.

At nine o'clock, being pretty near the shore, I sent three armed boats, under the command of Lieutenant Williamson, to look for a landing-place, and for fresh water. I ordered him, that if he should find it necessary to land in search of the latter, not to suffer more than one man to go with him out of the boats. Just as they were putting off from the ship, one of the natives having stolen the butcher's cleaver, leaped overboard, got into

The precise use of this small but elegant wooden bowl is not known, but its fine workmanship suggests that it was made for and used by Hawaiians of high status.

his canoe, and hastened to the shore, the boats pursuing him in vain.

The order not to permit the crews of the boats to go on shore was issued, that I might do every thing in my power to prevent the importation of some fatal disease into this island, which I knew some of our men now laboured under, and which, unfortunately, had been already communicated by us to other islands in these seas. With the same view, I ordered all female visiters to be excluded from the ships. Many of them had come off in the canoes. Their size, colour, and features did not differ much from those of the men; and though their countenances were remarkably open and agreeable, there were few traces of delicacy to be seen, either in their faces, or other proportions. The only difference in their dress, was their having

The Voyage pushed northward and made landfall in present-day Oregon at a spot Cook named Cape Foulweather before continuing on to Nootka Sound.

a piece of cloth about the body, reaching from near the middle, to half-way down the thighs, instead of the *maro* worn by the other sex. They would as readily have favoured us with their company on board as the men; but I wished to prevent all connection, which might, too probably, convey an irreparable injury to themselves, and, through their means, to the whole nation. Another necessary precaution was taken, by strictly enjoining, that no person, known to be capable of propagating the infection, should be sent upon duty out of the ships.

Whether these regulations, dictated by humanity, had the desired effect, or no, time only can discover. I had been equally attentive to the same object, when I first visited the Friendly Islands; yet I afterward found, with real concern, that I had not succeeded. And I am much afraid, that this will always be the case, in such voyages of ours, whenever it is necessary to have a number of people on shore. The opportunities and inducements to an intercourse between the sexes are then too numerous to be guarded against; and however confident we may be of the health of our men, we are often undeceived too late. It is even a matter of doubt with me, if it be always in the power of the most skilful of the faculty to pronounce, with any certainty, whether a person who has been under their care, in certain stages of this malady, is so effectually cured, as to have no possibility of his being still capable of communicating the taint. I think I could mention some instances which justify my presuming to hazard this opinion. It is, likewise, well known, that, amongst a number of men, there are, generally, to be found some so bashful as to endeavour to conceal their labouring under any symptoms of this disorder. And there are others, again, so profligate, as not to care to whom they communicate it. Of this last, we had an instance at Tongataboo, in the gunner of the *Discovery*, who had been stationed on shore to manage the trade for that ship. After he knew that he had contracted this disease, he continued to have connections with different women, who were supposed not to have already contracted it. His companions expostulated with him without effect, till Captain Clerke, hearing of this dangerous irregularity of conduct, ordered him on board.

Chapter 7

IN NOOTKA SOUND

This phase of the expedition brought Cook into contact for the first time with the native people of the American northwest coast, who were unrelated to the peoples of the Pacific Islands with whom familiarity had grown over the course of the three voyages. The people of Nootka Sound were, however, like Islanders in being keenly interested in making contact and in barter that periodically broke down into theft. The elaborate houses and ceremony interested the Europeans, who were the first to record and represent the great art traditions of this civilization.

THE SHIPS HAVING FOUND SO EXCELLENT SHELTER in an inlet, the coasts of which appeared to be inhabited by a race of people, whose inoffensive behaviour promised a friendly intercourse, the next morning after coming to anchor, I lost no time in endeavouring to find a commodious harbour where we might station ourselves during our continuance in the Sound. Accordingly, I sent three armed boats, under the command of Mr. King, upon this service; and soon after, I went myself, in a small boat, on the same search. I had very little trouble in finding what we wanted. On the North West of the arm we were now in, and not far from the ships, I met with a convenient snug cove well suited to our purpose. Mr. King was equally successful; for he returned about noon, which an account of a still better harbour, which he had seen and examined, lying on the North West side of the land. But as it would have required more time to carry the ships thither, than to the cove where I had been, which was immediately within our reach; this reason operated to determine my choice in favour of the latter situation. But being apprehensive, that we should not be able to transport our ships to it, and to moor them properly, before night came on, I thought it best to remain where we were till next morning; and, that no time might be lost, I employed the remainder of the day to some useful purposes, ordering the sails to be unbent, the top-masts to be struck, and the fore-mast of the *Resolution* to be unrigged, in order to fix a new bib, one of the old ones being decayed.

OPPOSITE: Though unrelated to the peoples of the South Pacific, the inhabitants of Nootka Sound had similarly complex societies with structures of inherited rank and status.

A great many canoes, filled with natives, were about the ships all day; and a trade commenced betwixt us and them, which was carried on with the strictest honesty on both sides. The articles which they offered to sale were skins of various animals, such as bears, wolves, foxes, deer, rackoons, polecats, martins; and, in particular, of the sea otters, which are found at the islands East of Katchatka. Besides the skins in their native shape, they also brought garments made of them, and another sort of clothing made of the bark of a tree, or some plant like hemp; weapons, such as bows, arrows, and spears; fish-hooks, and instruments of various kinds; wooden vizors of many different monstrous figures; a sort of woollen stuff, or blanketing; bags filled with red ochre; pieces of carved work; beads; and several other little ornaments of thin brass and iron, shaped like a horse-shoe, which they hang at their noses; and several chissels, or pieces of iron, fixed to handles. From their possessing which metals, we could infer that they had either been visited before by some civilized nation, or had connections with tribes on their continent, who had communication with them. But the most extraordinary of all the articles which they brought to the ships for sale, were human skulls, and hands not yet quite stripped of the flesh, which they made our people plainly understand they had eaten; and, indeed, some of them had evident marks that they had been upon the fire. We had but too much reason to suspect, from this circumstance, that the horrid practice of feeding on their enemies is as prevalent here, as we had found it to be at New Zealand and other South Sea islands. For the various articles which they brought, they took in exchange knives, chissels, pieces of iron and tin, nails, looking-glasses, buttons, or any kind of metal. Glass beads they were not fond of; and cloth of every sort they rejected.

We employed the next day in hauling our ships into the cove, where they were moored head and stern, fastening our hawsers to the trees on shore. On heaving up the anchor of the *Resolution*, we found, notwithstanding the great depth of water in which it was let go, that there were rocks at the

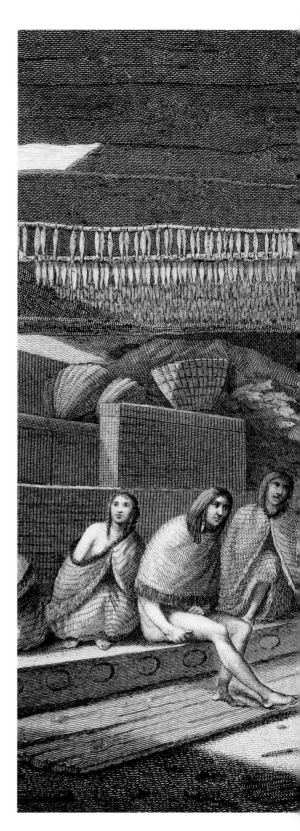

The impressive architecture and art of America's northwest coast were visually documented by Europeans for the first time during Cook's third voyage.

A view of Nootka Sound today. The inhabitants encountered here were keenly interested in barter.

bottom. These had done some considerable damage to the cable; and the hawsers that were carried out, to warp the ship into the cove, also got foul of rocks; from which it appeared that the whole bottom was strewed with them. The ship being again very leaky in her upper works, I ordered the carpenters to go to work to caulk her, and to repair such other defects as, on examination, we might discover.

The fame of our arrival brought a great concourse of the natives to our ships in the course of the day. We counted above a hundred canoes at one time, which might be supposed to contain, at an average, five persons each; for few of them had less than three on board; great numbers had seven, eight, or nine; and one was manned with no less than seventeen. Amongst these visiters, many now favoured us with their company for the first time, which we could guess, from their approaching the ships with their orations and other ceremonies. If they had any distrust or fear of us, they now appeared to have laid it aside; for they came on board the ships, and mixed with our people with the greatest freedom. We soon discovered, by this nearer intercourse, that they were as light-fingered as any of our friends in the islands we had visited in the course of the voyage. And they were far more dangerous thieves; for, possessing sharp iron instruments, they could cut a hook from a tackle, or any other piece of iron from a rope, the instant that our backs were turned. A large hook, weighing between twenty and thirty pounds, several smaller ones, and other articles of iron, were lost in this manner. And as to our boats, they stripped them of every bit of iron that was worth carrying away, though we had always men left in them as a guard. They were dexterous enough in effecting their purposes; for one fellow would contrive to amuse the boat-keeper, at one end of the boat, while another was pulling out the iron work at the other. If we missed a thing immediately after it had been

A man of Nootka Sound, with elaborate ornaments and tattoos, depicted by John Webber.

stolen, we found little difficulty in detecting the thief, as they were ready to impeach one another. But the guilty person generally relinquished his prize with reluctance; and sometimes we found it necessary to have recourse to force.

The ships being securely moored, we began our other necessary business of the next day. The observatories were carried ashore, and placed upon an elevated rock on one side of the cove, close to the *Resolution*. A party of men, with an officer, was sent to cut wood, and to clear a place for the conveniency of watering. Others were employed to brew spruce-beer, as pine trees abounded here. The forge was also set up, to make the iron-work wanting for the repairs of the fore-mast.

Handheld rattles were employed in dance and ritual by the people around Nootka Sound. This example collected during the voyage is now in the Museum of Archaeology and Anthropology in Cambridge.

For, besides one of the bibs being defective, the larboard trestle-tree, and one of the cross-trees were sprung.

A considerable number of the natives visited us daily; and, every now and then, we saw new faces. On their first coming, they generally went through a singular mode of introducing themselves. They would paddle, with all their strength, quite round both ships, a Chief, or other principal person in the canoe, standing up with a spear, or some other weapon, in his hand, and speaking, or rather hollowing, all the time. Sometimes the orator of the canoe would have his face covered with a mask, representing either a human visage, or that of some animal; and, instead of a weapon, would hold a rattle in his hand, as before described. After making this circuit round the ships, they would come along-side, and begin to trade without further ceremony. Very often, indeed, they would first give us a song, in which all in the canoe joined, with a very pleasing harmony.

During these visits, they gave us not other trouble, than to guard against their thievish tricks. But, in the morning of the 4th, we had a serious alarm. Our party on shore, who were employed in cutting wood, and filling water, observed that the natives all around them were arming themselves in the best manner they could; those, who were not possessed of proper weapons, preparing sticks, and collecting stones. On hearing this, I thought it prudent to arm also; but, being determined to act upon the defensive, I ordered all our workmen to retreat to the rock, upon which we had placed our observatories; leaving the natives in quiet possession of the ground where they had assembled, which was within a stone's throw of the *Resolution*'s stern. Our fears were ill-grounded: these hostile preparations were not directed against us, but against a body of their own countrymen, who were coming to fight them; and our friends of the Sound, on observing our apprehensions, used their best endeavours to convince us that this was the case. We could see, that they had people looking out, on each point of the cove, and canoes frequently passed between them and the main body assembled near the ships. At length, the adverse party, in about a dozen large canoes, in about a dozen large canoes, appeared off the South point of the cove, where they stopped, and lay drawn up in line of battle, a negociation having commenced. Some people in canoes, in conducting the treaty, passed between the two parties, and there was some speaking on both sides. At length, the difference, whatever it was, seemed to be compromised; but the strangers were not allowed to come along-side the ships, nor to have any trade or intercourse with us. Probably we were the cause of the quarrel; the strangers, perhaps, being desirous to share in the advantages of a trade with us; and our first friends, the inhabitants of the Sound, being determined to engross us entirely to themselves. We had proofs of this on several other occasions; nay, it appeared, that even those who lived in the Sound were not united in the same cause; for the weaker were frequently obliged to give way to the stronger party, and plundered of every thing, without attempting to make the least resistance.

We resumed our work in the afternoon, and, the next day, rigged the fore-mast; the head of which being rather too small for the cap, the carpenter went to work, to fix a piece on one side, to fill up the vacant space. In cutting into the mast-head for this purpose, and examining the state of it, both cheeks were found to be so rotten, that there was no possibility of repairing them; and it became necessary to get the mast out, and to fix new ones upon it. It was evident, that one of the cheeks had been defective at the first, and that the unfound part had been cut out, and a piece put in; which had not only weakened the mast-head, but had, in a great measure, been the occasion of rotting every other part of both cheeks. Thus, when we were almost ready to put to sea, we had all our work to do over again; and, what was still more provoking, an additional repair was to be undertaken, which would require some time to be completed. But, as there was no remedy, we immediately set about it. It was fortunate for the voyage, that these defects were discovered, when we were in a place, where the materials requisite were to be procured. For, amongst the driftwood, in the cove where the ships lay, were some small seasoned trees very fit for our purpose. One of these was pitched upon; and the carpenters began, without lots of time, to make out of it two new cheeks.

In the morning of the 7th, we got the fore-mast out, and hauled it ashore; and the carpenters of the ships were set to work upon it. Some parts of the lower standing rigging having been found to be very much decayed, as we had time now to put them in order, while the carpenters were repairing the fore-mast, I ordered a new set of main-rigging to be fitted, and a more perfect set of fore-rigging to be selected out of the best parts of the old.

From the time of our putting into the Sound till now, the weather had been exceedingly fine, without either wind or rain. That comfort, at the very moment when the continuance of it would have been of most service, was withdrawn. In the morning of the 8th, the wind freshened at South East, attended with thick hazy weather and rain. In the afternoon the wind increased; and, toward the evening, it blew very hard indeed. It came, in excessively heavy squalls, from over the high land on the opposite shore, right into the cove; and, through the ships were very well moored, put them in some danger. These tempestuous blasts succeeded each other pretty quick; but they were of short duration; and in the intervals between them we had a perfect calm. According to the old proverb, Misfortunes seldom come single; the mizzen was now the only mast on board the *Resolution* that remained rigged, with its top-mast up. The former was so defective, that it could not support the latter during the violence of the squalls, but gave way at the head under the rigging. About eight o'clock the gale abated; but the rain continued with very little intermission for several days; and, that the carpenters might be enabled to proceed in their labours, while it prevailed, a tent was erected over the fore-mast, where they could work with some degree of convenience.

The bad weather which now came on, did not, however, hinder the natives from visiting us daily; and, in such circumstances, their visits were very advantageous to us. For they frequently brought us a tolerable supply of fish, when we could not catch any ourselves with hook and line;

and there was not a proper place near us where we could draw a net. The fish which they brought us were either sardines; or what resembled them much, a small kind of bream; and sometimes small cod.

On the 11th, notwithstanding the rainy weather, the main-rigging was fixed and got over head; and our employment, the day after, was to take down the mizen-mast, the head of which proved to be so rotten, that it dropped off while in the slings. In the evening we were visited by a tribe of natives whom we had never seen before; and who, in general, were better looking people than our old friends, some of whom attended them. I prevailed upon these visiters to go down into the cabin for the first time; and observed, that there was not a single object that fixed the attention of most of them for a moment; their countenances marking, that they looked upon all our novelties with the utmost indifference. This, however, was not without exception; for a few of the company shewed a certain degree of curiosity.

In the afternoon of the next day, I went into the woods with a party of our men, and cut down a tree for a mizen-mast. On the day following, it was brought to the place where the carpenters were employed upon the fore-mast. In the evening the wind, which had been, for some time, Westerly, veered to South East, and increased a very hard gale, with rain, which continued till eight o'clock the next morning, when it abated, and veered again to the West.

The fore-mast being, by this time, finished, we hauled it along-side; but the bad weather prevented our getting it in till the afternoon; and we set about rigging it with the greatest expedition, while the carpenters were going on with the mizen-mast on shore. They had made very considerable progress in it on the 16th; when they discovered, that the stick upon which they were at work had sprung, or wounded; owing, as supposed, to some accident in cutting it down. So that all their labour was thrown away; and it became necessary to get another tree out of the woods, which employed all hands above half a day. During these various operations, several of the natives, who were about the ships, looked on with an expressive silent surprize, which we did not expect, from their general indifference and inattention.

On the 18th, a party of strangers, in six or eight canoes came into the cove, where they remained, looking at us for some time; and then retired, without coming alongside either ship. We supposed, that our old friends, who were more numerous, at this time, about us, than these new visiters, would not permit them to have any intercourse with us. It was evident, upon this and several other occasions, that the inhabitants of the adjoining parts of the Sound engrossed us entirely to themselves; or if, at any time, they did not hinder strangers from trading with us, they contrived to manage the trade for them in such a manner, that the price of their commodities was always kept up, while the value of ours was lessening every day. We also found, that many of the principal natives, who lived near us, carried on a trade with more distant tribes, in the articles they had procured from us. For we observed, that they would frequently disappear for four or five days at a time, and then return with fresh cargoes of skins and curiosities, which our people were so passionately fond of, that they always came to a good market. But we received most benefit from such of the natives that visited us daily. These, after disposing of all their little trifles, turned their attention to fishing; and we never failed to partake of what they caught. We also got from these people a considerable quantity of very good animal oil, which they had reserved in bladders. In this traffic some would attempt to cheat us, by mixing water with the oil; and, once or twice,

A north Pacific sea otter, also painted by Webber, would have already been familiar to Russian fur traders of the time. The Pacific Northwest hosted several competing interests by the late eighteenth century, and Nootka Sound was the site of a 1789 clash between the British and the Spanish.

they had the address to carry their imposition so far, as to fill their bladders with mere water, without a single drop of oil. It was always better to bear with these tricks, than to make them the foundation of a quarrel; for our articles of traffic consisted, for the most part, of mere trifles; and yet we were put to our shifts to find a constant supply even of these. Beads, and such other toys, of which I had still some left, were in little estimation. Nothing would go down with our visiters but metal; and brass had, by this time, supplanted iron; being so eagerly sought after, that before we left this place, hardly a bit of it was left in the ships, except what belonged to our necessary instruments. Whole suits of clothes were stripped of every button; bureaus of their furniture; and copper kettles, tin cannisters, candlesticks, and the like, all went to wreck; so that our American friends here got a greater medley and variety of things from us, than any other nation whom we had visited in the course of the voyage.

❧ Chapter 8 ❧

PROBING ARCTIC WATERS

Cook coasted Bering Strait and visited a native Chukchi community in Siberia communities, his realization growing that the charts with which he had been provided, and particularly that of Stahlin, which had indicated navigable routes to the north and east, appeared concocted. He ventured farther into Arctic seas, risking the ships. The cold was acute and the ice floes highly dangerous, but at least the men were able to hunt and feast on "sea horses" (walruses). It became clearer to Cook that, contrary to much geographical thought at the time, ice could form at sea, and sea ice could, and indeed was, renewed, thus making it less likely that open water might be found, irrespective of the distance from land or from frozen rivers that had previously been considered the probable sources of Arctic ice.

AT FIRST, WE SUPPOSED this land to be a part of the island of Alaschka, laid down in Mr. Stæhlin's map, before mentioned. But from the figure of the coast, the situation of the opposite shore of America, and from the longitude, we soon began to think that it was, more probably, the country of the Tschutski, or the Eastern extremity of Asia, explored by Beering in 1728. But to have admitted this, without farther examination, I must have pronounced Mr. Stæhlin's map, and his account of the new Northern Archipelago, to be either exceedingly erroneous, even in latitude, or else to be a mere fiction; a judgment which I had no right to pass upon a publication so respectably vouched, without producing the clearest proofs.

After a stay of between two and three hours, with these people, we returned to our ships; and, soon after, the wind veering to the South, we weighed anchor, stood out of the bay, and steered to the North East, between the coast and the two islands. The next day, at noon, the former extended from South 80° West, to North 84° West; the latter bore South 40° West; and the peaked mountain, over Cape Prince of Wales, bore South 36° East; with land extending from it as far as South 75° East. The latitude of the ship was 66° 5 ¼'; the longitude 191° 19'; our depth

John Webber depicted a "white bear" encountered in Alaska.

of water twenty-eight fathoms; and our position nearly in the middle of the channel between the two coasts, each being seven leagues distant.

From this station we steered East, in order to get nearer the American coast. In this course the water shoaled gradually, and there being little wind, and all our endeavours to increase our depth failing, I was obliged at last to drop anchor in six fathoms; the only remedy we had left to prevent the ships driving into less. The nearest part of the Western land bore West, twelve leagues distant; the peaked hill over Cape Prince of Wales, South 16° West; and the Northernmost part of the American continent in sight, East South East, the nearest part about four leagues distant. After we had anchored, I sent a boat to sound, and the water was found to shoal gradually toward the land. While we lay at anchor, which was from six to nine in the evening, we found little or not current; nor could we perceive that the water either rose or rell.

A breeze of wind springing up at North, we weighed, and stood to the Westward, which course soon brought us into deep water; and, during the 12th, we plied to the North, both coasts being in sight; but we kept nearest to that of America.

At four in the afternoon of the 13th, a breeze springing up at South, I steered North East by North, till four o'clock next morning, when, feeling no land, we directed our course East by North; and between nine and ten, land, supposed to be a continuation of continent, appeared. It extended from East by South to East by North; and, soon after, we saw more land, bearing North by East. Coming pretty suddenly into thirteen fathoms water, at two in the afternoon, we made a trip off till four, when we stood in again for the land; which was seen, soon after, extending from North to South East; the nearest part three or four leagues distant. The coast here forms a point, named *Point Mulgrave*, which lies in the latitude of 67° 45'; and in the longitude of 194° 51'. The land appeared very low next the sea; but, a little back, it rises into hills of a moderate height. The whole was free from snow; and, to appearance, destitute of wood. I now tacked, and bore away

Cruises through the Arctic ice brought many challenges, but also the possibility of hunting "sea horses."

North West by West; but, soon after, thick weather with rain coming on, and the wind increasing, I hauled more to the West.

Next morning, at two o'clock, the wind veered to South West by South, and blew a strong gale, which abated at noon; and the sun shining out, we found ourselves, by observation, in the latitude of 68° 18'. I now steered North East, till six o'clock the next morning, when I steered two points more Easterly. In this run we met with several seahorses, and flights of birds; some like land-sharks, and others no bigger than hedge-sparrows. Some shags were also seen; so that we judged ourselves to be not far from land. But as we had a thick fog, we could not expect to see any; and, as the wind blew strong, it was not prudent to continue a course which was most likely to bring us to it. From the noon of this day, to six o'clock in the morning of the following, I steered East by North; which course brought us into sixteen fathoms water. I now steered North East by East, thinking, by this course, to deepen our water. But, in the space of six leagues, it shoaled to eleven fathoms; which made me think it proper to haul close to the wind, that now blew at West. Toward noon, both sun and moon were seen clearly at intervals, and we got some flying observations for the longitude; which, reduced to noon, when the latitude was 70° 33', gave 197° 41'. The time-keeper for the same time, gave 198°; and the variation was 35° 1' 22" East. We had, afterward, reason to believe, that the observed longitude was within a very few miles of the truth.

Some time before noon, we perceived a brightness in the Northern horizon, like that reflected from ice, commonly called the blink. It was little noticed, from a supposition that it was improbable we should meet with ice so soon. And yet, the sharpness of the air, and gloominess of the weather, for two or three days past, seemed to indicate some sudden change. About an hour after, the sight of a large field of ice, left us no longer in doubt about the cause of the brightness of the horizon. At half past two, we tacked, close to the edge of ice, in twenty-two fathoms water, being then in the latitude of 70° 41'; not being able to stand on any farther. For the ice was quite impenetrable, and extended from West by South, to East by North, as far as the eye could reach. Here were abundance of sea-horses; some in the water; but far more upon the ice. I had thoughts of hoisting out the boats to kill some; but the wind freshening, I gave up the design; and continued to ply to the Southward, or rather to the Westward; for the wind came from that quarter.

We gained nothing; for, on the 18th at noon, our latitude was 70° 44'; and we were near five leagues father to the Eastward. We were, at this time, close to the edge of the ice, which was as compact as a wall; and seemed to be ten or twelve feet high at least. But, farther North, it appeared much higher. Its surface was extremely rugged; and here and there, we saw upon it pools of water.

We now stood to the Southward; and, after running six leagues, shoaled the water to seven fathoms; but it soon deepened to nine fathoms. At this time, the weather, which had been hazy, clearing up a little, we saw land extending from South to South East by East, about three or four miles distant. The Eastern extreme forms a point, which was much incumbered with ice; for which reason it obtained the name of *Icy Cap*. Its latitude is 70° 29', and its longitude 198° 20'. The other extreme of the land was loft in the horizon; so that there can be no doubt of its being a continuation

Walruses provided the explorers with a welcome supply of fresh meat.

of the American continent. The *Discovery* being about a mile astern, and to leeward, found less water than we did; and tacking on that account, I was obliged to tack also, to prevent separation.

Our situation was now more and more critical. We were in shoal water, upon a lee shore; and the main body of the ice to windward, driving down upon us. It was evident that, if we remained much longer between it and the land it would force us ashore; unless it should happen to take the ground before us. It seemed nearly to join the land to leeward; and the only direction that was open, was to the South West. After making a short board to the Northward I made a signal for the *Discovery* to tack, and tacked myself at the same time. The wind proved rather favourable so that we lay up South West, and South West by West.

At eight o'clock in the morning of the 19th, the wind veering back to the West, I tacked to the Northward; and, at noon, the latitude was 70° 6', and the longitude 196° 42'. In this situation, we had a good deal of drift-ice about us; and the main ice was about two leagues to the North. At half past one, we got in with the edge of it. It was not so compact as that which we had seen to the Northward; but it was too close, and too large pieces, to attempt forcing the ships through it. On the ice, lay a prodigious number of sea-horses; and, as we were in want of fresh provisions, the boats from each ship were sent to get some.

By seven o'clock in the evening, we had received, on board the *Resolution*, nine of these animals; which, till now, we had supposed to be sea-cows; so that we were not a little disappointed, especially

On August 18, 1778, the ships were in a critical situation, very nearly trapped among broken ice.

Contacts with the people of Unalaska were sufficiently friendly to involve visits to local houses such as this.

some of the seamen, who, for the novelty of the thing, had been feasting their eyes for some days past. Nor would they have been disappointed now, nor have known the difference, if we had not happened to have one or two on board, who had been in Greenland, and declared what animals these were, and that no one ever eat of them. But, notwithstanding this, we lived upon them as long as they lasted; and there were few on board who did not prefer them to our salt meat.

* * *

THE FOG BEING VERY THICK, and the wind Easterly, I now hauled to the Southward; and, at ten o'clock the next morning, the fog clearing away, we saw the continent of America, extending from South by East, to East by South; and at noon, from South West half South, to East; the nearest part five leagued distant. At this time we were in the latitude of 69° 32', and in the longitude of 195° 48'; and as the main ice was at no great distance from us, it is evident, that it now covered a part of the sea, which, but a few days before, had been clear; and that it extended farther to the South, than where we first fell in with it. It must not be understood, that I supposed any part of this ice which we had seen, to be fixed; on the contrary, I am well assured, that the whole was a moveable mass.

Having but little wind, in the afternoon, I sent the Master in a boat, to try if there was any current; but he found none. I continued to steer in for the American land, until eight o'clock, in order to get a nearer view of it, and to look for a harbour; but seeing nothing like one, I stood again to the North, with a light breeze Westerly. At this time, the coast extended from South

West to East; the nearest part four or five leagues distant. The Southern extreme seemed to form a point, which was named *Cape Lisburne*. It lies in the latitude of 69° 5', and in the longitude of 194° 42', and appeared to be pretty high land, even down to the sea. But here may be low land under it, which we might not see, being not less than ten leagues from it. Every where else, as we advanced Northward, we had found a low coast, from which the land rises to a middle height. The coast now before us was without snow, except in one or two places; and had a greenish hue. But we could not perceive any wood upon it.

On the 22d, the wind was Southerly, and the weather mostly foggy, with some intervals of sunshine. At eight in the evening it fell calm, which continued till midnight, when we heard the surge of the sea against the ice, and had several loose pieces about us. A light breeze now sprung up at North East; and, as the fog was very thick, I steered to the Southward, to clear the ice. At eight o'clock next morning, the fog dispersed, and I hauled to the Westward. For finding that I could not get to the North near the coast, on account of the ice, I resolved to try what could be done at a distance from it; and as the wind seemed to be settled at North, I thought it a good opportunity.

As we advanced to the West, the water deepened gradually to twenty-eight fathoms, which was the most we had. With the Northerly wind the air was raw, sharp, and cold; and we had fogs, sunshine, showers of snow and sleet, by turns. At ten in the morning on the 26th, we fell in with the ice. At noon, it extended from North West to East by North, and appeared to be thick and compact. At this time, we were, by observation, in the latitude 69° 36', and in the

A tufted puffin colony. The colorful birds, spotted on an island in the Bering Sea, inspired someone among the men to name the island Bird Island. In fact, it was Saint Matthew Island, named a decade earlier by the Russian Ivan Sindt.

The Russian fur trade actually beat Cook and his men to the Aleutian Islands by almost two decades.

longitude of 184°; so that it now appeared we had no better prospect of getting to the North here, than nearer the shore.

I continued to stand to the Westward, till five in the afternoon, when we were in a manner embayed by the ice, which appeared high, and very close in the North West and North East quarters, with a great deal of loose ice about the edge of the main field. At this time, we had baffling light winds; but it soon fixed at South, and increased to a fresh gale, with showers of rain. We got the tack aboard, and stretched to the Eastward; this being the only direction in which the sea was clear of ice.

At four in the morning of the 27th, we tacked and stood to the West, and at seven in the evening we were close in with the edge of the ice, which lay East North East, and West South West, as far each way as the eye could reach. Having but little wind, I went with the boats, to examine the state of the ice. I found it consisting of loose pieces, of various extent, and so close together, that I could hardly enter the outer edge with a boat; and it was as impossible for the ships to enter it, as if it had been so many rocks. I took particular notice, that it was all pure transparent ice, except for the upper surface, which was a little porous. It appeared to be entirely composed of frozen snow, and to have been all formed at sea. For, setting aside the improbability, or rather impossibility, of such huge masses floating out of rivers, in which there is hardly water for a boat, none of the productions of the land were found incorporated, or fixed in it; which must have unavoidably been the case, had it been formed in rivers, either great or small. The pieces of ice that formed the outer edge of the field, were from forty or fifty yards in extent, to four or five; and I judged, that the larger pieces reached thirty feet, or more, under the surface of the water. It also appeared to me very improbable, that this ice could have been the production of the preceding

7.

W: W: Ellis ad viv: delin:
1779.

Oriental Falcon Lath. p. 34* p. 7ᵉ

winter alone. I should suppose it rather to have been the production of a great many winters. Nor was it less improbable, according to my judgment, that the little that remained of the summer, could destroy the tenth part of what now subsisted of this mass; for the sun had already exerted upon it the full influence of his rays. Indeed I am of the opinion, that the sun contributes very little toward reducing these great masses. For although that luminary is a considerable while above the horizon, it seldom shines out for more than a few hours at a time; and often is not seen for several days in succession. It is the wind, or rather the waves raised by the wind, that brings down the bulk of these enormous masses, by grinding one piece against another, and by undermining and washing away those parts that lie exposed to the surge of the sea. This was evident, from our observing, that the upper surface of many pieces had been partly washed away, while the base or under part remained firm for several fathoms round that which appeared above water, exactly like a shoal round an elevated rock. We measured the depth of water upon one, and found it to be fifteen feet; so that the ships might have sailed over it. If I had not measured this depth, I would not have believed, that there was sufficient weight of ice above the surface, to have sunk the other so much below it. Thus it may happen, that more ice is destroyed in one stormy season, than is

ABOVE: An etching of Snug Corner Cove in Prince William Sound first appeared in *A New, Genuine and Complete History of the Whole of Captain Cook's Voyages* (1781).

OPPOSITE: A Siberian peregrine falcon was painted by the voyage surgeon William Ellis, who was also a fine natural history artist.

formed in several winters, and an endless accumulation is prevented. But that there is always a remaining store, every one who has been upon the spot will conclude, and none but closet-studying philosophers will dispute.

* * *

THE SEASON WAS now so far advanced, and the time when the frost is expected to set in so near at hand, that I did not think it consistent with prudence, to make any farther attempts to find a passage into the Atlantic this year, in any direction; so little was the prospect of succeeding. My attention was now directed toward finding out some place where we might supply ourselves with wood and water; and the object uppermost in my thoughts was, how I should spend the winter, so as to make some improvements in geography and navigation, and, at the same time, be in a condition to return to the North, in farther search of a passage, the ensuing summer.

ABOVE: This extraordinary cuirass, from a wooden suit of armor, was collected during the short visit to Prince William Sound on the Alaskan coast.

RIGHT: Cascade Glacier at Prince William Sound.

~ Chapter 9 ~

AT KEALAKEKUA

One mystery of Cook's final voyage concerns the loss of whatever journal he may have written from the time of arrival at Kealakekua Bay until his death. It is unthinkable that he would not have written about the drama and richness of the encounter, but equally difficult to believe that one of his successor commanders or subordinates would have suppressed or destroyed such a record. In any case, for these events we rely on the narrative of James King, a humane and intelligent officer who later wrote the final volume of the official voyage publication, which appeared under the title A Voyage to the Pacific Ocean *(1784). Of all Cook's meetings in the Pacific, none was more extraordinary than the arrival King described at Kealakekua Bay, when the mariners were met by a vast concourse of people. Cook proceeded, it appeared, to be treated as a deity, and for his willingness to enter into pagan worship and idolatry he was censured by many readers of the published account, some of whom even saw his subsequent death as a divine punishment.*

KARAKAKOOA BAY IS SITUATED ON THE WEST SIDE of the island of Owhyhee, in a district called Akona. It is about a mile in depth, and bounded by two low points of land, at the distance of half a league, and bearing South South East and North North West from each other. On the North point, which is flat and barren, stands the village of Kowrowa; and in the bottom of the bay, near a grove of tall cocoa-nut trees, there is another village of a more considerable size, called Kakooa: between them, runs a high rocky cliff, inaccessible from the sea shore. On the South side, the coast, for about a mile inland, has a rugged appearance; beyond which the country rises with a gradual ascent, and is overspread with cultivated inclosures and groves of cocoa-nut trees, where the habi-

OPPOSITE: Sculpted out of gourds, the unusual ceremonial helmets worn by Hawaiian warriors have been attributed by some to early Spanish influence, but there is no firm evidence for any European visit before Cook's.

Cook participated in rites on this *heiau* (temple) on the shores of Kealakekua Bay.

tations of the natives are scattered in great numbers. The shore, all around the bay, is covered with a black coral rock, which makes the landing very dangerous in rough weather; except at the village of Kakooa, where there is a find sandy beach, with a *Morai*, or burying-place, at one extremity, and a small well of fresh water, at the other. This bay appearing to Captain Cook a proper place to refit the ships, and lay in an additional supply of water and provisions, we moored in the North side, about a quarter of a mile from the shore, Kowrowa bearing North West.

As soon as the inhabitants perceived our intention of anchoring in the bay, they came off from the shore in astonishing numbers, and expressed their joy by singing and shouting, and exhibiting a variety of wild and extravagant gestures. The sides, the decks, and rigging of both ships were soon completely covered with them; and a multitude of women and boys, who had not been able to get canoes, came swimming round us in shoals; many of whom, not finding room on board, remained the whole day playing in the water.

Among the chiefs who came on board the *Resolution*, was a young man, called Pareea, whom we soon perceived to be a person of great authority. On presenting himself to Captain Cook, he told him, that he was *Jakanee*[1] to the king of the island, who was at the time engaged on a military expedition at Mowee, and was expected to return within three or four days. A few presents from Captain Cook attached him entirely to our interests, and he became exceedingly useful to us in the management of his countrymen, as we had soon occasion to experience. For we had not been long at anchor, when it was observed that the *Discovery* had such a number of people hanging on one side, as occasioned her to heel considerably; and that the men were unable to keep off the crowds which continued pressing into her. Captain Cook, being apprehensive that she might suffer some injury, pointed out the danger to Pareea, who immediately went to their assistance, cleared the ship of its incumbrances, and drove away the canoes that surrounded her.

---

1   We afterward met with several others of the same denomination; but whether it be an office, or some degree of affinity, we could never learn with certainty.

The authority of the chiefs over the inferior people appeared, from this incident, to be of the most despotic kind. A similar instance of it happened the same day on board the *Resolution* where the crowd being so great, as to impede the necessary business of the ship, we were obliged to have recourse to the assistance of Kancena, another of their chiefs, who had likewise attached himself to Captain Cook. The inconvenience we laboured under being made known, he immediately ordered his countrymen to quit the vessel; and we were not a little surprized to see them jump overboard, without a moment's hesitation; all except one man, who loitering behind, and shewing some unwillingness to obey, Kaneena took him up in his arms, and threw him into the sea.

Both these chiefs were men of strong and well-proportioned bodies, and of countenances remarkably pleasing. Kaneena especially, whose portrait Mr. Webber has drawn, was one of the finest men I ever saw. He was about six feet high, had regular and expressive features, with lively, dark eyes; his carriage was easy, firm, and graceful.

It has been already mentioned, that during our long cruize off this island, the inhabitants had always behaved with great fairness and honesty in their dealings, and had not shewn the slightest propensity to theft; which appeared to us the more extraordinary, because those with whom we had hitherto held any intercourse, were of the lowest rank, either servants or fishermen. We now found the case exceedingly altered. The immense crowd of islanders, which blocked up every part of the ships, not only afforded frequent opportunity of pilfering without risk of discovery, but our inferiority in number held forth a prospect of escaping with impunity in case of detection. Another circumstance, to which we attributed this alteration in their behaviour, was the presence and encouragement of their chiefs; for generally tracing the booty into the possession of some men of consequence, we had the strongest reason to suspect that these depredations were committed at their instigation.

Looking from the Hikiau *heiau* toward the point where Cook met his death, Kealakekua Bay.

ABOVE: Cook arrived in Hawaii just at the time the god Lono normally appeared in the Hawaiian ritual calendar and was treated as an embodiment of the god. He was accordingly feted and presented with sacrifices. Cook's willingness to go along with this treatment fascinated and horrified those who later read accounts of the voyage back in England. The more pious considered Cook to have been complicit in idolatry.

OPPOSITE: Hawaiians wore some of the most impressive articles of costume the mariners had encountered in Oceania. This man wears a feather helmet and cape.

Soon after the *Resolution* had got into her station, our two friends, Pareea and Kaneena, brought on board a third chief, named Koah, who, we were told, was a priest, and had been, in his youth, a distinguished warrior. He was a little old man, of an emaciated figure; his eyes exceedingly sore and red, and his body covered with a white leprous scurf, the effects of an immoderate use of the *ava*. Being led into the cabin, he approached Captain Cook with great veneration, and threw over his shoulders a piece of red cloth, which he had brought along with him. Then stepping a few paces back, he made an offering of a small pig, which he held in his hand, whilst he pronounced a discourse that lasted for considerable time. This ceremony was frequently repeated during our stay at Owhyhee, and appeared to us, from many circumstances, to be a sort of religious adoration. Their idols we found always arrayed with red cloth, in the same manner as was done to Captain Cook; and a small pig was their usual offering to the *Eatooas*. Their speeches, or prayers, were uttered too with a readiness and vocabulary that indicated them to be according to some formulary.

Chapter 10

THE DEATH OF COOK

In Hawaiian religion, two gods, Lono and Ku, take turns being supreme. Cook had been associated with Lono but returned during the period of Ku's ascendancy, which threatened the balance of the customary order and generated tension. Following relatively minor incidents, a boat was stolen and Cook thought of taking the Hawaiian king hostage to secure its return. The precise causes of the violence in which Cook fell have been much debated. While Cook has been seen as a distant, authoritarian, and discipline-minded commander, he seems also to have been deeply admired by his men, who were traumatized by his death. James King concluded his narrative with an overview of Cook's life, achievements, and character.

WE WERE EMPLOYED THE WHOLE OF THE 11TH, and part of the 12th, in getting out the foremast, and sending it, with the carpenters, on shore. Besides the damage which the head of the mast had sustained, we found the heel exceedingly rotten, having a large hold up the middle of it, capable of holding four or five cocoa-nuts. It was not, however, thought necessary to shorten it; and fortunately, the logs of red toa-wood, which had been cut at Eimeo, for anchor-stocks, were found fit to replace the sprung parts of the fishes. As these repairs were likely to take up several days, Mr. Bayly and myself, got the astronomical apparatus on shore, and pitched our tents in *Morai*; having with us a guard of a corporal and six marines. We renewed our friendly correspondence with the priests, who, for the greater security of the workmen, and their tools, *tabooed* the place where the mast lay, sticking their wands round it, as before. The sailmakers were also sent on shore, to repair the damages which had taken place in their department, during the late gales. They were lodged in a house adjoining the *Morai*, that was lent us by the priests. Such were our arrangements on shore. I shall now proceed to the account of those other transactions with the natives, which led, by degrees, to the fatal catastrophe of the 14th.

Upon coming to anchor, we were surprised to find our reception very different from what it had been on our first arrival; no shouts, no bustle, no confusion; but a solitary bay, with only here and there a canoe stealing close along the shore. The impulse of curiosity, which had before

This scene of Cook's death, based on a painting by John Webber, would be one of the most prolifically reproduced images associated with eighteenth-century travel. But Webber was not a witness, and the scene was heroically contrived rather than precisely represented.

operated to so great a degree, might now indeed be supposed to have ceased; but the hospitable treatment we had invariably met with, and the friendly footing on which we parted, gave us some reason to expect, that they would again have flocked about us with great joy, on our return.

We were forming various conjectures, upon the occasion of this extraordinary appearance, when our anxiety was at length relieved by the return of a boat, which had been sent on shore, and brought us word, that Terreeoboo was absent, and had left the bay under the *taboo*. Though this account appeared very satisfactory to most of us; yet others were of opinion, or rather, perhaps, have been led, by subsequent events, to imagine, that there was something, at this time, very suspicious in the behavior of the natives; and that the interdiction of all intercourse with us, on pretence of the king's absence, was only to give him time to consult with his Chiefs, in what manner it might be proper to treat us. Whether these suspicions were well founded, or the account given by the natives was the truth, we were never able to ascertain. For though it is not improbable, that our sudden return, for which they could see no apparent cause, and the necessity of which we afterward found it very difficult to make them comprehend, might occasion some alarm; yet the unsuspicious conduct of Terreeoboo; who, on his supposed arrival, the next morning, came immediately to visit Captain Cook, and the consequent return of the natives to their former friendly intercourse with us, are strong proofs, that they neither meant, nor apprehended, any change of conduct.

The site of Cook's death today.

In support of this opinion, I may add the account of another accident, precisely of the same kind, which happened to us, on our first visit, the day before the arrival of the king. A native had sold a hog on board the *Resolution*, and taken the price agreed on, when Pareea, passing by, advised the man not to part with the hog, without an advanced price. For this, he was sharply spoken to, and pushed away; and the *taboo* being soon after laid on the bay, we had at first no doubt, but that it was in consequence of the offence given to the Chief. Both these accidents serve to shew, how very difficult it is to draw any certain conclusion from the actions of people, with whose customs, as well as language, we are so imperfectly acquainted; at the same time, some idea may be formed from them, of the difficulties, at the first view, perhaps, not very apparent, which those have to encounter, who, in all their transactions with these strangers, have to steer their course amidst so much uncertainty, where a trifling error may be attended with even the most fatal consequences. However true or false our conjectures may be, things went on in their usual quiet course, till the afternoon of the 13th.

Toward the evening of that day, the officer who commanded the watering-party of the *Discovery*, came to inform me, that several Chiefs had assembled at the well near the beach, driving away the natives, whom he had hired to assist the sailors rolling down the casks to the shore. He told me, at the same time, that he thought their behavior extremely suspicious, and that they meant to give some farther disturbance. At his request, therefore, I sent a marine along with him, but suffered him to take only his side-arms. In a short time, the officer returned, and on his acquainting me, that the islanders had armed themselves with stones, and were grown very tumultuous, I went myself to the spot, attended by a marine, with his musquet. Seeing us approach, they threw away their stones, and, on speaking to some of the Chiefs, the mob were driven away, and those who chose it, were suffered to assist in filling the casks. Having left things quiet here, I went to meet Captain Cook, whom I saw coming on shore, in the pinnace. I related to him what had just passed; and he ordered me, in case of their beginning to throw stones, or behave insolently, immediately to fire a ball at the offenders. I accordingly gave orders to the corporal, to have the pieces of the sentinels loaded with ball, instead of a small shot.

Soon after our return to the tents, we were alarmed by a continued fire of musquets, from the *Discovery*, which we observed to be directed at a canoe, that we saw paddling toward the shore, in great haste, pursued by one of our small boats. We immediately concluded, that the firing was in consequence of some theft, and Captain Cook ordered me to follow him with a marine armed, and to endeavor to seize the people, as they came on shore. Accordingly we ran toward the place where we supposed the canoe would land, but were too late; the people having quitted it, and made their escape into the country before our arrival.

We were at this time ignorant, that the goods had been already restored; and as we thought it probably, from the circumstances we had at first observed, that they might be of importance, were unwilling to relinquish our hopes of recovering them. Having therefore inquired of the natives, which way the people had fled, we followed them, till it was near dark, when judging ourselves to be about three miles from the tents, and suspecting, that the natives, who frequently encouraged us in the pursuit, were amusing us with false information, we thought it in vain to continue our search any longer, and returned to the beach.

During our absence, a difference, of a more serious and unpleasant nature, had happened. The officer, who had been sent in the small boat, and was returning on board, with the goods which had been restored, observing Captain Cook and me engaged in the pursuit of the offenders, thought it his duty to seize the canoe, which was left drawn up on the shore. Unfortunately, this canoe belonged to Pareea, who arriving, at this same moment, from on board the *Discovery*, claimed his property, with many protestations of his innocence. The officer refusing to give it up, and being joined by the crew of the pinnace, which was waiting for Captain Cook, a scuffle ensued, in which Pareea was knocked down, by a violent blow to the head, with an oar. The natives, who were collected about the spot, and had hitherto been peaceable spectators, immediately attacked our people with such a shower of stones, as forced them to retreat, with great precipitation, and swim off to a rock, at some distance from the shore. The pinnace was immediately ransacked by the islanders; and, but for the timely interposition of Pareea, who seemed to have recovered from the blow, and forgot it at the same instant, would soon have been entirely demolished. Having driven away the crowd, he made signs to our people, that they might come and take possession of the pinnace, and that he would endeavour to get back the things which had been taken out of it. After their departure, he followed them in his canoe, with a midshipman's cap, and some other trifling articles of the plunder, and, with much apparent concern at what had happened, asked, if the *Orono* would kill him, and whether he would permit him to come on board the next day? On being assured, that he should be well received, he joined noses (as their custom is) with the officers, in token of friendship, and paddled over to the village of Kowrowa.

When Captain Cook was informed of what had passed, he expressed much uneasiness at it, and as we were returning on board, "I am afraid," said he, "that these people will oblige me to use some violent measures; for," he added, "they must not be left to imagine, that they have gained an advantage over us." However, as it was too late to take any steps this evening, he contented himself with giving orders, that every man and woman on board should be immediately turned out of the ship. As soon as this order was executed, I returned on shore; and our former confidence in the natives being now much abated, by the events of the day, I posted a double guard on the *Morai,* with orders to call me, if they saw any men lurking about the beach. At about eleven o'clock, five islanders were observed creeping round the bottom of the *Morai,* ; they seemed very cautious in approaching us, and, at last, finding themselves discovered, retired out of sight. About midnight, one of them venturing up close to the observatory, the sentinel fired over him; on which the men fled, and we passed the remainder of the night without further disturbance.

Next morning, at day-light, I went on board the *Resolution* for the time-keeper, and, in my way, was hailed by the *Discovery,* and informed, that their cutter had been stolen, during the night, from the buoy where it was moored.

When I arrived on board, I found the marines arming, and Captain Cook loading his double-barrelled gun. Whilst I was relating to him what had happened to us in the night, he interrupted me, with some eagerness, and acquainted me with the loss of the *Discovery*'s cutter, and with the preparations he was making for its recovery. It had been his usual practice, whenever any thing of consequence was lost, at any of the islands in this ocean, to get the king, or some of the principal *Erees*, on board, and to keep them as hostages, till it was restored. This method, which had always attended with success, he meant to pursue on the present occasion; and, at the same time, had given orders to stop all the canoes that should attempt to leave the bay, with an intention of seizing and destroying them, if he could not recover the cutter by peaceable means. Accordingly, the boats of both ships, well manned and armed, were stationed across the bay; and, before I left the ship, some great guns had been fired at two large canoes, that were attempting to make their escape.

It was between seven and eight o'clock when we quitted the ship together; Captain Cook in the pinnace, having Mr. Phillips, and nine marines with him; and myself in the small boat. The last orders I received from him were, to quiet the minds of the natives, on our side of the bay, by assuring them, they should not be hurt; to keep my people together; and to be on my guard. We then parted; the Captain went toward Kowrowa, where the king resided; and I proceeded to the beach. My first care, on going ashore, was to give strict orders to the marines to remain within the tent, to load their pieces with ball, and not to quit their arms. Afterward I took a walk to the huts of old Kaoo, and the priests, and explained to them, as well as I could, the object of the hostile preparations, which had exceedingly alarmed them. I found, that they had already

The mariners were impressed by the methods used by people in the vicinity of Kamchatka to preserve fish by drying it on racks in the open air.

heard of the cutter's being stolen, and I assured them, that though Captain Cook was resolved to recover it, and to punish the authors of the theft, yet that they, and the people of the village on our side, need not be under the smallest apprehension of suffering any evil from us. I desired the priests to explain this to the people, and to tell them not to be alarmed, but to continue peaceable and quiet. Kaoo asked me, with great earnestness, if Terreeoboo was to be hurt? I assured him, he was not; and both he and the rest of his brethren seemed much satisfied with this assurance.

In the mean time, Captain Cook, having called off the launch, which was stationed at the North point of the bay, and taken it along with him, proceeded to Kowrowa, and landed with the Lieutenant and nine marines. He immediately marched into the village, where he was received with the usual marks of respect; the people prostrating themselves before him, and bringing their accustomed offerings of small hogs. Finding that there was no suspicion of his design, his next step was, to inquire for Terreeoboo, and the two boys, his sons, who had been his constant guests on board the *Resolution*. In a short time, the boys returned along with the natives, who had been sent in search of them, and immediately led Captain Cook to the house where the king had slept. They found the old man just awoke from sleep; and, after short conversation about the loss of the cutter, from which Captain Cook was convinced he was in no wise privy to it, he invited him to

In Kamchatka, news of the voyage's tragic outcome, as well as other reports and specimens, were dispatched by land for England.

return in the boat, and spend the day on board the *Resolution*. To this proposal the king readily consented, and immediately got up to accompany him.

Things were in this prosperous train, the two boys being already in the pinnace, and the rest of the party having advanced near the water-side, when an elderly woman called Kanee-kabareea, the mother of the boys, and one of the king's favourite wives, came after him, and with many tears, and entreaties, besought him not to go on board. At the same time, two Chiefs, who came along with her, laid hold of him, and insisting, that he should go no farther, forced him to sit down. The natives, who were collecting in prodigious numbers along the shore, and had probably been alarmed by the firing of the great guns, and the appearances of hostility in the bay, began to throng round Captain Cook and their king. In this situation, the Lieutenant of marines, observing that his men were huddled close together, and thus incapable of using their arms, if any occasion should require it, proposed to the Captain, to draw them up along the rocks, close to the water's edge; and the crowd readily making way for them to pass, they were drawn up in a line, at the distance of about thirty yards from the place where the king was sitting.

All this time, the old king remained on the ground, with the strongest marks of terror and dejection in his countenance; Captain Cook, not willing to abandon the object for which he had come on shore, continuing to urge him, in the most pressing manner, to proceed; whilst, on the other hand, whenever the king appeared inclined to follow him, the Chiefs, who stood round him, interposed, at first with prayers and entreaties, but afterward, having recourse to force and violence, and insisting on his staying where he was. Captain Cook therefore finding, that the alarm had spread too generally, and that it was in vain to think any longer of getting him off, without bloodshed, at last gave up the point; observing to Mr. Phillips, that it would be impossible to compel him to go on board, without the risk of killing a great number of the inhabitants.

Though the enterprize, which had carried Captain Cook on shore had now failed, and was abandoned, yet his person did not appear to have been in the least danger, till an accident happened, which gave a fatal turn to the affair. The boats, which had been stationed across the bay, having fired at some canoes, that were attempting to get out, unfortunately had killed a Chief of the first rank. The news of his death arrived at the village where Captain Cook was, just as he had left the king, and was walking slowly toward the shore. The ferment it occasioned was very conspicuous; the women and children were immediately sent off; and the men put on their war-mats, and armed themselves with spears and stones. One of the natives, having in his hands a stone, and a long iron spike (which they call a *pahooa*) came up to the Captain, flourishing his weapon, by way of defiance, and threatened to throw the stone. The Captain desired him to desist; but the man persisting in his insolence, he was at length provoked to fire a load of small-shot. The man having his mat on, which the shot were not able to penetrate, this had no other effect than to irritate and encourage them. Several stones were thrown at the marines; and one of the *Erees* attempted to stab Mr. Phillips with his *pahooa*; but failed in the attempt, and received from him a blow with the but end of his musquet. Captain Cook now fired his second barrel, loaded with ball, and killed one of the foremost of the natives. A general attack with stones immediately followed, which was answered by a discharge of musquetry from the marines, and the people on the boats. The islanders, contrary to the expectations of every one, stood the fire with great firmness; and before the marines had time to reload, they broke in upon them with dreadful shouts and yells. What followed was a scene of the utmost horror and confusion.

Four of the marines were cut off amongst the rocks in their retreat, and fell a sacrifice to the fury of the enemy; three more were dangerously wounded; and the Lieutenant, who had received a stab between the shoulders with a *pahooa*, having fortunately reserved his fire, shot the man who had wounded him just as he was going to repeat his blow. Our unfortunate Commander, the last time he was seen distinctly, was standing at the water's edge, and calling out to the boats to cease firing, and to pull in. If it be true, some of those who were present have imagined, that the marines and boat-men had fired without his orders, and that he was desirous of preventing any further bloodshed, it is not improbable, that his humanity, on this occasion, proved fatal to him. For it was remarked, that whilst he faced the natives, none of them had offered him any violence, but that having turned about, to give his orders to the boats, he was stabbed in the back, and fell with his face into the water. On seeing him fall, the islanders set up a great shout, and his body was immediately dragged on shore, and surrounded by the enemy, who snatching the dagger out of each other's hands, shewed a savage eagerness to have a share in his destruction.

Thus fell our great and excellent Commander! After a life of so much distinguished and successful enterprize, his death, as far as regards himself, cannot be reckoned premature; since he lived to finish the great work for which he seems to have been designed; and was rather removed from the enjoyment, than cut off from the acquisition, of glory. How sincerely his loss was felt and lamented, by those who had so long found their general security in his skill and conduct, and every consolation, under their hardships, in his tenderness and humanity, it is neither necessary nor possible for me to describe; much less shall I attempt to paint the horror with which we were struck, and the universal dejection and dismay, which followed so dreadful and unexpected a calamity. The reader will not be displeased to turn from so sad a scene, to the contemplation of his character and virtues, whilst I am paying my last tribute to the memory of a dear and honoured friend, in a short history of his life, and public services.

Captain James Cook was born near Whitby, in Yorkshire, in the year 1727; and, at an early age, was put apprentice to a shopkeeper in a neighbouring village. His natural inclination not having been consulted on this occasion, he soon quitted the counter from disgust, and bound himself, for nine years, to the matter of a vessel in the coal trade. At the breaking out of war in 1755, he entered into the king's service, on board the Eagle, at that time commanded by Captain Hamer, and afterward by Sir Hugh Pallifer, who soon discovered his merit, and introduced him on the quarter-deck.

In the year 1758, we find him master of the Northumberland, the flag ship of Lord Colville, who had then the command of the squadron stationed on the coast of America. It was here, as I have often heard him say, that, during a hard winter, he first read Euclid, and applied himself to the study of mathematics and astronomy, without any other assistance, than what a few books, and his own industry, afforded him. At the same time, that he thus found means to cultivate and improve his mind, and to supply the deficiencies of an early education, he was engaged in most of the busy and active scenes of the war in America. At the siege of Quebec, Sir Charles Saunders committed to his charge the execution of services, of the first importance in the naval department. He piloted the boats to the attack of Montmorency; conducted the embarkation to the Heights of Abraham; examined the passage, and laid buoys for the security of the large ships in proceeding up the river. The courage and address with which he acquitted himself in these services, gained him the warm friendship of Sir Charles Saunders and Lord Colville, who continued to patronize him, during the rest of their lives, with the greatest zeal and affection. At the conclusion of the war, he was appointed, through the recommendation of Lord Colville and Sir Hugh Pallifer, to survey the Gulf of St. Lawrence, and the coasts of Newfoundland. In this employment he continued till the year 1767, when he was fixed on by Sir Edwarde Hawke, to command an expedition to the South Seas; for the purpose of observing the transit of *Venus*, and prosecuting discoveries in that part of the globe.

From this period, as his services are too well known to require a recital here, so his reputation has proportionably advanced to a height too great to be affected by my panegyrick. Indeed, he appears to have been most eminently and peculiarly qualified for this species of enterprize. The earliest habits of his life, the course of his services, and the constant application of his mind, all conspired to fit him for it, and gave him a degree of professional knowledge, which can fall to the lot of very few.

The constitution of his body was robust, inured to labour, and capable of undergoing the severest hardships. His stomach bore, without difficulty, the coarsest and most ungrateful food. Indeed, temperance in him was scarcely a virtue; so great was the indifference with which he submitted to every kind of self-denial. The qualities of his mind were of the same hardy, vigorous kind with those of his body. His understanding was strong and perspicacious. His judgment, in whatever related to the services he was engaged in, quick and sure. His designs were bold and manly; and both in the conception, and in the mode of execution, bore evident marks of a great original genius. His courage was cool and determined, and accompanied with an admirable presence of mind in the moment of danger. His manners were plain and unaffected. His temper might perhaps have been justly blamed, as subject to hastiness and passion, had not these been disarmed by a disposition the most benevolent and humane.

Such were the outlines of Captain Cook's character; but its most distinguishing feature was, that unremitting perseverance in the pursuit of his object, which was not only superior to the opposition of dangers, and the pressure of hardships, but even exempt from the want of ordinary relaxation. During the long and tedious voyages in which he was engaged, his eagerness and activity were never in the least abated. No incidental temptation could detain him for a moment; even those intervals of recreation, which sometimes unavoidably occurred, and were looked for by us with a longing, that persons who have experienced the fatigue of service, will readily excuse, were submitted to by him with a certain impatience, whenever they could not be employed in making further provision for the more effectual prosecution of his designs.

It is not necessary, here, to enumerate the instances in which these qualities were displayed, during the great and important enterprizes in which he was engaged. I shall content myself with stating the result of those services, under the two principal heads to which they may be referred, those of geography and navigation, placing each in a separate and distinct point of view.

Perhaps no science ever received greater additions from the labours of a single man, than geography has done from those of Captain Cook. In his first voyage to the South Seas, he discovered the Society Islands; determined the insularity of New Zealand; discovered the straits which separate the two islands, and are called after his name; and made a complete survey of both. He afterward explored the Eastern coast of New Holland, hitherto unknown; an extent of twenty-seven degrees of latitude, or upward of two thousand miles.

In his second expedition, he resolved the great problem of a Southern continent; having traversed that hemisphere between the latitudes of 40° and 70°, in such a manner, as not to leave a possibility of its existence, unless near the pole, and out of reach of navigation. During this voyage, he discovered New Caledonia, the largest island in the Southern Pacific, except New Zealand; the island of Georgia; and an unknown coast, which he named Sandwich Land, the *thule* of the Southern hemisphere; and having twice visited the tropical seas, he settled the situations of the old, and made several new discoveries.

But the voyage we are now relating, is distinguished, above all the rest, by the extent and importance of its discoveries. Besides several smaller islands in the Southern Pacific, he discovered, to the North of the equinoctial line, the group called the Sandwich Islands; which, from their situation and productions, bid fairer for becoming an object of consequence, in the system of European navigation, than any other discovery in the South Sea. He afterward explored what had hitherto remained unknown of the Western coast of America, from the latitude of 43° to 70° North, containing an extent of three thousand five hundred miles; ascertained the proximity of the two great continents of Asia and America; passed the straits between them, and surveyed the coast, on each side, to such a height of Northern latitude, as to demonstrate the impracticability of a passage, in that hemisphere,

The ships called also at the island of Krakatoa, now part of Indonesia, where Webber drew and painted dwellings, inhabitants, and plants, including the plantain tree.

from the Atlantic into the Pacific Ocean, either by an Eastern or a Western course. In short, if we accept the sea of Amur, and the Japanese Archipelago, which still remain imperfectly known to Europeans, he has completed the hydrography of the habitable globe.

As a navigator, his services were not perhaps less splendid; certainly not less important and meritorious. The method which he discovered, and so successfully pursued, of preserving the

health of seamen, forms a new era in navigation, and will transmit his name to future ages, amongst the friends and benefactors of mankind.

Those who are conversant in naval history, need not be told, at how dear a rate the advantages, which have been sought, through the medium of long voyages at sea, have always been purchased. That dreadful disorder which is peculiar to this service, and whose ravages have marked the tracks of discoverers with circumstances almost too shocking to relate, must, without exercising an unwarrantable tyranny over the lives of our seamen, have proved an insuperable obstacle to the prosecution of such enterprizes. It was reserved for Captain Cook to shew the world, by repeated trials, that voyages might be protracted to the unusual length of three or even four years, in unknown regions, and under every change and rigour of climate, not only without affecting the health, but even without diminishing the probability of life, in the smallest degree. The method he pursued has been fully explained by himself, in a paper which was read before the Royal Society, in the year 1776[2]; and whatever improvements the experience of the present voyage has suggested, are mentioned in the proper places.

With respect to his professional abilities, I shall leave them to the judgment of those who are best acquainted with the nature of the services in which he was engaged. They will readily acknowledge, that to have conducted three expeditions of so much danger and difficulty, of so unusual a length, and in such a variety of situation, with uniform and invariable success, must have required not only a thorough and accurate knowledge of his business, but a powerful and comprehensive genius, fruitful in resources, and equally ready in the application of whatever the higher and inferior calls of the service required.

Having given the most faithful account I have been able to collect, both from my own observation, and the relations of others, of the death of my ever honoured friend, and also of his character and services; I shall now leave his memory to the gratitude and admiration of posterity; accepting, with melancholy satisfaction, the honour, which the loss of him hath procured me, of seeing my name joined with his; and of testifying that affection and respect for his memory, which, whilst he lived, it was no less my inclination, than my constant study, to shew him.

---

2   Sir Godfrey Copley's gold medal was adjudged to him, on that occasion.

IMAGE CREDITS

Mark Bentley Adams: p.7; pp.42–43; p.63; p.66; p.71; p.121; p.296; p.297. **Bridgeman Images:** front dustjacket, *Lost in the Clouds*, Robin Brooks / Private Collection; front board, *Astronomical telescope used on the Pacific voyages of Captain James Cook* / Heath & Wing of London / Museum of New Zealand Te Papa Tongarewa, Wellington, New Zealand / Purchased 1953; endpapers, *The Discoveries of Captain Cook and de la Perouse*, Jacques Grasset de Saint-Sauveur / © National Library of Australia, Canberra, Australia; p.2, Nathaniel Dance / National Maritime Museum, London, UK / De Agostini Picture Library / G. Dagli Orti; pp.4–5, *HMS Resolution and HMS Adventure in Matavai Bay*, William Hodges / Pictures from History; pp.8–9, *Landing of Captain Cook at Botany Bay in 1770*, Emmanuel Phillips Fox / National Gallery of Victoria, Melbourne, Australia / Gilbee Bequest; p.13, National Maritime Museum, London, UK / De Agostini Picture Library / G. Nimatallah; pp.14–15, *The Progress of Human Culture and Knowledge*, James Barry / © RSA, London, UK; p.18, *Woman from Tierra del Fuego*, Alexander Buchan / De Agostini Picture Library; p.21, Thomas Phillips / National Portrait Gallery, London, UK; p.22, Universal History Archive/UIG; pp.24–25, Natural History Museum, London, UK; p.26, De Agostini Picture Library; p.28, John Hall / Bibliotheque Nationale, Paris, France / Archives Charmet; p.31; Rigobert Bonne / De Agostini Picture Library; p.32, British Library, London, UK / © British Library Board. All Rights Reserved; p.36, Private Collection / Ken Welsh; p.44, De Agostini Picture Library; p.47, Giulio Ferrario / The Stapleton Collection; p.49, Antonio Zatta / De Agostini Picture Library; p.50, T. Chambers (after Sydney Parkinson) / British Library, London, UK; p.51, British Library, London, UK; p.52, G. Smith (after Sydney Parkinson) / Alecto Historical Editions, London, UK; p.55, Fred Polydore Nodder (after Sydney Parkinson) / Natural History Museum, London, UK; p.68, Sydney Parkinson / Natural History Museum, London, UK; p.75, after Sydney Parkinson / Natural History Museum, London, UK; p.77, Private Collection; pp.80–81, Private Collection / © Look and Learn; p.82, James Gillray / Private Collection / The Stapleton Collection; p.83, Museum of New Zealand Te Papa Tongarewa, Wellington, New Zealand / Gift of the Australian Government, 1970; pp.84–85, John Hamilton Mortimer / © National Library of Australia, Canberra, Australia; p.86, Fred Polydore Nodder (after Sydney Parkinson) / Natural History Museum, London, UK; p.88, Natural History Museum, London, UK; p.89, Sydney Parkinson / Natural History Museum, London, UK; p.90, Sydney Parkinson / Natural History Museum, London, UK; p.91, Natural History Museum, London, UK; p.92, John Frederick Miller (after Sydney Parkinson) / Natural History Museum, London, UK; pp.100–101, William Hodges / National Maritime Museum, London, UK / De Agostini Picture Library; p.104, *The Resolution, c.1775* / Henry Roberts / Mitchell Library, State Library of New South Wales; p.106, Nathaniel Hodges / Pictures from History; p.109, Georg Forster / Natural History Museum, London, UK; p.111, Richard Westall / Private Collection; p.112, *South Africa: Table Mountain and Cape Town* / William Hodges / Pictures from History; pp.114–115, *The Ice Islands on the 9th January 1773* / B. T. Pouney (after William Hodges) / Private Collection; p.119, Universal History Archive / UIG; p.122, *Waterfall in Dusky Bay* / William Hodges / Pictures from History; p.126, Charles Howard Hodges / Private Collection; pp.128–129, *A View of Cape Stephens in Cook's Straits New Zealand with Waterspout* / William Hodges / Pictures from History; p.130, Georg Forster / Natural History Museum, London, UK; p.133, *HMS Resolution and HMS Adventure in Matavai Bay* / William Hodges / Pictures from History; pp.134–135, *Oaitepeha Bay* / William Hodges / Pictures from History; p.137, John Hall (after William Hodges) / Private Collection; p.144, Francesco Bartolozzi (after William Hodges) / De Agostini Picture Library; pp.146–147, *Chile: A View of the Monuments of Easter Island, Rapanui (Easter Island)* / William Hodges / Pictures from History; p.148, De Agostini Picture Library; p.151, Private Collection; p.153, *Tahitian War Canoes* / William Hodges / National Maritime Museum, London, UK; pp.154–155, *Tahiti, Bearing South-East* / William Hodges / Pictures from History; p.161, Georg Forster / Natural History Museum, London, UK; pp.166–167, *James Cook landing in Middleburgh, Tonga in 1778* / after Benard / Bibliotheque Nationale, Paris; pp.170–171, William Hodges in 1773 / Pictures from History; pp.176–177, *James Cook Disembarking on the Island of Tanna in New Hebrides* / William Hodges / De Agostini Picture Library; pp.182–183, William Hodges / National Maritime Museum, London, UK / De Agostini Picture Library; p.186, Benard / Bibliotheque des Arts Decoratifs, Paris; p.192, Benard / Bibliotheque des Arts Decoratifs, Paris; pp.196–197, after John Webber / De Agostini Picture Library; p.206, Nathaniel Dance-Holland / De Agostini Picture Library; p.208, Georg Forster / Natural History Museum, London, UK; pp.212–213, *Captain Burney Discovering His Murdered Shipmates* / Isaac Cruikshank / Private Collection / Photo ©

Christie's Images; pp.216–217, *The Death of Captain James Cook* / Johann Zoffany / National Maritime Museum, London, UK / Bridgeman Images; p.221, John Webber / Museum of New Zealand Te Papa Tongarewa, Wellington, New Zeland / Gift of the New Zealand Government, 1960; pp.222–223, Photo © Tallandier; p.224, Private Collection / © Look and Learn; p.227, William Ellis / Natural History Museum, London, UK; p.228, William Ellis / Natural History Museum, London, UK; p.231, *Captain Cook's Interview with Natives in Adventure Bay, Van Diemen's Land, 29th January 1777* / John Webber / © Royal Naval Museum, Portsmouth, Hampshire, UK; p.232, Photo © Tallandier; p.234, Nathaniel Dance-Holland / De Agostini Picture Library; pp.236–237, *View in Queen Charlotte's Sound*, New Zealand / James Webber / Private Collection / Photo © Bonhams, London, UK; p.244, William Ellis / Natural History Museum, London, UK; p.246, M. Seemulle / De Agostini Picture Library; p.249, *Native Inhabitants of the Friendly Islands Dancing in Hapee* / John Webber / Bibliotheque Nationale, Paris / Archives Charmet; p.250, after John Webber / British Library, London, UK / De Agostini Picture Library; p.254, John Webber / De Agostini Picture Library; p.256, *View of Huaheine* / Cleveley, John the Younger / Mark and Carolyn Blackburn Collection of Polynesian Art; p.257, *Poedua (Poetua), Daughter of Oreo, Chief of Ulaietea, One of the Society Isles* / John Webber / Private Collection / Photo © Christie's Images; p.260, *Polynesia, View of Otaheite (Tahiti)* / John Webber / De Agostini Picture Library; p.261, *View of Port of Moorea with* Resolution *and* Discovery, *Society Islands, October 1777* / af ter John Webber / De Agostini Picture Library; p.262 (left), *A Toopapaoo of a Chief with a Priest Making his Offering to the Morai in Huoheine* / John Webber / Private Collection; p.262 (right), *Funeral with Deceased under Canopy, Tahiti, Society Islands* / John Webber / De Agostini Picture Library; pp.264–265, Universal History Archive / UIG; p.266, William Ellis / Natural History Museum, London, UK; p.268, after John Webber / Private Collection / Prismatic Pictures; p.272, after John Webber / National Archives of Canada, Ottawa / De Agostini Picture Library; pp.274–275, after John Webber / De Agostini Picture Library; p.277, John Webber / De Agostini Picture Library; p.281, after John Webber / National Gallery of Australia, Canberra / De Agostini Picture Library; p.284, J. Heath and E. Scott (after John Webber) / Private Collection / The Stapleton Collection; p.286, *The* Resolution *Beating Through the Ice with the* Discovery *in the Most Imminent Danger in the Distance* / John Webber / Private Collection; p.287, after John Webber / De Agostini Picture Library;

p.290, William Ellis / Natural History Museum, London, UK; p.294, *A Man of the Sandwich Islands in a Mask* / Thomas Cook (after John Webber) / Private Collection; p.298, *An Offering before Captain Cook in the Sandwich Islands* / Samuel Middiman and John Hall (after John Webber) / © National Library of Australia, Canberra, Australia; p.299, after John Webber / De Agostini Picture Library; p.301, *The Death of Captain Cook* / John Webber / Museum of New Zealand Te Papa Tongarewa, Wellington, New Zeland / Gift of Horace Fildes; p.305, *Balagans or Summer Habitations, with the Method of Drying Fish at St. Peter and Paul, Kamtschatka* / John Webber / Private Collection; p.306, *The Narta, or Sledge for Burdens in Kamtschatka* / John Webber / Private Collection; pp.310–311, *View in the Island of Cracatoa* / John Webber / Private Collection; pp.318–319, National Geographic Creative / National Geographic Creative / Bridgeman Images.
Cambridge University Museum of Archaeology and Anthropology: p.20, accession number: D 1914.77; p.30, D 1914.34; p.38, D 1914.20–21; p.39, D 1914.35–36; p.41, D 1914.10; p.53, D 1914.56; p.54, D 1914.49 (above) and D 1914.38 (left); p.150, Z 5954 (D 1903.69); p.160, 1922.988–989; p.165, D1914.79; p.168, 1922.929 (left) and 1922.943 (right); p.169, 1925.379; p.175, 1922.987; p.189, 1922.986; p.269, 1922.915; p.270, 1922.916; p.278, 1922.948; p.292, 1922.950 A–B; back dustjacket (bottom), 1922.987; back board, 1922.917. **Creative Commons:** p.97, Collectie Stichting Nationaal Museum van Wereldculturen / Tropenmuseum, Amsterdam; pp.258–259, evilkalla / GNU Free Documentation License; p.271, Kirt Edblom, CC BY-SA 2.0; p.276, Tim Gage, CC Attribution-Share Alike 2.0 Generic. **Getty Images:** p.283, after John Webber / De Agostini Picture Library; p.291, The LIFE Picture Collection. **Glenn Jowitt Estate:** p.59; pp.94–95; p.136; p.159; p.162; p.163 (both); p.184; p.238 (both); p.241; p.242; p.248; p.253 (both); p.263. **Library of Congress:** p.46. **National Maritime Museum, London, UK:** spine, object ID: BHC2628.
Nicholas Thomas Collection: pp.34–35; p.67; p.149; p.181, George Williams Anders (London, 1784). **Shutterstock:** p.56, Mike Fennell; p.60, Nokuro; p.64, Leah-Anne Thompson; pp.72–73, Kathie Nichols; pp.78–79, electra; p.107, Max Studio; p.120, Dmitry Naumov; p.125, Dmitry Komarov; pp.140–141, Dmytro Pylypenko; p.142, Skreidzeleu; p.172, Robert Szymanski; p.173, Michal Durinik; p.202, artincamera; p.285, tryton2011; p.288, tryton2011; p.289, photomatz; pp.292–293, Wildnerdpix; p.302, kuma. **State Library of New South Wales:** back cover (top right), watercolor on ivory with gold frame / call number: DL Pa 24.

INDEX

Page numbers followed by *ph* indicate illustrations and their captions.

This cutaway painting of Cook's *Endeavour* was created by Robert Nicholson for
National Geographic. In spring 2016, as this book was going to press, archaeologists
believed they discovered the sunken Endeavour in U.S. waters off the coast of Rhode Island.
In 1775, the ship had been sold into private and later leased to the British navy. Renamed *Lord Sandwich*, the
ship was scuttled in August 1778 along with twelve other British vessels in an attempt to scuttle the French
navy coming to the aid of the colonies. At the same time, Cook's third voyage was sailing through the Bering
Strait, unaware of the fate of his erstwhile vessel.

Quarto is the authority on a wide range of topics.

Quarto educates, entertains and enriches the lives of our readers—enthusiasts and lovers of hands-on living.

www.quartoknows.com

First published in 2016 by Voyageur Press, an imprint of Quarto Publishing Group USA Inc., 400 First Avenue North, Suite 400, Minneapolis, MN 55401 USA. Telephone: (612) 344-8100 Fax: (612) 344-8692

quartoknows.com
Visit our blogs at quartoknows.com

Voyageur Press titles are also available at discounts in bulk quantity for industrial or sales-promotional use. For details contact the Special Sales Manager at Quarto Publishing Group USA Inc., 400 First Avenue North, Suite 400, Minneapolis, MN 55401 USA.

10 9 8 7 6 5 4 3 2 1

ISBN: 978-0-7603-5029-4

Library of Congress Cataloging-in-Publication Data

Names: Cook, James, 1728-1779, author.
Title: The voyages of Captain James Cook : the illustrated accounts of three
    epic Pacific voyages / James Cook.
Description: Minneapolis, Minnesota : Voyageur Press, 2016.
Identifiers: LCCN 2016017380 | ISBN 9780760350294 (hardback)
Subjects: LCSH: Cook, James, 1728-1779--Travel--Pacific Area. | Cook, James,
    1728-1779--Diaries. | Voyages around the world--Early works to 1800. |
    Oceania--Discovery and exploration--Early works to 1800. | BISAC: HISTORY
    / Modern / 18th Century. | HISTORY / World. | HISTORY / Oceania.
Classification: LCC G420.C65 C672 2016 | DDC 910.9182/3--dc23
LC record available at https://lccn.loc.gov/2016017380

Acquiring Editor: Dennis Pernu
Project Manager: Jordan Wiklund
Art Director & Cover Designer: James Kegley
Layout Designer: Ashley Prine